Cognitive Technologies

Editor-in-chief

Daniel Sonntag, DFKI, Saarbrücken, Saarland, Germany

The series Cognitive Technologies encompasses artificial intelligence and its subfields and related areas, such as natural-language processing and technologies, high-level computer vision, cognitive robotics, automated reasoning, multiagent systems, symbolic learning theories and practice, knowledge representation and the semantic web, and intelligent tutoring systems and AI and education. Cognitive science, including human and animal cognition and artificial life, is within the scope of this series, as is the integration of symbolic and subsymbolic computation. The series includes textbooks, monographs, coherent thematic state-of-the-art collections, and multiauthor anthologies.

More information about this series at http://www.springer.com/series/5216

Yohei Murakami · Donghui Lin
Toru Ishida

Editors

Services Computing
for Language Resources

 Springer

Editors
Yohei Murakami
Kyoto University
Kyoto
Japan

Toru Ishida
Kyoto University
Kyoto
Japan

Donghui Lin
Kyoto University
Kyoto
Japan

ISSN 1611-2482   ISSN 2197-6635   (electronic)
Cognitive Technologies
ISBN 978-981-13-4001-7   ISBN 978-981-10-7793-7   (eBook)
https://doi.org/10.1007/978-981-10-7793-7

This Springer imprint is published by the registered company Springer Nature Singapore Pte Ltd. part of Springer Nature
The registered company address is: 152 Beach Road, #21-01/04 Gateway East, Singapore 189721, Singapore

Preface

We started working on a service-oriented language infrastructure called the Language Grid in 2006. Our vision remains to shift from language resources to language services. The research goal is not to repackage language resources but to interconnect them flexibly as Web services. Since language is used everywhere in our daily life in different ways, attempting to develop complete general translation packages will not overcome all language barriers: We need to encourage end users to create their own customized multilingual environments to cover the various situations they actually face. Our first Springer book titled "The Language Grid: service-oriented collective intelligence for language resource interoperability" in 2011 focused on our research goal, system architecture, and applications, and the final part was titled Towards Federation of Service Grids. This book summarizes the technologies developed in recent years to actually realize the federation of service grids as well as the designs of applications and analyses of future issues likely to arise in language service networks.

This book includes 13 chapters in four parts. The first part describes two types of language service platforms to interconnect language services across service grids. One platform federates heterogeneous as well as homogeneous language service platforms on the cloud. To share language service registries and compose language services across platforms, a federated grid architecture with upper-level ontology for a service grid has been proposed and illustrated with a case study of a federated operation involving the Language Grid. The other platform connects a language service platform on a user's device to a public one on the cloud to efficiently construct personalized multilingual applications. This architecture allows users to combine language services regardless of the policy of the service grid operator.

The second part details various language service composition technologies that improve the reusability, efficiency, accuracy, and fault tolerance of composite services. One technology allows users to dynamically bind atomic language services to a language service workflow for reusing it. Another predicts and maximizes the parallel processing efficiency of a composite language service under parallel execution policies of atomic language services. A third optimizes a language service workflow consisting of crowd workers by using various performance models of crowd workers. The last one analyzes the robustness of composite language services to cascading failure, a frequent cause of failure in dependent language services.

The third part reports research work and activities on creating language resources and services. One aspect addresses language service creation for low-resource languages. To provide an efficient, robust, and accurate bilingual lexicon creation method for low-resource languages, a constraint approach to pivot-based lexicon induction has been introduced, where a new bilingual lexicon of a closely related language pair is induced from two existing dictionaries using a distant language as a pivot. Another aspect is to create complicated language services suitable for real-world demands. To consider how to compose different language services to meet the requirements posed by various users, a user-centered service design approach has been proposed and illustrated with a field study of a multi-language communication service.

The fourth part provides various applications and tools for understanding and designing language services that well support intercultural collaboration. Researchers proposed a series of mechanisms and guidelines to address the issue of content inconsistency in knowledge sharing among multi-language communities. In parallel, controlled experiments have been conducted to understand how various language services can effectively support the listening comprehension of non-native speakers, which is useful for designing real-time adaptive systems with greater listening comprehension. To support the users in multilingual communication, the translation agent metaphor is proposed as a novel interactive way to promote the efficiency of communication and reduce the communication breaks caused by translation errors. Moreover, a multiagent-based gaming simulation environment was developed to understand the strategies of various stakeholders in the language service infrastructure. Furthermore, an intercultural communication environment was developed by an international NPO to support agricultural knowledge transfer in rural areas in Vietnam.

The Language Grid has been contributing to the research into language resources for ten years as a concrete example of an effective language service infrastructure and its applications. In June 2017, we launched the Language Grid Association, a nonprofit organization, as a legal entity to continue to support the research and development of language services. We are grateful to the many researchers, students, and field-workers who have collaborated with, and supported our project.

Kyoto, Japan   Yohei Murakami
August 2017   Donghui Lin
                                                                                             Toru Ishida

Contents

Part IV   Understanding and Designing Language Services

Contributors

Xun Cao Department of Social Informatics, Kyoto University, Kyoto, Japan

Shinsuke Goto Department of Social Informatics, Kyoto University, Kyoto, Japan

Reiko Hishiyama Faculty of Science and Engineering, Waseda University, Tokyo, Japan

Toru Ishida Department of Social Informatics, Kyoto University, Kyoto, Japan

Kemas M. Lhaksmana School of Computing, Telkom University, Bandung, Indonesia

Donghui Lin Department of Social Informatics, Kyoto University, Kyoto, Japan

Trang Mai Xuan Department of Social Informatics, Kyoto University, Kyoto, Japan

Yumiko Mori NPO Pangaea, Kyoto, Japan

Yohei Murakami Unit of Design, Kyoto University, Kyoto, Japan

Takao Nakaguchi Department of Web Business Technology, School of Applied Information Technology, The Kyoto College of Graduate Studies for Informatics, Kyoto, Japan; Department of Social Informatics, Kyoto University, Kyoto, Japan

Yuu Nakajima Faculty of Science, Toho University, Chiba, Japan

Nguyen Cao Hong Ngoc Department of Social Informatics, Kyoto University, Kyoto, Japan

Naoyuki Oda Faculty of Science, Toho University, Chiba, Japan

Masayuki Otani Department of Informatics, Faculty of Science and Engineering, Kindai University, Osaka, Japan

Ryutaro Otsuka Faculty of Science and Engineering, Waseda University, Tokyo, Japan

Amit Pariyar Institute of Social Informatics and Technological Innovations, University Malaysia Sarawak, Sarawak, Malaysia

Chunqi Shi Department of Social Informatics, Kyoto University, Kyoto, Japan

Toshiyuki Takasaki NPO Pangaea, Kyoto, Japan

Mairidan Wushouer Department of Computer Science, Xinjiang University, Urumqi, Xinjiang Uyghur Autonomous Region, People's Republic of China

Naomi Yamashita NTT Communication Science Labs, Kyoto, Japan

Part I
Language Service Platform

Federated Grid Architecture for Language Services

Yohei Murakami, Takao Nakaguchi, Donghui Lin and Toru Ishida

Abstract The existing platforms designed to ensure interoperability of language services define their own data format and annotation vocabularies. To construct a comprehensive language service infrastructure, various types of language services supporting different languages need to be connected to the platforms. However, it is difficult for a single operator to collect and organize services for two key reasons: what kinds of language services are registered depends on the purpose of the platforms, and the language resources are characterized by their locality. Therefore, federation of the platforms across regions is essential to establish the comprehensive infrastructure desired. In this chapter, we extend the existing service grid architecture to federate heterogeneous as well as homogeneous language service platforms. To this end, we introduce an upper-level ontology for a service grid that facilitates the semantic integration of domain ontologies and guides the development of new domain ontologies. Moreover, we also introduce a federated grid architecture that can share language service registries, and compose language services across service grids.

Keywords Service grid · Federated grid · Upper-level ontology

Y. Murakami (✉)
Unit of Design, Kyoto University, 91 Chudoji Awata-cho,
Kyoto 600-8815, Japan
e-mail: yohei@i.kyoto-u.ac.jp

T. Nakaguchi · D. Lin · T. Ishida
Department of Social Informatics, Kyoto University,
Kyoto 606-8501, Japan
e-mail: ta_nakaguchi@kcg.edu

D. Lin
e-mail: lindh@i.kyoto-u.ac.jp

T. Ishida
e-mail: ishida@i.kyoto-u.ac.jp

T. Nakaguchi
Department of Web Business Technology, The Kyoto College of Graduate
Studies for Informatics, Kyoto, Japan

© Springer Nature Singapore Pte Ltd. 2018
Y. Murakami et al. (eds.), *Services Computing for Language Resources,*
Cognitive Technologies, https://doi.org/10.1007/978-981-10-7793-7_1

3

1   Introduction

There are many language resources (both data and programs) on the Internet. To reuse the resources, many efforts have been made to combine language resources in some previous platforms based on web services. These efforts focus on wrapping the resources as services, and defining own data formats that are exchanged between language services and own annotation vocabularies to be embedded in the format. The format and vocabularies are used to communicate between language services developed by different providers. To construct a global language service infrastructure, the platforms need to connect to various types of language services supporting different languages.

However, a single platform operator has great difficulties in collecting and organizing various types of language services for two reasons: each platform has its own policy about what kinds of language services need to be registered, and the language resources have characterized by their locality. The former means that a platform for text analysis needs text processing tools like word segmentation and dependency parsers, while another platform for communication support aggregates multilingual resources like machine translators, parallel corpora, and bilingual dictionaries. On the other hand, the latter forces the platform operator to negotiate with language resource providers in the same country or region. For example, META-SHARE [17], an information-sharing infrastructure for language resources or language processing software in Europe, provides almost half (46.4%) of the language resources available in 5 European languages (English, Spanish, French, German and Finnish). In the Language Grid [6], a multilingual service platform operated in Japan, language resources that support Japanese occupy 71.6% of all resources.

Federation of the platforms operating in different regions and for different purposes is, therefore, essential to establish the truly global language service infrastructure. In this chapter, we extend the existing service grid architecture so that it provides functionalities to compose services, in order to federate heterogeneous as well as homogeneous language service platforms. To this end, we had to address the following research issues.

Design an upper-level ontology for service grid   To construct a service grid for each domain, we need an upper-level ontology that facilitates the semantic integration of domain ontologies and guides the development of new domain ontologies. By inheriting the upper-level ontology, service grid operators can manage services specialized for a certain domain while maintaining consistency with the other service grids.

Develop federated grid architecture to access services across service grids   We need a federation architecture to coordinate service grids. Since each service grid is operated by an individual operator, operation policies vary with the operator. The federation architecture must clarify the responsibilities and authority of shared information and services.

The rest of this chapter is organized as follows. Section 2 compares existing language service platforms and introduces our service grid architecture. Section 3 presents an upper-level ontology for service grids to instantiate domain-specific service grids. Section 4 introduces a federated grid architecture that can share information and compose services across service grids. Section 5 illustrates how to federate heterogeneous as well as homogeneous platforms with the proposed architecture by using a case study of the Language Grid.

2 Language Service Platforms

There are two types of platforms that support developers in combining language resources: those that take the pipeline processing approach such as GATE [3] and UIMA [4] (U-Compare [8] and DKPro [2]), and those that take the service composition approach such as PANACEA [18], LAPPS Grid [5], and the Language Grid. The former focus on using the pipeline technique to process huge amounts of local data. The latter aim to share language resources distributed on the Internet as web services and combine them in a workflow manner. Table 1 summarizes the features of these platforms.

2.1 Pipeline Processing Approach

This approach uses a common interface and common data format to permit exchanges between language resources. The resources are combined in a pipeline to analyze documents. Each resource, called a processing resource or analysis engine, annotates a document flowing in the pipeline in the stand-off annotation manner.

Table 1 Comparison among platforms

	Pipeline processing approach			Service composition approach		
	GATE	U-Compare	DKPro	LAPPS Grid	PANACEA	Language Grid
Standardized interface	✓	✓	✓	✓	✓	✓
	(Common)	(Common)	(Common)	(Common)	(Each type)	(Each type)
Common format	✓	✓	✓	✓	✓	
	(GATE)	(CAS)	(CAS)	(LIF)	(TO)	
Format converter				✓	✓	
Type system	✓	✓	✓	✓		✓
RPC protocol				✓	✓	✓
				(SOAP)	(SOAP)	(SOAP)

The document together with annotations follow a common data format, such as GATE format or CAS (Common Analysis Structure). The annotations comply with a predefined annotation type system. GATE provides annotation schemas to define annotation type for each case, while U-Compare and DKPro contain pre-defined annotation types based on the UIMA type system. By employing a common data format and a predefined annotation type system, the pipeline-based platforms ensure interoperability of language resources.

2.2 Service Composition Approach

This approach wraps language resources as web services, called *language services*, and uses workflows to combine the language services. To realize interoperability of language services on a platform, the language service interfaces are standardized. LAPPS Grid employs Galaxy as a workflow engine, PANACEA Taverna, and Language Grid ActiveBPEL. LAPPS Grid provides a single common method as in the pipeline processing approach, while PANACEA and Language Grid define the interfaces according to language service types. They do not have to employ a common interface because the workflow can freely assign outputs of a service to the inputs of another.

Web service technologies also allow users to invoke language services on a different platform because they provide remote procedure call protocols independent from service implementations. All the platforms use SOAP as the protocol.

Moreover, to achieve consistency of data, LAPPS Grid and PANACEA present several format converters between different formats and their own formats like LIF (LAPPS Interchange Format) and TO (Travelling Object). In addition, LAPPS Grid defines LAPPS Web Service Exchange Vocabulary, an ontology of terms for a core of linguistic objects and features exchanged among language services that consume and produce linguistically annotated data. It is used for service description and input/output interchange to support service discovery and composition. On the other hand, Language Grid requires service providers to wrap their resources with the standardized interfaces that expose every annotation data type, in order to avoid the need to enforce a common format and the use of converters [11]. To bridge other service-based platforms and Language Grid, we have developed adapters that can link Heart of Gold and UIMA component to our standardized interfaces [1, 19].

In this way, all the platforms technically establish data flows between language services. However, the platforms cannot always know what services are available and whether they can access language services on a different platform. Therefore, it is necessary to share language service information across platforms. In this chapter, we propose an upper-level ontology to define language service information to be exchanged between platforms, and a federated grid architecture to share it in a federation of platforms by extending the existing service grid architecture.

2.3 Service Grid Architecture

In constructing the Language Grid, we introduced the service grid in a previous work [12]. Figure 1 shows that the service grid architecture consists of five parts: Service Manager, Service Supervisor, Grid Composer, Service Database, and Composite Service Container.

The Service Manager manages node, user, service and resource information registered in the service grid. The service information includes access control settings and access logs. Since the information is registered through the Service Manager, it plays a front-end role for any functions other than service invocation. The Service Supervisor controls service invocations according to the access control settings registered by the service providers. Before invoking the services on the Composite Service Container, it verifies whether the request satisfies the providers' access control settings. The Grid Composer connects the nodes within the service grid to realize a P2P grid network. The Service Database is a repository of various types of information registered through the Service Manager and service invocation logs. The Composite Service Container provides a workflow engine that combines not only atomic services corresponding to resources but also composite services.

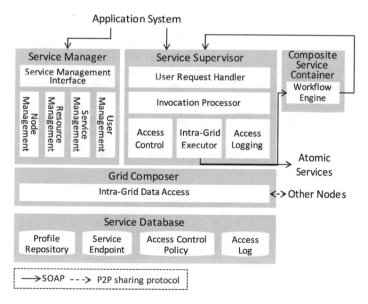

Fig. 1 Service grid architecture [12]

3   Upper-Level Ontology for Service Grid

The interoperability of language services requires standardization of service interfaces and metadata to suit their functionalities. To this end, we proposed a service grid
ontology as the upper-level ontology [13]. This ontology allows operators to organize services in their domain. As illustrated with VOWL (Visual Notation for OWL
Ontologies) [9] in Fig. 2, the service grid ontology is not just an ontology of data
exchanged between services, but an ontology to define service metadata and resource
metadata. *ServiceGrid* class has more than one *Resource* class and more than one *Ser-*
vice class that is provided from each *Resource* class. *Resource* and *Service* class have
more than one attributes (*hasResourceAttribute* and *hasServiceAttribute*) to describe
features of their instances. The attributes can have any individuals, represented by
Thing class. Also, *Service* class has at least one service interface to describe a method,
and an endpoint that allows users to access the service instances via a protocol. This
interface is used to wrap service providers' resources as a web service and describe
service composition workflows. A service grid operator can define his/her domain
service grid ontology by inheriting *ServiceGrid*, *Resource*, and *Service* class.

Service grid operators can add a new service type to suit their purposes. As the
number of service types increases, the reusability of workflows, however, decreases
because the service grid may have many close but not the identical interfaces for
the common functionalities. To increase the reusability of workflows, it is important
to verify which services are compatible with the existing workflows. Our solution
was to introduce semantic matching that guarantees substitutability of services in an
abstract workflow, into a domain service grid ontology.

Semantic matching was proposed to discover a service whose capability satisfies a
user's request [16]. Since the goal of the previous research was to fulfill users' request
as much as possible, the semantic matching prefers services that output a superclass
of users' required class. However, our goal is to find services whose capabilities
are compatible with the current workflow. If a service that outputs a superclass of

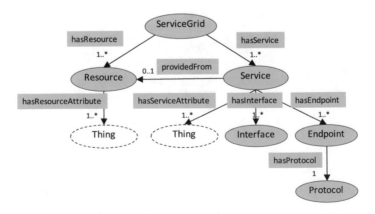

Fig. 2 Upper-level ontology for service grid

the workflow's required class is bound to the workflow, the subsequent service in a workflow may fail to run because the service may receive an input different from its expected input, such as a sibling class. This semantic mismatching triggers the issue of type-unsafety. Therefore, we modify the semantic matching rules by considering type-safety in binding services to a workflow.

First, we define notations relevant to the input-output of a service, and then modify the semantic matching rules.

Definition 3.1 (*Input-output of a service*) Service s is defined as the tuple $s = (Input_s, Output_s) \in S$ where $Input_s$ is the set of inputs required to invoke s, $Output_s$ is the set of outputs returned by s after its execution, and S is the set of all services registered in a service grid. Each input and output is also a class.

Exact   Input $i_s \in Input_s$ and output $o_s \in Output_s$ of service s in the set of services S match input $i_w \in Input_w$ and output $o_w \in Output_w$ of service w in a workflow with the degree of exact match if the input and output classes are equivalent ($i_s \equiv i_w, o_s \equiv o_w$).

Plug-in   Input $i_s \in Input_s$ and output $o_s \in Output_s$ of service s in the set of services S match input $i_w \in Input_w$ and output $o_w \in Output_w$ of service w in a workflow with the degree of plugin if i_s is a superclass of i_w ($i_s \sqsupseteq i_w$) and o_s is a subclass of o_w ($o_s \sqsubseteq o_w$).

Subsume   Input $i_s \in Input_s$ and output $o_s \in Output_s$ of service s in the set of services S match input $i_w \in Input_w$ and output $o_w \in Output_w$ of service w in a workflow with the degree of subsume if either i_s is a subclass of i_w ($i_s \sqsubset i_w$) or o_s is a superclass of o_w ($o_s \sqsupset o_w$).

Fail   When none of the previous matches are found, then both concepts are incompatible and the match has the degree of fail.

Note that, valid degrees of match are *exact* and *plug-in* to discover type safe services that satisfy the data flow in a workflow. Based on the *exact* match, a domain service grid ontology introduces the inheritance of service interfaces, which guarantees that an inherited interface provides the same methods as the superclass of a service. A service grid operator constructs a hierarchy of *Service* classes using the inheritance of service interfaces.

When many service users need more additional detailed information, a new service class can be derived by inheriting the service interface of the superclass, i.e., not created from scratch. The inherited service interface can add other interfaces while maintaining consistency with the existing one. This inheritance of service interfaces constructs a hierarchy of homogeneous services. This is similar to an OWL-S profile hierarchy [10] and WSMO capability [20]. However, they use property aspects to organize the service hierarchy like existing taxonomies of service categories, which is different from our approach of basing the domain service grid ontology on interface inheritance.

4   Federated Grid Architecture

The service grid ontology allows a service grid operator to define a hierarchy of services and metadata as a domain service grid ontology while maintaining consistency with other domains. Next, we proposed a federated grid architecture to share service instances compliant with each domain service grid ontology among the other service grids [14]. Note that this architecture provides the transparent access to services in the federation when users' requirements are not satisfied by their own service grid.

Figure 3 shows an extended federated grid architecture created from the service grid architecture in Fig. 1. Inter-Grid Executor and Inter-Grid Data Access, indicated by white rectangles, are added to Service Supervisor and Grid Composer of the existing architecture, respectively. In addition, a database for domain definitions and a federation list are newly deployed as the Service Database, in order to store the domain service grid ontology and a list of federated service grids.

The Inter-Grid Executor invokes services across service grids. This contrasts to the Intra-Grid Executor, which is responsible for service invocation only within the same service grid. Invocation Processor uses the two executors differently depending on the types and destination of service invocation requests. The requests are classified into local or remote requests: *local request* refers to the request submitted by application systems or composite service containers in the same service grid, whereas *remote request* refers to an incoming request from another federated service grid. The local requests whose destination is another federated service grid are sent to Inter-Grid Executor, the other requests including every remote request are passed to Intra-Grid Executor.

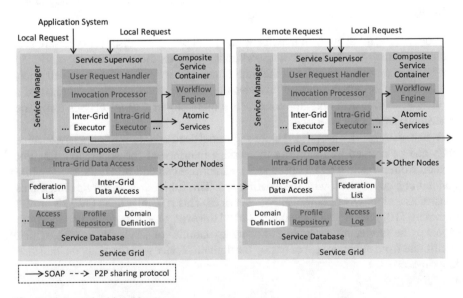

Fig. 3 Federated grid architecture

The Inter-Grid Data Access is responsible for sharing information with the other federated service grids. The shared information is related to user, resource, and service profiles, and service domain definition, which are open to every stakeholder. This is in contrast to Intra-Grid Data Access which shares information only with other nodes in the same service grid. The shared information is private one for each stakeholder, such as service endpoints, access logs, and access control policies for service providers, usage histories for service users, and a federated service grid list for operators. By replacing a part of the implementations of Intra-Grid Data Access with Inter-Grid Data Access, Grid Composer can write profile information and domain definitions to Service Database in the other federated service grids without having to modify Service Manager or Service Supervisor.

In this section, we present the details of information sharing and service composition in the federation.

4.1 Information Sharing

Once a federation is established between service grids, they swap certificates with each other. These certificates are used to certify a member of the federation and so permit information sharing and service composition across the service grids. A service grid requesting federation obtains the service domain definition and profile information including users, resources, and services from the target service grid. The service grid publishes the information to its service users so that the users can invoke services registered in the target service grid.

On the other hand, the target service grid obtains only user profile information registered in the requesting service grid, and publishes it to its service providers so that they can control access from the users of the requesting service grid. Such an asymmetric information sharing excludes services that exceed the scope of the target service grid from its service list. Therefore, bidirectional federation is necessary if both of the service users are to invoke services across the service grids.

After establishing the federation, information is shared via Inter-Grid Data Access based on the above information sharing policy. Meanwhile, private information, such as access control policy, access log, service endpoint information, user authentication information, and so on, is not shared among service grids.

4.2 Service Composition on Federated Grid

In composing services across service grids, Invocation Processor decides whether to use Intra-Grid Executor or Inter-Grid Executor according to the destination of the service request. If the destination is the same service grid, it selects the Intra-Grid Executor. Otherwise, it selects Inter-Grid Executor to forward the request to the federated service grid where the service is deployed.

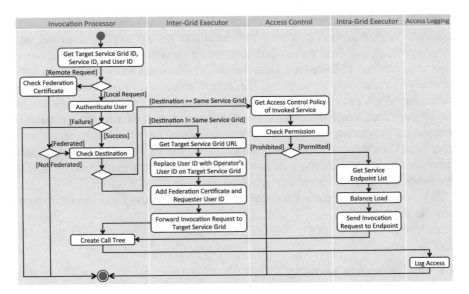

Fig. 4 Service composition process in service supervisor

Figure 4 shows details of the processing flow among Invocation Processor, Inter-Grid Executor, Access Control, Intra-Grid Executor, and Access Logging. When Invocation Processor receives a service request, it checks whether it is a local request or a remote request, and authenticates the requester. Next, Invocation Processor performs access control, service execution, and access logging sequentially. Since user passwords and access control policies are not shared in the federation, it skips the user authentication if the request is a remote one, and access control if the destination is another federated service grid. In executing the service, it selects Intra-Grid Executor if the destination is the same service grid. Otherwise, it selects Inter-Grid Executor to forward the request to the other federated service grid.

Intra-Grid Executor obtains a list of endpoints related to the service to be invoked, and then chooses one while taking instruction from a load balancing component such as round-robin, least connections, and fastest response time. The load balancing components are pluggable, which enables a variety of load balancing mechanisms to be used. On the other hand, Inter-Grid Executor simply forwards the request to the other federated service grid where the service is deployed. The access control and endpoint selection are delegated to the federated service grid. In forwarding the request, Inter-Grid Executor has to attach the federation certificate to certify that the requester is a member of the federation, and replace the requester's user ID with the operator's user ID of the federated service grid. This is because the federated service grid does not share user authentication information of the requester for security reasons. Moreover, Inter-Grid Executor inserts the requester's user ID into the request header so that the federated service grid can identify the requester and control access from the requester. By separating user authentication and access control between the two service grids, user passwords do not have to be shared.

5   Case Study: The Language Grid

In this section, we show how to define a domain service grid and federate service grids by applying it to the Language Grid.

5.1   *Language Grid Ontology*

By inheriting the service grid ontology, we constructed the language grid ontology shown in Fig. 5. This ontology defines LanguageGrid, LanguageResource, and LanguageService classes as subclasses of ServiceGrid, Resource, and Service classes, respectively. Moreover, the LanguageResource and LanguageService classes derive 15 types of language resource classes and 18 types of language service classes such as text to speech engines, translator, and so on.

Table 2 shows the 18 language service classes defined in the language grid ontology. These service classes are characterized with the sub-property of *hasServiceAttribute* property, indicating which objects a service processes and which methods a service presents. The former covers *hasSupportedLanguages*, *hasSupportedLanguagePairs*, *hasSupportedLanguagePaths*, *hasSupportedImageTypes*, *hasSupportedAudioTypes*, and *hasSupportedVoiceTypes*, which specify languages, images, and audio files to be processed by services. The latter covers *hasSupportedMatchingMethods*, which indicates matching mechanisms are available to search language data resources such as bilingual dictionaries, concept dictionaries, and so on.

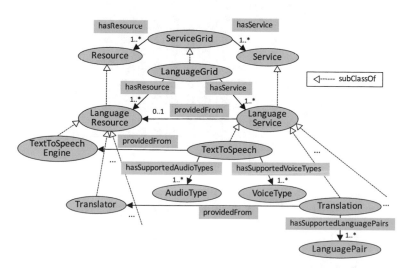

Fig. 5 Domain ontology inheriting upper-level ontology

Table 2 Language service classes

Service class	hasServiceAttribute property	Thing class	Interface class
BackTranslation	hasSupportedLanguagePaths	LanguagePath	backtranslate
BilingualDictionary	hasSupportedLanguagePairs, hasSupportedMatchingMethods	LanguagePair, MatchingMethod	search
BilingualDictionaryWith LongestMatchSearch	hasSupportedLanguagePairs, hasSupportedMatchingMethods	LanguagePair, MatchingMethod	search searchWithLongestMatch
ConceptDictionary	hasSupportedLanguages, hasSupportedMatchingMethods	Language, MatchingMethod	search, getRelatedConcepts
DependencyParse	hasSupportedLanguages	Language	parseDependency
DialogCorpus	hasSupportedLanguages, hasSupportedMatchingMethods	Language, MatchingMethod	search
LanguageIdentification	hasSupportedEncodings, hasSupportedLanguages	Encoding, Language	identify
MorphologicalAnalysis	hasSupportedLanguages	Language	analyze
MultihopTranslation	hasSupportedLanguagePaths	LanguagePath	translate multihopTranslate
NamedEntityTagging	hasSupportedLanguages	Language	tag

(continued)

Table 2 (continued)

Service class	hasServiceAttribute property	Thing class	Interface class
ParalleText	hasSupportedLanguagePairs, hasSupportedMatchingMethods	LanguagePair, MatchingMethod	search
Paraphrase	hasSupportedLanguages	Language	paraphrase
PictogramDictionary	hasSupportedLanguages, hasSupportedMatchingMethods, hasSupportedImageTypes	Language, MatchingMethod, ImageType	search
SimilarityCalculation	hasSupportedLanguages	Language	calculate
SpeechRecognition	hasSupportedLanguages, hasSupportedAudioTypes, hasSupportedVoiceTypes	Language, AudioType, VoiceType	recognize
TextToSpeech	hasSupportedLanguages, hasSupportedAudioTypes, hasSupportedVoiceTypes	Language, AudioType, VoiceType	speak
Translation	hasSupportedLanguagePairs	LanguagePair	translate
TranslationWith TemporalDictionary	hasSupportedLanguagePairs	LanguagePair	translate translateWithDict

Refer to http://langrid.org/service_manager/service-type for the WSDL files and more information

Moreover, we defined a service interface for each service class. To standardize the interface, we extracted common parameters of language resources belonging to the same resource type. For the morphological analyzers, we introduced five morphological analysis services: TreeTagger, MeCab, Juman, KLT, and ICTCLAS. All set source text and source language for input parameters. On the other hand, many formats are provided for the morphemes for output parameters. Every analyzer returns word, lemma, and part of speech tag, except for ICTCLAS. Therefore, we defined the output of a morphological analysis service as the tuple of word, lemma, and POS tag. Furthermore, we enumerated POS tags available in the output of the analysis service. Since POS tags depends on the languages, we selected a minimal set of POS tags common in all languages: noun, proper noun, pronoun, verb, adjective, adverb, unknown, and other. This interface is designed for interoperability instead of completeness. As a result, some of the information details generated by the original morphological analyzers can be lost.

Figure 6 illustrates our hierarchy of language services based on interface inheritance. First, LanguageService class is classified into four classes: SpeechService class processes speech data, DataService class deals with linguistic data resources

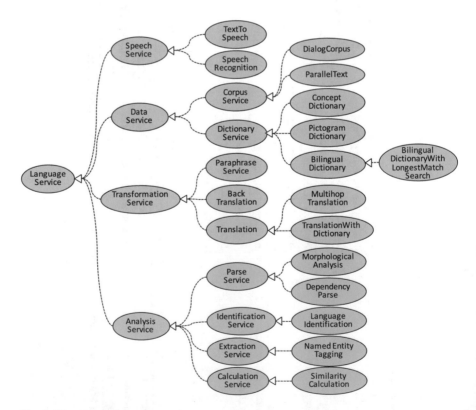

Fig. 6 Hierarchy of language services

like lexical and corpus data, TransformationService class transforms input texts to output texts, while AnalysisService class analyzes input data like parsing, calculating, extracting, and identifying and outputting analysis results. All the service instances directly belong to any subclass of the class whose name suffixes "service". These subclasses correspond to language service classes shown in Table 2.

MultihopTranslation and TranslationWithDictionary class, and BilingualDictionaryWithLongestMatchSearch class are derived from Translation class and BilingualDictionary class, respectively. Hence, they have the same interface as their superclass. For example, Translation class provides a translate method whose input parameters are source language, target language, and source text (denoted by sLang, tLang, source, respectively). By extending this interface, TranslationWithDictionary and MultihopTranslation class are defined as a subclass of Translation class. The former introduces simple dictionary data into its input parameters in order to replace words in the translated text with translated words in the dictionary. This aims at improving translation quality by restricting context within the dictionary. Without the dictionary, this service returns a translated text like Translation class. On the other hand, the latter introduces an array of intermediate languages to cascade several translation services. Without intermediate languages, this service behaves like Translation class by using default languages as intermediate languages.

Based on this hierarchy, we can bind any subclasses to an abstract workflow including the superclass's interface. For instance, backtranslation workflow connects two translation interfaces to translate the translated text into the source language again. Therefore, we can select JServer, an instance of Translation class, and DictTrans, an instance of TranslationWithDictionary, for forward translation and backward translation, respectively. To dynamically bind these services when invoking the backtranslation service, we introduced a hierarchical service composition description using higher-order function [15].

5.2   Federated Operation of Language Grid

We have been operating the Language Grid[1] since 2007. The lessons drawn from our operation experience are highly instructive in designing the federated operation. Even though we promoted international cooperation, 70–80% of language grid users are from Japan because the operator is located in Japan. To expand the Language Grid, we federated it with NECTEC in Thai, University of Indonesia in Indonesia, and Xinjiang University in China in 2010, 2011, and 2014, respectively. Figure 7 illustrates the federation relations among 7 service grids. Ovals represent service grids and its operator: language grids are shown in gray, while LAPPS grids are show in white. As shown in Fig. 7, the language grid federation was established by the mutual interconnections of service grids. They employ the same language service platform and language grid ontology, which easily enables interoperability of

---

[1] http://langrid.org/service_manager/.

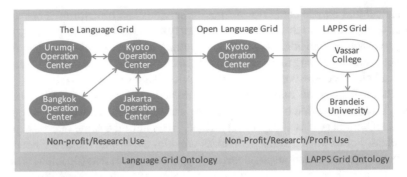

Fig. 7 Federated operation of service grids

language services among the 4 language service grids. As of 2017, this homogeneous federation links 225 services (176 services from Kyoto Language Grid, 37 services from Bangkok Language Grid, 4 services from Jakarta Language Grid, and 8 services from Urumqi Language Grid).

Apart from the Language Grid, we also started the Open Language Grid [7] to allow users to access language services for profit use as well as non-profit and research use. This operation policy conflicts with that of the Language Grid as the latter limits service use to only non-profit and research users. The difference between the policies prevents access from the Open Language Grid to the Language Grid. Consequently, the federation is unidirectional.

On the other hand, we established a heterogenous federation for Open Language Grid and LAPPS Grid. Although they employ the same operational policy, LAPPS Grid was constructed with different technologies from Language Grid: LIF for a common data format, LAPPS Web Service Exchange Vocabulary for annotations, and Galaxy for a workflow engine. LAPPS Grid ontology based on service grid ontology makes the metadata of language services in LAPPS Grid interoperable with those of Language Grid. Furthermore, to ensure interoperability of language services based on different design philosophies, we developed several service adapters that enable users to access LIF-based language services through the standard Language Grid service interfaces and vice versa. For example, a morphological analysis adapter is implemented in a workflow combining tokenizer and POS tagger in LAPPS Grid. This resulted in shared access to 20 service types (18 service types from Open Language Grid and 2 service types from LAPPS Grid).

6   Conclusion

In this chapter, we proposed a method that builds a language service infrastructure by the federation of various platforms. To this end, we addressed the following two research issues.

Design an upper-level ontology for service grid To make service grid specific to a certain domain, we constructed an upper-level ontology called *service grid ontology*. This allows service grid operators to freely define resource type and service type, their unique attributes, and service interface while maintaining consistency with the other service grids. This also guarantees substitutability of language services in an abstract workflow by introducing interface inheritance to a hierarchy of language services.

Develop federated grid architecture to access services across service grids We developed a federated grid architecture to realize unidirectional and bidirectional coordination between homogeneous service grids or heterogeneous service grids. The direction of federation reflects the compatibility of operational policies between service grids. Homogeneous service grid federation increases the number of services belonging to the same service types, whereas heterogeneous service grid federation diversifies service types.

Acknowledgements This research is partially supported by a Grant-in-Aid for Young Scientists (A) (17H04706, 2017–2020) and a Grant-in-Aid for Scientific Research (A) (17H00759, 2017–2020) from Japan Society for the Promotion of Science (JSPS).

References

1. Bramantoro, A., Tanaka, M., Murakami, Y., Schäfer, U., Ishida, T.: A hybrid integrated architecture for language service composition. In: Proceedings of the Sixth International Conference on Web Services (ICWS'08), pp. 345–352 (2008)
2. Eckart de Castilho, R., Gurevych, I.: A broad-coverage collection of portable NLP components for building shareable analysis pipelines. In: Proceedings of the Workshop on Open Infrastructures and Analysis Frameworks for HLT, pp. 1–11 (2014)
3. Cunningham, H., Maynard, D., Bontcheva, K., Tablan, V.: GATE: an architecture for development of robust HLT applications. In: Proceedings of the Fortieth Annual Meeting on Association for Computational Linguistics (ACL'02), pp. 168–175 (2002)
4. Ferrucci, D., Lally, A.: UIMA: an architectural approach to unstructured information processing in the corporate research environment. J. Nat. Lang. Eng. **10**, 327–348 (2004)
5. Ide, N., Pustejovsky, J., Cieri, C., Nyberg, E., Wang, D., Suderman, K., Verhagen, M., Wright, J.: The language application grid. In: Proceedings of the Ninth International Conference on Language Resources and Evaluation (LREC'14), pp. 22–30 (2014)
6. Ishida, T. (ed.): The language grid: Service-oriented collective intelligence for language resource interoperability. Springer Science & Business Media, Berlin (2011)
7. Ishida, T., Murakami, Y., Lin, D., Nakaguchi, T., Otani, M.: Open language grid - towards a global language service infrastructure. In: Proceedings of the Third ASE International Conference on Social Informatics (2014)
8. Kano, Y., Baumgartner, W., McCrohon, L., Ananiadou, S., Cohen, K., Hunter, L., Tsujii, J.: U-Compare: share and compare text mining tools with UIMA. Bioinformatics **25**(15), 1997–1998 (2009)
9. Lohmann, S., Negru, S., Haag, F., Ertl, T.: Visualizing ontologies with VOWL. Semant. Web **7**(4), 399–419 (2016)
10. Martin, D., Burstein, M., McDermott, D., McIlraith, S., Paolucci, M., Sycara, K., McGuinness, D.L., Sirin, E., Srinivasan, N.: Bringing semantics to web services with OWL-S. World Wide Web **10**(3), 243–277 (2007)

11. Murakami, Y., Lin, D., Ishida, T.: Service-oriented architecture for interoperability of multi-language services. In: Buitelaar, P., Cimiano, P. (eds.) Towards the Multilingual Semantic Web: Principles, Methods and Applications, pp. 313–328. Springer Science & Business Media, Berlin (2014)

12. Murakami, Y., Lin, D., Tanaka, M., Nakaguchi, T., Ishida, T.: Service grid architecture. In: Ishida, T. (ed.) The Language Grid: Service-oriented Collective Intelligence for Language Resource Interoperability, pp. 19–34. Springer Science & Business Media, Berlin (2011)

13. Murakami, Y., Nakaguchi, T., Lin, D., Ishida, T.: An ontology for language service composability. In: Proceedings of the Third International Workshop on Worldwide Language Service Infrastructure and Second Workshop on Open Infrastructures and Analysis Frameworks for Human Language Technologies (WLSI/OIAF4HLT'16), pp. 61–69 (2016)

14. Murakami, Y., Tanaka, M., Lin, D., Ishida, T.: Service grid federation architecture for heterogeneous domains. In: Proceedings of the Ninth International Conference on Services Computing (SCC'12), pp. 539–546 (2012)

15. Nakaguchi, T., Murakami, Y., Lin, D., Ishida, T.: Higher-order functrions for modeling hierarchical service bindings. In: Proceedings of the Thirteenth International Conference on Services Computing (SCC'16), pp. 798–803 (2016)

16. Paolucci, M., Kawamura, T., Payne, T.R., Sycara, K.: Semantic matching of web services capabilities. In: Proceedings of the First International Semantic Web Conference (ISWC'02), pp. 333–347 (2002)

17. Piperidis, S.: The meta-share language resources sharing infrastructure: principles, challenges, solutions. In: Proceedings of the 8th International Conference on Language Resources and Evaluation Conference (LREC'12), pp. 36–42 (2012)

18. Toral, A., Pecina, P., Way, A., Poch, M.: Towards a user-friendly webservice architecture for statistical machine translation in the PANACEA project. In: Proceedings of the 15th Conference of the European Association for Machine Translation (EAMT'11), pp. 63–70 (2011)

19. Trang, M.X., Murakami, Y., Lin, D., Ishida, T.: Integration of workflow and pipeline for language service composition. In: Proceedings of the 9th International Conference on Language Resources and Evaluation Conference (LREC'14), pp. 3829–3836 (2014)

20. Wang, H.H., Gibbins, N., Payne, T.R., Redavid, D.: A formal model of the Semantic Web Service Ontology (WSMO). Inf. Syst. 37(1), 33–60 (2012)

Language Mashup: Personalized Language Service Platform

Masayuki Otani, Nguyen Cao Hong Ngoc, Takao Nakaguchi
and Donghui Lin

Abstract The aim of the Language Grid is to enable users to develop new language services by sharing and combining any existing language resources as language services. To implement this concept, we had to address the following problems: (1) only organization agents can register and invoke services, i.e., private users cannot invoke services on the Language Grid directly. Private users are able to use only the applications that have been developed and published non-commercially; (2) using the resources of mobile devices and services in the cloud is hindered by mismatches such as different communication protocols and different input and output methods. This chapter introduces a language service infrastructure for personal use called Language Mashup. It enables users to develop and install domain-specific multi-lingual applications on their smart personal devices by combining various kinds of language services created from the language resources provided by both academia and industry, and located on cloud servers or on mobile devices.

Keywords Mobile service mashup · Private and public services · Mobile and cloud services

M. Otani (✉)
Department of Informatics, Faculty of Science and Engineering,
Kindai University, 3-4-1 Kowakae, Osaka 577-8502, Japan
e-mail: otani@info.kindai.ac.jp

N. C. H. Ngoc · D. Lin
Department of Social Informatics,
Kyoto University, Kyoto 606-8501, Japan
e-mail: nchngoc@ai.soc.i.kyoto-u.ac.jp

D. Lin
e-mail: lindh@i.kyoto-u.ac.jp

T. Nakaguchi
Department of Web Business Technology, School of Applied Information
Technology, The Kyoto College of Graduate Studies for Informatics,
7 Monzen-cho Tanaka, Sakyo, Kyoto 606-8225, Japan
e-mail: ta_nakaguchi@kcg.edu

© Springer Nature Singapore Pte Ltd. 2018
Y. Murakami et al. (eds.), *Services Computing for Language Resources*,
Cognitive Technologies, https://doi.org/10.1007/978-981-10-7793-7_2

1   Introduction

The Language Grid [5] is a language service platform that uses the Service Grid [6] and so enables users to register and developing new service by combining them. The goal of the Language Grid is to enable users to develop new language applications that are specific to some community by utilizing any existing language resources as language services and combining them. However, the original Language Grid has not yet achieved its full potential. Since language services on the Language Grid are shared among unspecified people via the web, it is forbidden to register commercial services that can be used only by authorized users. In order to realize sharing and combining any existing language resources, we need a framework that enables users to make composite services which can invoke not only shared public services but also the services for authorized users.

This chapter introduces *Language Mashup* [9], a mobile extension of the Language Grid in Sect. 2 that can solve the above problem. Language Mashup is installed in users' mobile devices and enables users to combine the language services that are permitted to be invoked by authorized users with the public services which are shared on the Language Grid.

Furthermore, Language Mashup has another extension [8]. It can combine not only language resources that includes the resources permitted to be used by authorized users, but also the functions of the user's device. By combining the language services with the device functions, people can make real-world-oriented language services; for example, the optical character recognition (OCR) functions of the device can be used to create live video translator applications. In Sect. 3, we detail the service composition that combines language services and device functions. The latter are wrapped as services.

2   Language Service Platform for Personal Use

2.1   Intellectural Property Problems in Language Grid

The Language Grid is the web service platform that shares existing language resources from all over the world as language services and develops new services by combining them [5]. Its motivation is to enable the users to customize existing language resources without expert knowledge, e.g., natural language processing, web programming, etc.

Our original intent was to create an institutional framework for a public service grid operated by non-profit organizations such as universities or research institutes. However, we found several potential problems that hindered private users from using this framework to develop specific multilingual environments. To collect a lot of services from various providers, the Language Grid had to establish strict agreements to protect intellectual property rights. Its users have to be organizations, not individuals. It also prohibits commercial use of the language services. Unfortunately, these limitations restricted the participation to those few users associated with universities and non-profit organizations that have developed language resources or want to use such resources. These agreements shut out companies who were interested in commercial use of the language services, and individuals who wanted to use them for their personal use.

Moreover, the operation model of Language Grid assumes that the operation centers, which are located at various regions of the world, should reach agreement with each other to permit federated operation [7]; the users register the language services that they have developed with the servers so that the third parties can use them. The server software of Language Grid prevented private users from accessing free commercial language services in Language Grid because access from the Language Grid is regarded as invocation for third party use not personal use. Moreover, the service providers need to keep their services stable to satisfy this operation model.

The following problems summarize the above analysis, and should be solved to enable private users to develop multi-language applications by invoking and combining commercial services with non-commercial services (i.e., services registered with Language Grid).

- Private users are not able to invoke services directly from the Language Grid since only organizational users can register and invoke services on Language Grid.
- The services registered with Language Grid have to be for non-profit use although many of the services were created for commercial use by authorized users.

2.2 Mashup Framework

Language Mashup [9] is a language service platform for private users that is incorporated to a mobile mashup framework that solves the problems explained in the previous section. Since Language Mashup was developed as a mobile application, it assumes that it is used by private users, i.e., the owner of the mobile device on which Language Mashup is installed. By using this framework, private users can develop multi-language communication environments that are appropriate for their problem domain by combining the following services: (i) Commercial language services installed in their own devices or that can be invoked from the individual devices. (ii) Non-commercial language services registered on the language platform for open access called *Open Language Grid*; private users can invoke services developed as open source resources by universities or research institutes.

The following subsections provide an overview of Open Language Grid and the details of Language Mashup.

Open Language Grid

Open Language Grid was proposed to remove the limitation pointed out in Sect. 2.1 that prevents the participation of potential users like individuals and companies. It allows individuals to use language services for commercial purpose by registering with it as a user, to start operation of grid servers easily, and to connect their servers to other servers freely. In the rest of this section, we call the existing language platform (i.e., the Language Grid) the *contractual grid*, and the Open Language Grid the *open grid*, in order to distinguish these two types of platform.

The main points impacted by these changes are the legal agreement and the registered language services. The open grid allows private users to invoke or register language services on the platform while contractual grid allows just organization users to do so. In terms of agreement, these two policies are not compatible. Therefore, it is forbidden to access language services on the contractual grid to be accessed from the open grid but the reverse is allowed.

In regard to available language resources, the open grid permits users to register only those language resources that can be freely provided to other users as services, such as open-source language resources. Open-source language services registered with the open grid so far include Stanford POS Tagger for English, SVMTool for Spanish, and Japanese morphological analysis, e.g., MeCab, ChaSen, and Juman. These language resources are published by academic communities as freely available resources. People are able to find these resources easily using LRE Map [3], which provides the possibility of search based on a fixed set of metadata and to view the details of the resources so found.

Language Mashup

Both the contractual grid and open grid allow their users to register their language services with the servers so that these services can be used from third party applications. However, free commercial language services usually permit only personal use and access to such services from either grid is regarded as an invocation for third party use, not private use.

To solve this problem, we proposed Language Mashup (hereafter referred to as the *mashup*). The mashup aims at combining useful commercial language resources which are open to the public but limited to just private use. A lot of language resources on the Web are of this style, for example, Bing Translator, Google Translate, Baidu Translation, and SYSTRANet. Although they often provide higher quality services if users pay for them, even if the users pay for them, they cannot register the services with either the contractual or the open grid unless the users receive special permission from the providers. To solve such intellectual property right problems, grid operators must spend long periods in negotiation and to implement special functionality to control access in a more secure manner. It is hard for the operators to deal with each case where they have to cope with too many types, interfaces, and licenses of the language resources.

Figure 1 shows the design concept of the mashup, where the user operates a grid server on his/her smart device(s) for private use and register language resources that are necessary to implement their environment by themselves.

By invoking the mashup on the user's smart device, the user can make a composite language service by invoking language services that are pre-installed on the users'

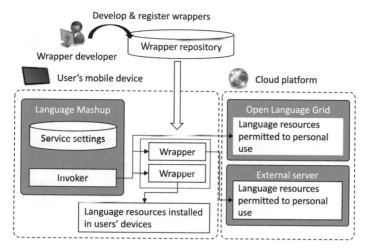

Fig. 1 The concept of Language Mashup

mobile device, located at an external server as private-use only language resources, or registered with contractual/open grids as open access language services, without considering where the service is located and what kind of device the service is installed on. The mashup implements the following functions in order to realize the framework whereby users can invoke a service without being concerned about the location of the service or the device in which the service is installed.

Virtualization of Local or Cloud Resources
The mashup manages the settings of service invocation and handles invocation requests from users' applications to combine services that are located on external servers, installed in users' devices, and/or registered with contractual/open grids without considering their locations. Concretely, it manages the following settings: setting name, device information (on user's device, on contractual/open grids), and service location (URL of the service). User applications installed on the user's device can invoke one or more services by referring to setting name and parameters; i.e. specifying location and device is not needed. This service invocation controller allows other invocation methods to be implemented as long as these methods become components which mediate between the invocation component of the mashup and composite/atomic services by employing the invocation interface of the mashup.

Automatic Wrapping of Local Resources
We have developed a wrapper repository that is a framework for downloading and deploying wrappers in order to apply wrappers to language resources accessible for only private use and located on the user's device or external servers. The wrapper repository enables the users to upload or download wrappers to/from it and to install them in the users' devices as services which can be invoked from the mashup.

Table 1 Comparisons between three kinds of grid servers

Grid type	Agreement	Operator/user	Purpose	Language resources (LRs)
Contractual grid	Strict	Organization/organization	Non-profit, research	LRs provided under the agreement
Open grid	Relaxed	Organization/individual	Non-profit, research, profit	Open-source LRs (e.g. MeCab, Stanford POS Tagger)
Mashup	None	Individual/individual	Personal use	LRs permitted for private use (e.g. Bing Trans.)

2.2.1 Mashup Services on Different Grids

Table 1 compares the features of contractual grid, open grid, and mashup. This table shows that they can complement each other in various situations. The most important point is the ranges of the language resources that are handled by each grid differ with grid type. The contractual grid can make various language resources available if their providers reach agreement. The open grid allows to register and provide just open-source language resources to avoid complex legal negotiations. The mashup can combine language resources that are permitted only for private use with academic language resources for the user's private access.

The users can create multilingual environments to suit various situations by coordinating these three kind of grid servers. Figure 2 indicates how this is achieved. Each arrow represents the direction of a service invocation. Since the open grid employs simple Terms of Use, an abbreviated form of the full agreement, individuals can easily register as users. Users of the contractual grid can combine language services on both grids. On the other hand, Mashup users can combine commercial language services on mashup and academic language services on the open grid by registering the former with the mashup server.

3 Language Service Platform for Mobile Device

3.1 Combination of Language Services and Mobile Functions

The previous section introduced the framework for the mashup of commercial and non-commercial language services on users' mobile devices. Needless to say, this framework only focuses on *language* services. However, in many scenarios com-

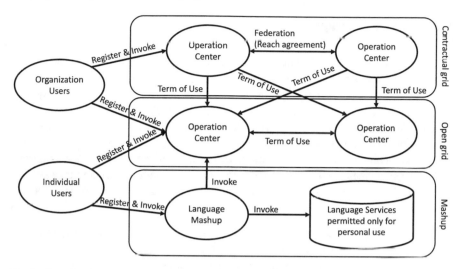

Fig. 2 Coordination among contractual grid, open grid, and mashup

bining not only language services but also the functions of the mobile devices will greatly benefit users.

Mobile devices now offer many sophisticated functions due to the rapid growth in hardware complexity and services, e.g., speech recognition, text-to-speech, Bluetooth low energy (BLE) links, gesture recognition, camera, text service, etc. Nowadays, the use of mobile devices to help people to overcome language barriers has become popular such as translating an image of an unknown word, spoken words, and gestures. There are many such applications that take advantage of the display screen, microphone, speaker, camera, gesture for translation purposes. By using the functions implemented in mobile devices as well as language services, we create several advantages such as providing more alternatives in selecting a service, and utilizing unique functions that are available on-site as sensor services, e.g., camera, gesture, or BLE. These functions cannot be replaced by cloud language services.

Thus, it is essential to well utilize resources and services on mobile devices as well as language resources and services on the cloud. Currently, however, each developer has to work hard to find his or her own solution for creating such applications since there is no framework that can support those tasks easily. To solve the similar problem, several types of mobile cloud computing have been proposed [1, 11, 12]. These papers describe that the mobile device can use the cloud for data processing, where several mobile cloud applications are available, e.g., Google Map, Gmail for iPhone, Cisco's WebEx on iPad. However, developers must have expertise knowledge of both cloud computing techniques and mobile device programming techniques to implement such applications. In addition, it is not easy for all developers to compose and integrate different types of services

3.2   Design Concept

We extended Language Mashup to realize the efficient combination of cloud language services and mobile function services [8]. Extended Language Mashup allows users to invoke existing language resources which are registered on the language platform such as Google translation service, Bing translation service, Baidu translation service, SYSTRANet, Standford POS Tagger, and SVMTool. Moreover, they can combine those existing language resources with not only their own language resources installed in their mobile devices, but also their mobile device functions wrapped as services to create the composite services required. The language service infrastructure for mobile environments that fulfills our design concept is described in Fig. 3.

- Resource includes two types of resources, i.e., the resources installed in users' mobile devices and those published on the cloud (e.g., Open Language Grid). The former include the device functions and user's data (e.g., parallel texts made by users). The latter are published on the web like existing cloud resources.
- Atomic Service includes mobile atomic services that wrap the mobile resources of the user's device and published language services in the cloud.
- Composite Service, users of extended Language Mashup can make composite services by combining atomic services on both the mobile devices and the cloud.
- Application can be easily developed by invoking services that include composite and atomic services. These applications should run on the mobile device as the services are invoke for private use.

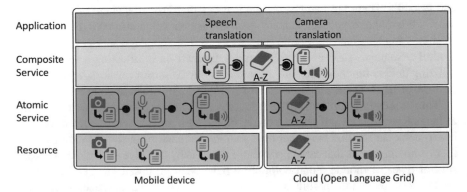

Fig. 3   Design concept of language service platform for mobile environments

3.3 Architecture

The main motivation of this design concept is to realize an appropriate infrastructure to combine cloud/mobile language services and the services that wrap mobile devices functions. These services, however, have different characteristics, for example, the input and output methods and the communication protocols. While language services on the cloud usually require input and output parameters, services on mobile devices sometimes does not require all those parameters because services on mobile devices use device components as input and output. The input component can be a microphone, camera, geoloc, compag, and gestures; the output component can be the display screen, speaker, and vibrator. With regard to the communication protocol, mobile services use intra-device connections while cloud services need an Internet protocol like SOAP, JSON-RPC, HTTP REST, etc. Therefore, our proposed framework includes appropriate modules to deal with those issues.

Overall Framework

The language service infrastructure for mobile environments consists of four main components: Service Supervisor, Grid Composer, Service Database and Service Container. The idea of Grid Composer Component and Service Database Component are almost the same as found in the Language Grid [5] but some unnecessary modules are omitted. Service Supervisor Component and Service Container Component are the main extensions as they need to deal with mobile functions.

- Service Supervisor for mobile environments controls service invocation by service users. This component executes inter-grid and intra-grid services.
- Grid Composer creates a grid network within its services grid. Although Language Grid supports the inter-grid network so as to share service information across grids, our framework does not support it and we omit the inter-grid data access module to make it lightweight.
- Service Database is a repository to store various types of service information.
- Service Container consists of all services such as composite services, mobile atomic services, and some modules which control the execution of those services.

Figure 4 describes the overall framework of the language service infrastructure for mobile environments.

Service Supervisor

To extend the Service Supervisor of Language Grid to the mobile environment, this component includes the two modules, Inter-Grid Executor and Intra-Grid Executor, that are required to establish method invokers for both cloud services and mobile services. The Intra-Grid Executor creates method invokers for services on Service Container while Inter-Grid Executor creates method invokers for cloud services. The Inter-Grid Executor has the same modules as the original Service Grid, i.e., SOAP Method Invoker (SOAP MI) and JSON-RPC Method Invoker (JSRPC MI).

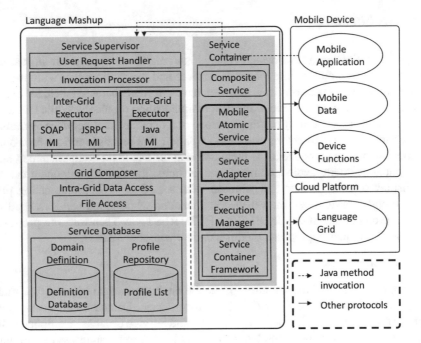

Fig. 4 Overall framework

In our framework, both Intra-Grid Executor and Inter-Grid Executor play important roles because the communication methods of cloud and mobile services are different. For example, Java Method Invoker (Java MI) is used when speech recognition services in mobile devices are invoked while SOAP MI is used if the translation service lies in the cloud such as Bing translation service. A composite service that consists of a speech recognition service and Bing translation service to translate voice messages into another language has to work with the different communication methods of its two atomic services. The service composition of different communication methods are realized by combining Intra-Grid Executor and Inter-Grid Executor.

Grid Composer

Since the framework for the mobile environment should be lightweight and compact, some functionalities of Grid Composer have been dropped or reduced, i.e., the Inter-Grid Data Access module has been deleted. Instead of this module, the Intra-Grid Data Access module provides read and write interfaces for the Service Database to keep compatibility.

Service Container

In order to execute composite services and atomic services in mobile environment, the Service Container includes the following additional components.

- The Mobile Atomic Service executes atomic services by wrapping mobile resources (including mobile data and device functions) as services with standard interfaces.
- The Service Adapter deals with the adaptation of device functions wrapped as services on mobile devices to suit ordinary cloud services.
- Service Execution Manager executes Composite Services (cloud services combined with mobile atomic services), especially monitoring or event detecting services. To detect events during their own life cycles, these services run continuously while normal services work only when invoked. For example, the BLE detection service that uses Bluetooth connection to detect beacons near the mobile device (i.e., invocation of BLE detection) and returns the beacon list, needs to update beacon information every few seconds. To deal with event-detecting services without event processing middle-ware, the execution model is simplified by the introduction of periodic execution of composite services and a queue for each event detecting service instead of centralizing all these operations in shared event-queue middle-ware.

3.4 Implementation

To implement the language service infrastructure for mobile environments the following issues should be resolved: (1) for atomic services: how to utilize services in both the cloud and mobile devices, which include mobile data and device functions wrapped as services, and (2) for composite services: how to handling the differences of services in the cloud and services on mobile devices and the different execution demands of those services.

The framework of extended Language Mashup provides some special modules including Inter-Grid Executor, Mobile Atomic Services, Service Adapter, Service Execution Manager in order to fulfill these requirements. Of particular interest, we focus on the modules of Mobile Atomic Services and the Service Adapter as they are the most important parts to realize the language service infrastructure for mobile devices.

Mobile Atomic Services

This is a module included in Service Container component, and consists of mobile data wrapped as services and device functions wrapped as services. Mobile data may include user's dictionaries, parallel texts, or any other user data which can be wrapped as services with wrappers that are compatible with the proposed framework. The compatible interfaces (Table 2) are provided using device native APIs in order to utilize the device functions.

Service Adapter

This module is also used by the Service Container component to deal with the adaptation of device functions wrapped as services on mobile devices. Usually services in the cloud require input and output parameters while services on mobile devices sometimes does not require all those parameters because services on mobile devices use device components as input and output. This means the interfaces of services on mobile devices and cloud have to be different even if these services have the same functionality. For instance, the interface of a speech recognition service on a mobile device does not include speech as input while the interface of the same service in Language Grid requires speech. Such different interfaces complicate the developers' task when creating composite services. They have to make two composite services which interfaces are corresponded to different concrete services. It is more convenient for developers if they can write just one composite service and have it bound to many concrete services that have the same functionality. Service Adapter in the framework is the bridge between the developer view and concrete services. Concretely, Service Adapter can handle the following differences.

- The difference in service names (for example, the composite service requires DeviceTextToSpeechService but the concrete service is TextToSpeechService)
- The difference in service input and output parameters (for example, DeviceTextToSpeechService requires only language as input parameter but TextToSpeechService requires both language and speech as input parameters).

Our proposed solution selects the Service Adapter automatically by Service Container when adaptation is needed. Figure 5 shows an example how service adaptation proceeds. A composite service translates some sentences by invoking a translation

Table 2 Interfaces of device functions

Service interface	Input	Output	Function
DeviceSpeechRecognitionService	Language	Text	Receive speech via the microphone and convert to text
DeviceTextToSpeechService	Language Text VoiceType AudioType	N/A	Read a text
DeviceGestureService	Language	Text	Recognize text from hand-writing on screen
DeviceLocationService	N/A	Position	Return current position (latitude, longitude)
DeviceTextService	Language	ListOfSuggestion	Check spelling
DeviceBLEService	N/A	ListOfBeacons	Detect nearby beacons
DeviceCameraService	CaptureRequest	CaptureResult	Capture a single image from the image sensor

service (the service type is TranslationService) and reads aloud the translated text by invoking a text-to-speech service (the service type is DeviceTextToSpeechService, see Table 2). At first, Google Translation Service is invoked as the concrete service of TranslationService. Then, a text-to-speech service on the user's device should be invoked. However, if the system can assign DeviceTextToSpeechService but not TextToSpeechService, the Service Container selects the Service Adapter that adapts latter service type to former service type by complementing its interface. The service names are obviously different. Moreover, the text-to-speech service on Android devices does not need the output parameter (because the speech is passed directly to the speaker) whereas the text-to-speech service in Language Grid requires *speech* as the output parameter. Therefore, Service Adapter has to deal with two differences (the difference in service names and the difference in service input and output parameters). The difference in service name is fixed in the process of returning the actual wrapper by Service Container. Instead of finding service by type, Service Container will find all services and return the compatible service by using the mapping table. The difference in service input and output parameters is fixed by adding more functions corresponding to each service adapter. For example, the adapter for DeviceTextToSpeechService needs a function to read the audio file from the output of TextToSpeechService on the mobile device.

3.5 Case Study: Mobile Shopping Translation System

Let us consider the scenario of a Japanese girl traveling in Vietnam with an American friend. While walking on the street, her smart phone receives notification of a special discount at a Vietnamese restaurant. The notification and further information on her phone are in Japanese while her friend (American) receives the same notification but

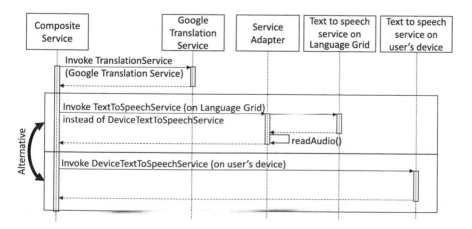

Fig. 5 An example of interface adaptation process for text-to-speech translation service

in English. It is very convenient for them because they do not know Vietnamese and the local people are not good at English or Japanese. It is good for both travelers and the businesses since without the notification and translation, travelers may miss out on a good experience and the restaurant may miss out on potential customers.

The above scenario requires a beacon system to advertise the restaurant's information. The travelers' mobile devices will capture the beacon close to the restaurant. The summary or detailed information of the restaurant is passed to travelers by showing it on their device or speaking it via their headphone in their own language. The beacon only advertises the store's information; the system server will make information associated with existing translation services provided in the cloud available to the user's mobile device. The stores can promote themselves in any language, and language translation is transparent to the customer. The customer can choose the desired language.

The composite service in Mobile Shopping Translation System is a combination of BLE service and speech translation service. BLE service is initially implemented on the mobile devices. The speech translation service is composed of translation service and text-to-speech service. Any provided translation service in the cloud can be selected as the translation service such as Bing translation, Google translation, or Baidu translation. As the text-to-speech service, we can select a service in the cloud (for example, text-to-speech service of language grid) or a service on the mobile device (for example, text-to-speech function on an Android device wrapped as a service). This example application shows the necessity of composing cloud services and mobile services. Without using the proposed language service infrastructure, it is more complicated to combine the BLE function, the text-to-speech function with the translation service in the cloud since the device functions are not available as services which are able to be invoked via language grid. In addition, developers of the composite service have to write two different composite services, one for the text-to-speech function on the device and one for the text-to-speech service in the cloud. Furthermore, if someone else has to develop another application which requires BLE function or text-to-speech function, he or she has to write the complete description of the composite service from scratch. By using the proposed language service infrastructure, BLE function and text-to-speech function are treated as modular services, developers can easily combine them with other services and they need write only one composite service to use both text-to-speech service in the cloud and text-to-speech service on mobile devices. This composite flow is shown in Fig. 6.

4   Related Works

Several language platforms have been proposed to share language resources and thus enable users to access or publish language resources easily. Typical instances include the Language Grid [5], PANACEA [2], Meta-Share [10], and LAPPS Grid [4]. However, these platforms still do not satisfy the requirements of well utilizing language services in the cloud and device functions on mobile devices in an integrated

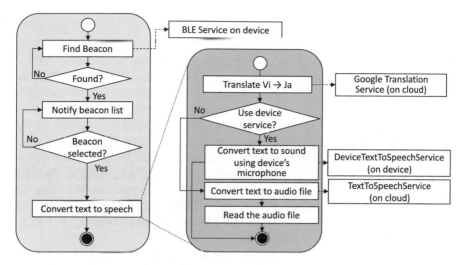

Fig. 6 The composite service of Mobile Shopping Translation System (MSTS)

manner. These platforms provide language resources and language tools. Some of them also provide workflow managers or composition tools. Since all of them are intended as web-service platforms, they cannot allow private users to freely access their resources. Moreover, none of these platforms focus on mobile device functions. The mashup framework introduced in this chapter permits the integrated utilization of services in the cloud and services on mobile devices.

To ensure the compatibility of services, Language Grid [5], Meta-Share [10] define their own standards. The core component of Meta-Share is resourceInfo, which contains all the information relevant for the description of a language resource. The LAPPS Grid [4] is a platform developed using Service Grid which is the server software of Language Grid. It defines a Web Service Exchange Vocabulary and establishes a Web Service Exchange Vocabulary Repository. Each service in the LAPPS Grid publishes metadata describing what it requires for input and what it produces as output. Web Service Exchange Vocabulary specifies a terminology for a core of linguistic objects and features exchanged among natural language processing tools. This means that it not only identifies a standard terminology, but also indicates the relations among them. PANACEA [2] is grounded on the use of existing standards for defining web service input and output formats, i.e. Traveling Objects. It offers converters to reduce most of the input and output format problems. Language Mashup aims at allowing users to ignore the differences between the interfaces of cloud services and mobile device services. Such services may have the same functionality but require different input and output parameters because mobile devices can interact directly with users via their device components such as the microphone or speaker. The Service Adapter module in the mashup framework resolves this issue. Thus, developers do not need to write different composite services for the same functional service on different devices, e.g., mobile device or cloud servers.

5   Conclusion

This chapter introduced Language Mashup, a language service infrastructure for personal use in mobile environments. We started by explaining the framework of the Language Mashup in Sect. 2. It represents a new solution where everyone can solve diversified communication problems in their domain since it provides the following attributes. (i) Language Mashup allows users to instantiate language service servers on the Open Language Grid, where users need accept only a simple open source Terms of Use instead of full legal agreements among providers, users and operators. Since Language Mashup enables users to avoid legal negotiations, usability is significantly improved. (ii) Language Mashup allows users to mashup commercial language services and services registered with the open grid on his/her devices. Since commercial services are often free for private use, users can compose various language services on their mobile devices.

Second, we explained how the architecture of Language Mashup realizes service composition of the language services that are usually located in the cloud platform and the services installed in mobile devices. For our infrastructure, we proposed the Inter-Grid Executor Module and Intra-Grid Executor Module to overcome the differences in communication protocols between cloud services and mobile services; Service Adapter deals with the differences in input and output methods between cloud services and mobile services, while Service Execution Manager deals with the execution of the composite service, especially those that include monitoring services. The proposed infrastructure not only allows users to use existing language resources in the cloud as well as their own language resources on their mobile devices, but also allows users to mashup cloud services and mobile services (services on the devices and device functions wrapped as services). In addition, it allows users to flexibly combine cloud services and/or mobile services in their composite services without implementing many different composite services that have the same functionality. Finally, a case study, Mobile Shopping Translation System, was presented to illustrate our proposed language service infrastructure.

Since some device functions place restriction on threads (for example, some of them need to be invoked in the user interface (UI) thread or non-UI thread) or direct execution (for example, some of them can be executed only from a single client), the framework should be enhanced to deal with this issue in future.

Acknowledgements This research was partially supported by a Grant-in-Aid for Scientific Research (S) (24220002, 2012–2016) and a Grant-in-Aid for Scientific Research (A) (17H00759, 2017–2020) from Japan Society for the Promotion of Science (JSPS).

References

1. Bahl, P., Han, R.Y., Li, L.E., Satyanarayanan, M.: Advancing the state of mobile cloud computing. In: Proceedings of the Third ACM Workshop on Mobile Cloud Computing and Services

(MCS '12), pp. 21–28. ACM, New York (2012)

2. Bel, N.: Platform for automatic, normalized annotation and cost-effective acquisition of language resources for human language technologies. panacea. Procesamiento del Lenguaje Natural **45**, 327–328 (2010)

3. Calzolari, N., Del Gratta, R., Francopoulo, G., Mariani, J., Rubino, F., Russo, I., Soria, C.: The LRE map. harmonising community descriptions of resources. In: LREC, pp. 1084–1089 (2012)

4. Ide, N., Pustejovsky, J., Cieri, C., Nyberg, E., DiPersio, D., Shi, C., Suderman, K., Verhagen, M., Wang, D., Wright, J.: The language application grid. In: International Workshop on Worldwide Language Service Infrastructure, pp. 51–70. Springer, Berlin (2015)

5. Ishida, T.: The Language Grid: Service-Oriented Collective Intelligence for Language Resource Interoperability. Springer Science & Business Media, Berlin (2011)

6. Murakami, Y., Lin, D., Ishida, T.: Service-Oriented Architecture for Interoperability of Multi-language Services, pp. 313–328. Springer, Berlin (2014)

7. Murakami, Y., Tanaka, M., Lin, D., Ishida, T.: Service grid federation architecture for heterogeneous domains. In: 2012 IEEE Ninth International Conference on Services Computing (SCC), pp. 539–546. IEEE, New York (2012)

8. Ngoc, N.C.H., Lin, D., Nakaguchi, T., Ishida, T.: Towards a language service infrastructure for mobile environments. In: LREC, pp. 4472–4478 (2016)

9. Otani, M., Nakaguchi, T., Lin, D., Murakami, Y., Ishida, T.: Language mashup: personal grid for language resources. In: International Workshop on Worldwide Language Service Infrastructure, pp. 99–110. Springer, Berlin (2015)

10. Piperidis, S.: The meta-share language resources sharing infrastructure: Principles, challenges, solutions. In: LREC, pp. 36–42 (2012)

11. Qureshi, S.S., Ahmad, T., Rafique, K., et al.: Mobile cloud computing as future for mobile applications-implementation methods and challenging issues. In: 2011 IEEE International Conference on Cloud Computing and Intelligence Systems (CCIS), pp. 467–471. IEEE, New York (2011)

12. Wang, Y., Chen, I.R., Wang, D.C.: A survey of mobile cloud computing applications: perspectives and challenges. Wirel. Pers. Commun. **80**(4), 1607–1623 (2015)

Part II
Language Service Composition

Language Service Composition Based on Higher Order Functions

Takao Nakaguchi, Yohei Murakami, Donghui Lin and Toru Ishida

Abstract To support multi-language activities, various composite services are created by a service composition that combines existing services or changes the combination of services composed by existing composite services. Multi-language activities have a wide variety of domains and their needs may change with the participants or situations, so service composition must be able to freely create various services to suit the languages of the participants and/or domains of the activity targets. Since existing service composition technologies relies on the deployment process of created composite services toward service infrastructure for users to find and execute them, delay and costs are expensive. To solve this problem, we propose a method that introduces the concept of higher order functions. In concrete, we regard services as functions and pass the functions invoked from composite services as runtime parameters of composite services to compose services without any deployment processes, this yields service composition that can efficiently support multi-language activities. We apply the proposals to Language Grid, designed to gather and provide language services, and evaluate the results. They show that our proposals can create various composite services at runtime with quite practical overheads.

T. Nakaguchi (✉) · D. Lin · T. Ishida
Department of Social Informatics, Kyoto University,
Kyoto 606-8501, Japan
e-mail: ta_nakaguchi@kcg.edu

D. Lin
e-mail: lindh@i.kyoto-u.ac.jp

T. Ishida
e-mail: ishida@i.kyoto-u.ac.jp

T. Nakaguchi
Department of Web Business Technology,
The Kyoto College of Graduate Studies for Informatics, Kyoto, Japan

Y. Murakami
Unit of Design, Kyoto University,
91 Chudoji Awata-cho, Kyoto 600-8815, Japan
e-mail: yohei@i.kyoto-u.ac.jp

© Springer Nature Singapore Pte Ltd. 2018
Y. Murakami et al. (eds.), *Services Computing for Language Resources*,
Cognitive Technologies, https://doi.org/10.1007/978-981-10-7793-7_3

Keywords Service composition · Higher order functions · Aspect oriented
programming

1 Introduction

As the internationalization of society advances, demands for multi-language support
have grown. Nowadays, composite service technology for the language processing
domain is being used to support international activities by easing language barriers. Composite services can be created by combining existing services through the
use of inter-service dependencies among component services in SOA-based service
infrastructures [3]. Services that don't offer such dependencies are called atomic
services.

A service infrastructure itself is a generic system but when used in a specific
domain it becomes specialized for that domain. Taverna [15], one such service infrastructure, has a unique workflow editor that allows web services or functions to be
executed on a local machine in various combinations that are controlled by workflows. HELIO [1] is a specialized version of Taverna for the solar physics domain
while BioVeL Project [2] provides services specific to the biodiversity domain. Natural Language Processing is another of the targets that tends to specialization. Service
Grid Server Software [13] is a service infrastructure that provides web services and
adopts WS-BPEL[1] as its workflow description language and ActiveBPEL[2] as its
workflow execution system. Specialized versions of this software for the language-
processing domain include LAPPS Grid [5] and Language Grid [6].

The language-processing domain can be the one of the most effective specializa-
tions of service infrastructures. While there are many data or processing programs
in this domain, that don't have well-standardized interfaces and are used most often
in isolation. Murakami et al. proposed a domain model and service architecture to
introduce SOA to this domain, which yield the Language Grid [12]. For the Language Grid, 27 key interfaces were standardized and they offer access to 227 atomic
services. To date, 22 composite services have been established. Since services that
are accessed through the same invocation interface can be switched, the number of
composite services that can be based on those services is potentially extremely large.
Unfortunately, complexity explodes if constituent services are nested in a circular
manner. The difficulty of registering and managing all possible composite service
variations statically makes it essential to create a mechanism that can identify the
possible variations dynamically at runtime. Our solution is a description method that
introduces higher-order functions into service composition and so can describe hierarchical service structures; we evaluate it by implementing and applying it to the Language Grid. The remainder of this chapter is organized as follows. Section 2 describes
the problem of composite service variations. In Sect. 3, we propose a hierarchical

---

[1]https://www.oasis-open.org/committees/wsbpel/.
[2]https://sourceforge.net/projects/activebpel502/.

service composition description, and in Sect. 4, we apply it to an existing service execution system. In Sect. 5, we evaluate the efficiency of our proposed method. In Sects. 6 and 7, we mention works related to this chapter to position this study. Finally, we conclude the chapter in Sect. 8.

2 Composite Services and Their Variations

Service composition is a technology that creates composite services by combining existing services. A service wraps data or programs and runs independently [3]. To increase the interoperability of services or to make application development easier, invocation interfaces must be unified. In the Language Grid, *Juman*[3] service and *TreeTagger*[4] service are provided through the *MorphologicalAnalysis* interface. *LifeScienceDict*[5] service and *KyotoTourismDict* service are accessed through the *BilingualDictionary* interface. *JServer*[6] service and *GoogleTranslate*[7] are accessed through the *Translation* interface. Each service runs independently and can be accessed by multiple clients simultaneously.

We turn our attention to composite services. *BackupTrans* can combine several translation services and allows making another service to be invoked as a backup service when a main service fails. *DictTrans* combines a translation service with a bilingual dictionary service. *DictCrossSearch* combines several bilingual dictionaries and provides unified search across all of them.

These services can be constructed as shown in Fig. 1. Double-line rectangle denotes composite services and single-lined denotes atomic services. In the figure, *BackupTrans* service combines *DictTrans* and *GoogleTrans* service. *DictTrans* combines the morphological analysis service *Juman*, a bilingual dictionary service *DictCrossSearch* and a translation service *JServer*, and increases translation quality by using the bilingual dictionary to supply the special words that the translation service is unaware of. Unfortunately, depending on several services constitutes a greater risk than invoking a single service because a service may fail to execute depending on the situation such as high CPU loads or network problems. That is why *BackupTrans* combines a composite translation service and a single *GoogleTranslate* service. *DictCrossSearch* service invokes *LifeScienceDict* service and *KyotoTourismDict* service through the *BilingualDictionary* interface and is accessed through the same interface. This is but one example of the services construction possible. Another user may need to invoke *DictTrans* directly, to use single bilingual dictionary service instead of *DictCrossSearch* or to combine other translation service with *JServer*. Because user needs may change depending on the situation,

---

[3] http://nlp.ist.i.kyoto-u.ac.jp/?JUMAN.
[4] http://www.cis.uni-muenchen.de/~schmid/tools/TreeTagger/
[5] http://lsd-project.jp/ja/index.html.
[6] http://www.kodensha.jp/platform/.
[7] https://cloud.google.com/translate/.

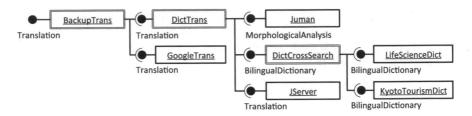

Fig. 1 Example construction of composite services

Fig. 2 Service invocation
graph

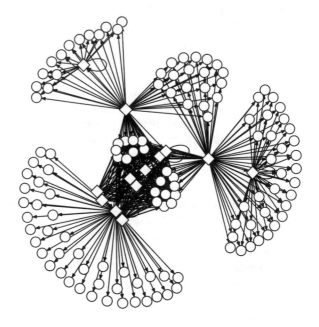

such like the languages used by the participants or the domains targeted by the user, a technology to create composite services must have a wide flexibility and a rapidity to create various combinations of services.

Figure 2 graphs the relationship between composite services and services that can be invoked from these composite services on Language Grid. Diamond nodes denote composite services and circle nodes denote atomic services. Edges denote a relation between services and services that share the same interface. The graph does not show atomic services that are not invoked from composite services. The number of nodes is 138 and the number of edges is 451. As the graph shows, the service-relationships form a complex graph structure. Since variations exist in each combination of edges yielding an explosion in variation number, it is not realistic to register and manage all of them. In this chapter, we focus on the hierarchical structuring of services and propose a method to describe service composition by introducing higher-order functions. In addition, we implement a function that realizes a hierarchical service composition, which is described by the method, as an extension of an existing service composition execution engine.

3 Description Language for Hierarchical Service Composition

A higher-order function receives functions as its parameters or returns functions as its result. Huges showed their importance and examples of usage in detail [4]. By introducing higher-order functions, we can modularize processes and express an entire process as a combination of functions. In this chapter, we regard services as functions and express hierarchical service composition by using higher-order functions.

To invoke services, we must send information about method names and its arguments. Executing a composite service invokes other services. We assume services, which described by proposed method, are atomic services or a variation of composite service consisting of ids of a composite service and services invoked from it. For the latter, we introduce the higher-order function *bind*. *bind* can create a variation of a composite service which can be invoked by another composite service, so *bind* can create hierarchical graph structures. Figure 3 shows the grammar of the description.

description is a root element and expresses hierarchical service composition and its invocation. *service* is *service_id* or *composition* created by *bind* function. *composition* consists of the identifier of a composite service and the list of *invocation*. *invocation* consists of *invocation_id*, which identifies all invocations in composite service, *conds*, which identifies conditions that must be satisfied to invoke the *service*. ?, + and * denote the occurrence zero or one, one or more and zero or more of preceding element. *LETTER* denotes normal characters other than white spaces.

Figure 4 shows an example description of the composition shown in Fig. 1. *bind* is used to specify the variation of *DictCrossSearch* and *BackupTrans* that *DictTrans* will invoke, and also *DictTrans* itself. As shown in Fig. 4, we can express the call graph structure of hierarchical service composition by introducing higher-order functions and invoke it. '清水寺は、京都にある寺院です' (KIYOMIZUDERA-HA, KYOTO-NI-ARU-JIIN-DESU) is a Japanese sentence meaning 'Kiyomizudera is a temple in Kyoto' in English.

```
description :== service "." method "(" args? ")"
service :== service_id | composition
method :== symbol
args :== ("'" symbol "'" ("," "'" symbol "'")* )
composition :== "bind(" service_id invocation+ ")"
invocation :== "," invocation_id ":" ("[" conds "]")? service
conds :== (cond ("," cond)* )
cond :== name ("==" | "<" | "<=" | ">=" | "!=") value
service_id :== symbol
invocation_id :== symbol
name :== symbol
value :== symbol
symbol :== LETTER+
```

Fig. 3 Grammar of hierarchical service composition description

```
bind(DictTrans,
  MorphologicalAnalysis: ['language'='ja'] Mecab,
  MorphologicalAnalysis: ['language'='en'] TreeTagger,
  BilingualDictionary: bind(DictCrossSearch,
    BilingualDictionary1: LifeScienceDict,
    BilingualDictionary2: KyotoTourismDict),
  Translation: bind(BackupTrans,
    MainTranslation: JServer, BackupTranslation: GoogleTrans)
  ).translate('ja','en', '清水寺は、京都にある寺院です。');
```

Fig. 4 Example of hierarchical service composition description

4 Implementation

The target of the implementation of the method proposed in this chapter is Language Grid. As we mentioned before, Language Grid adopts WS-BPEL as its description language of composite services and adopts ActiveBPEL as its composite service execution engine. To implement the proposed method, the following steps are needed: (1) Generate SOAP requests to invoke composite services from the description introduced in the preceding section and (2) to implement functions for determining services that the composite service actually invokes and generating the SOAP requests the composite service will send based on the hierarchical composite service description by extending the source code of ActiveBPEL.

4.1 Building SOAP Request

ActiveBPEL adopts SOAP[8] over HTTP[9] as its service invocation protocol. ActiveBPEL sends SOAP compliant requests to the services that will be executed. A SOAP request consists of *Header* and *Body*. *Header* can have any information while *Body* carries a method name and parameters. Thus, to implement the proposed method, we must generate the URL of services invoked and call graph information inserted into *Head* from the direct child element of the root element specified by the description. Moreover, we must generate information about the method and its parameters from the description that will be inserted into *Body*. Figure 5 shows the SOAP message generated from the description shown in Fig. 4. We omit namespaces and tag attributes for simplification.

Call graph information that will be used when the service is actually executed is generated in JSON[10] format, and added to the *Header* part of the SOAP messages, so that the service execution engine does not need to implement a description parser. *Body* carries a method name and parameters generated from the description. Though

---

[8]http://www.w3.org/TR/soap/.

[9]https://www.ietf.org/rfc/rfc2616.txt.

[10]http://json.org/.

```
<?xml version="1.0" encoding="UTF-8"?>
<Envelope>
<Header>
 <binding>[
  {"invocationId":"MorphologicalAnalysis",
   "conditions":[{"name":"language","op":"==","value":"ja"}],
   "serviceId":"Mecab"},
  {"invocationId":"MorphologicalAnalysis",
   "conditions":[{"name":"language","op":"==","value":"en"}],
   "serviceId":"TreeTagger"},
  {"invocationId":"BilingualDictionary",
   "serviceId":"DictCrossSearch", "children": [
    {"invocationId":"BilingualDictionary1", "serviceId":"LifeScienceDict"},
    {"invocationId":"BilingualDictionary2", "serviceId":"KyotoTourismDict"}
   ]},
  {"invocationId":"Translation",
   "serviceId":"BackupTrans", "children":[
    {"invocationId":"MainTranslation", "serviceId":"JServer"},
    {"invocationId":"BackupTranslation","serviceId":"GoogleTrans"}
   ]}]</binding>
</Header>
<Body>
 <translate>
  <sourceLang>ja</sourceLang>
  <targetLang>en</targetLang>
  <source>清水寺は、京都にある寺院です。</source>
 </translate>
</Body>
</Envelope>
```

Fig. 5 Example of SOAP message

parameter names and the URL of service are not shown in Fig. 4, they can be extracted from the information of service definition information (WSDL[11]) of the service. Invoking the search API of Language Grid, returns the WSDL of services.

4.2 Intercepting and Replacing Service Invocation

Next, we consider extending the service invocation process in the composite service execution engine. To realize the proposed method, the extension of composite service execution engine must extract information from the call graph, shown in the *Head* part in Fig. 5, sent by the client and use said information to trigger the service invoked. If the client ascribes a sub call graph to the invoked service, we have to insert a sub call graph into the request sent to the service. For example, in executing the *Dict-Trans* composite service based on the description shown in Fig. 4, the engine must switch the service to *DictCrossSearch* service and insert a sub call graph that specifies *BilingualDictionary1* and *BilingualDictionary2* into the SOAP request when the invocation identified by *BilingualDictionary* is executed. The service identifiers

---

[11] https://www.w3.org/TR/wsdl.html.

inside a composite service correspond to a partner link name inside the corresponding BPEL description.

To implement the proposed method, we could extend ActiveBPEL to reduce the cost. Direct modification of the source code of ActiveBPEL directly complicates subsequent source code revisions. Worse, when the source code is modified by version up, we must confirm the consistency of modification before fixing the change. For that reason, we use Aspect Oriented Programming (AOP) [8] to extend ActiveBPEL. By using AOP, we can isolate the extension codes from the original software. In implementing our proposed method, we used AspectJ [7] to apply AOP and inserted our extension codes into ActiveBPEL. ActiveBPEL receives the execution request for the composite service, then executes the composite service by executing the activities written in BPEL and returning the result. Because the call graph information inserted into the execution request and the extending service invocation based on that information are needed in order to realize our method, we extend the processes of *Receive* activity and *Invoke* activity. Figure 6 shows the class diagram that denotes classes related to this extension.

The package *org.activebpel.*** denotes all packages and classes under the package *org.activebpel* that represent modules associated with ActiveBPEL. *ActiveBPEL-Aspect* and *AspectBase* are the aspect and the base class that we implemented. The package *org.apache.axis.***, *java.*** and *javax.xml.soap.*** denote a third party library and Java standard libraries. Pointcuts in *ActiveBPELAspect* catch the executions of methods in ActiveBPEL that are needed to modify behavior of composite services and use methods in *AspectBase* to switch services as specified in the description. As shown in Fig. 6, the ActiveBPEL dependency is enclosed in *ActiveBPELAspect*, so *AspectBase* is independent from it.

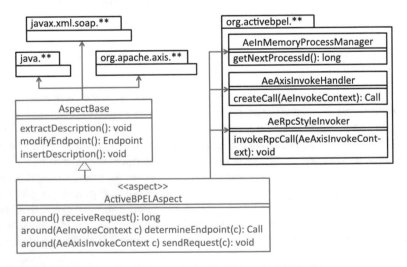

Fig. 6 A module structure of extension and related classes of ActiveBPEL

5 Evaluation

We evaluate the proposed method by applying it to the Language Grid. In more detail, we estimate the number of composite services that our method can realize by calculating the number of all variations of composite services using real services registered on the Language Grid and measure the execution overhead of our implementation by comparing the execution time of composite services with and without our method.

5.1 Number of Service Composition that Can Be Realized

The purpose of the proposed method is to realize various service compositions at runtime without deployment process to service execution engine. We measure the actual number of service compositions as the measure used to rate of the effectiveness of our proposed method. It is calculated as the product of the number of services conforming to the service invocation interfaces specified in a composite service. The services can be atomic services or composite services. Though the service invocations can be executed as long as the interface and the network protocol of the services match the specification of the service invocations, they could fail. To successfully complete the invocations, we should consider domain-specific constraints. In the case of the Language Grid, the constraints are that invoked services must support the languages specified as parameters from their invokers (composite services or client programs). For example, the *DictTrans* composite service invokes services conforming to *MorphologicalAnalysis* interface, *BilingualDictionary* interface and *Translation* interfaces, respectively. To invoke the *DictTrans*, the client sends the source language and target language as part of parameters. Then, the *DictTrans* passes the source language to the *MorphologicalAnalysis* service, and a pair of source language and target language to the *BilingualDictionary* service and the *Translation* service. These services must support the language(s) passed as parameters. We can determine whether a service supports certain language(s) or not by invoking the search API of the Language Grid. We count only those variations that have services that satisfy this constraint.

Further, because composite services can be nested like a layer and a composite service can be used in different layers, it is impossible to calculate the number in a simple brute-force manner. Therefore, we calculate the variations in each layer step-by-step. In the first calculation stage, we calculate the number of variations of all composite services from just the atomic services assigned to invocations and create variations of composite services. In the stages after the first stage, we calculate the number of variations according to atomic services and the variations created in the previous stage. In this way, we can calculate the summation of the variations at the calculation stage s: $ALLV_s$ by using the following formula. The number of first calculation stage is 1.

$$ALLV_s = \sum_{k=1}^{n} v(k, s)$$

n is the number of all services. $v(k, s)$ is the number of the variations of service k at stage s and can be calculated by the following formula.

$$v(k, s) = \begin{cases} 0, & s = 0 \text{ or service } k \text{ is ATOMIC} \\ \prod_{l=1}^{m_k} vi(k, l, s), & s \geq 1 \end{cases}$$

$v(k, s)$ becomes 0 when s is 0 or the service k is an atomic service, otherwise it becomes the product of $vi(k, l, s)$, which is the number of services that can be assigned to each service invocation l of the composite service k. m_k is the number of invocations of service k. Though the first calculation stage is 1, we define the number of variations at the stage 0 as 0 because $vi(k, l, s)$, described below, refers previous stage. $vi(k, l, s)$ can be calculated by the following formula.

$$vi(k, l, s) = \sum_{j=1}^{n} \begin{cases} 0, & \text{service } j \text{ does not satisfy } C_{kl} \\ 1, & \text{service } j \text{ is ATOMIC} \\ v(j, s - 1), & \text{service } j \text{ is COMPOSITE} \end{cases}$$

The calculation of $vi(k, l, s)$ considers only the those services that satisfy condition C_{kl}, which is that service j must conform to the interface of service invocation l and service j must support the language(s) passed from the composite service k. When the service j satisfies the condition and is an atomic service, $vi(k, l, s)$ is incremented by 1. If service j satisfies the condition and is a composite service, $vi(k, l, s)$ is incremented by the number of variations of service j at the former stage $s - 1$. At the calculation stage 1, $vi(k, l, s)$ becomes the number of atomic services that satisfy the condition C_{kl} because $s - 1$ is 0 so $v(j, s - 1)$ becomes 0.

Using the above formulas, we calculated the number of variations of composite services registered to the Language Grid that can translate Japanese (ja) to English (en). The number of atomic services that translate from ja to en is 65, the largest number of translation services among all the supported language pairs. Table 1 shows the results.

As shown in Table 1, the number of variations slightly increases with the stage number, and can easily explode when composite services are nested. We calculated the number of variations up to the 5th stage. In the Language Grid, 5-times nested service composition is practical as in nesting *BackTranslation* service which combines two *Translation* services to translate a translation result into source language, *BestTranslationSelection* service which combines several *Translation* services and *SimilarityCalculation* services to select a translation service whose result can be back-translated to yield a result most similar to the source text, *TranslationWith-Backup* service which combines two or more *Translation* services to realize a fallback function for translation, *DictTrans* service, and *DictCrossSearch* service. The vari-

Table 1 Calculation result

Calculation stage	ja → en
1	4.09×10^6
2	1.14×10^{33}
3	1.89×10^{165}
4	2.44×10^{826}
5	8.64×10^{4131}

ations of 5-times nested services which translate from ja to en were 8.64×10^{4131}. To deploy and use these variations, we must register and manage them in the service infrastructure. However, we can realize these compositions without paying this cost by using the proposed hierarchical service binding technique.

5.2 Execution Overhead

The proposed method is an extension to the existing workflow execution engines. It analyzes the *Head* part of SOAP request sent to a composite service, adds service binding information to the SOAP request from the composite service to component services, and modifies target URL of the SOAP request. These modifications might increase the execution time of composite services. However, each modification is not complex, and so overhead is insignificant. To confirm this, we prepare two configurations of ActiveBPEL, one is the existing system and the other is the system with our method. We use the same atomic services to execute a variation of *DictTrans* service which uses *DictCrossSearch* service in the both configurations, and compare the results. The call graph that is inserted into the SOAP request in the latter configuration is the same as that shown in Fig. 4. Figure 7 shows the sequence diagram of the composition we use for the evaluation. At each method invocation, a SOAP request is sent to target component. *Client* ran on a local machine and measured execution time, *DictTrans* and *DictCrossSearch* ran on ActiveBPEL in Language Grid and remaining services ran on a Language Grid server.

We extracted texts from two pages of Japanese Wikipedia, and translated them from Japanese to English using the both configurations of ActiveBPEL. One is the page for Kiyomizu Temple[12] and the other is the page for Life Science.[13] Twelve lines (A-L) were extracted from Kiyomizu Temple text and 7 (M-S) from Life Science. We translated each sentence 100 times. Figure 8 shows the result of execution. The left axis denotes the average execution time of 100 translations run for each sentence (A-S), while the right axis denotes the number of characters in each sentence. The filled and hollow rectangles denote the execution time by the existing method and the proposed method, respectively. The triangles denote the number of characters in

---

[12]https://ja.wikipedia.org/wiki/%E6%B8%85%E6%B0%B4%E5%AF%BA.
[13]https://ja.wikipedia.org/wiki/%E7%94%9F%E5%91%BD%E7%A7%91%E5%AD%A6.

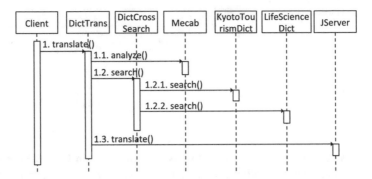

Fig. 7 Call sequence

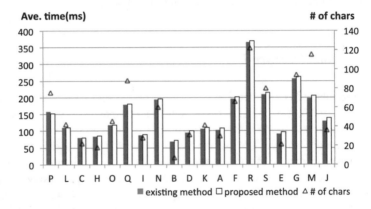

Fig. 8 Execution time (sorted by ascending order of overhead)

each sentence. These execution results are sorted in ascending order of the difference in execution time between the existing method and the proposed method. Although the execution time varies among invocations, which is caused by network delay and the different sentences length, the differences in execution times were small for all sentences and the average of the overhead is 2.12%. Thus the overhead penalty of the proposed method is limited.

6   Related Work

In this research, we use higher-order functions to express service composition consisting of hierarchical service combinations. The proposed method can be regarded as a novel service composition method, where a new composite service is executed by changing the call-relationship of existing composite services based on a given description. Moreover, the proposed method can be considered as a service reuse method since it does not produce new services, and simply uses existing atomic or composite services.

Some previous studies focused on automatic service composition methods. In the service composition methods that extend Golog [11] and McDermott [10], a user can describe his/her requirements in original languages (extended Golog language for former and extended PDDL for latter) and the service composition will be executed by selecting the appropriate services based on the description. However, when a user wants to conduct hierarchical service composition where other composite services are bound as a part of the overall composite service, these methods demand that concrete variations of composite services must be registered beforehand. In contrast, our method supports the description of hierarchical service composition without registering concrete composite service variations. Therefore, a user can invoke significantly many service composition variations without registering them beforehand and thus avoid paying the costs of managing them. QoS-based service selection [9] is one way to select services used in composite services; it involves the calculation of qualities of services that users prefer. The need of the user may change depends on the situation such as the domain of use or languages of other participants. The method proposed herein allows language service users to realize own service composition at runtime by calculating QoS and selecting services based on the results by using such selection technologies in combination.

The effort needed to improve the reusability of service composition has also been reported in some previous studies. For example, Fragmento [14] focuses on the reuse of process descriptions by extracting and sharing fragments of process descriptions that realize certain functions so that users can reuse them by searching a repository. In order to deploy composite services that use process fragments, the user must include the fragment of process description and related definitions such as WSDLs or XML Schemas into the services. If the fragment has some bugs, user must redo inclusion and deployment for all services that use the fragment. Our method uses existing composite services themselves as the unit of reuse and no modification is needed it, so we can receive the benefit of bug fix or other improvements of services without any additional works.

7 Discussion

As the proposed method provides for hierarchical service composition descriptions at runtime, we can now execute various variations of composite services without deploying new composite services. Moreover, developers can improve the reusability of composite services by providing fine granularity services that focus on simple problems. For example, developers can design the fallback function as a composite service that invokes alternate services when the main service fails where the invocation interface is the same for the main service and for the alternate services. When the invocation of the main service fails, this fallback composite service invokes alternate services until it succeeds or no more alternate service exists, and returns the result of successful invocation or error when no services succeed. Users can use this composite service by specifying a service with high quality and low availability to be the main service and services with relatively low quality and high availability to be the alternate services. Furthermore, as more services are created that offer fine granularity and high reusability, the more variations created by the combinations of these fine granularity services can be generated, and then other service composition methods, such like automated service composition, can become more robust.

Moreover, we can easily customize the service composition based on user requirements. Because services run independently from each other and provide certain functions to all users equally, it is difficult to change the behavior of existing services based on the requirements of each user or propagate information across services that is used in just one service composition. By using the proposed method, service composition can be customized flexibly by changing its construction based on the hierarchical description from different users. Since the customization of service composition is realized for each execution request, it does not affect the execution of requests from other users.

8   Conclusion

To well support the changing situations in which multi-language activities are used, service infrastructure must create various new services quickly by aggregating various services based on standardized invocation interfaces of them. In this chapter, we proposed a hierarchical service composition description and applied it to a real service infrastructure to dealt with this issue. The main contributions of this chapter are:

1. Propose a hierarchical service composition description by introducing higher-order functions.
2. Implement it by extending an existing service infrastructure.

For hierarchical service composition description, we introduced the *bind* function which can assign an atomic service or a variation of composite services to the service invocation in a composite service. This allows us to create service composition variations at runtime. For implementing the proposed method, we introduced AOP for modularizing codes by extending existing service infrastructures so as to reduce the dependency between workflow execution engine and our implementation. This extension enables composite service execution to recognize the hierarchical service composition description and transport the description as a part of the service invocation message.

Moreover, we applied the proposed method to an existing service infrastructure: the Language Grid, which is agglomeration of language resources and services, and evaluated the effect of the number of variations our method can realize under domain dependent constraints. We further evaluated the overhead of our method in terms of execution time. The results showed that various service compositions can be realized at runtime and the overhead of our method does not exceed 2.12%.

Acknowledgements This research was supported by a Grant-in-Aid for Scientific Research (S) (24220002, 2012–2016) and a Grant-in-Aid for Young Scientists (A) (17H04706, 2017–2020) from Japan Society for the Promotion of Science (JSPS). Most of this work was done while the first author was a researcher at Department of Social Informatics, Kyoto University.

References

1. Bentley, R., Csillaghy, A., Aboudarham, J., Jacquey, C., Hapgood, M., Bocchialini, K., Messerotti, M., Brooke, J., Gallagher, P., Fox, P., Hurlburt, N., Roberts, D., Duarte, L.S.: Helio: the heliophysics integrated observatory. Adv. Space Res. **47**, 2235–2239 (2011)
2. Donvito, G., Vicario, S., Notarangelo, P., Balec, B.: The Biovel Project: robust phylogenetic workflows running on the grid. In: EGICF12-EMITC2, pp. 26–30 (2012)
3. Erl, T.: Service-Oriented Architecture: Concepts, Technology, and Design. Pearson Education India, Delhi (2005)
4. Hughes, J.: Why functional programming matters. Comput. J. **32**(2), 98–107 (1989)
5. Ide, N., Pustejovsky, J., Cieri, C., Nyberg, E., Wang, D., Suderman, K., Verhagen, M., Wright, J.: The language application grid. In: Chair, N.C.C., Choukri, K., Declerck, T., Loftsson, H., Maegaard, B., Mariani, J., Moreno, A., Odijk, J., Piperidis, S. (eds.) Proceedings of the Ninth International Conference on Language Resources and Evaluation (LREC'14), pp. 22–30. European Language Resources Association (ELRA), Reykjavik, Iceland (2014)
6. Ishida, T. (ed.): The Language Grid: Service-Oriented Collective Intelligence for Language Resource Interoperability. Springer Science & Business Media, Berlin (2011)
7. Kiczales, G., Hilsdale, E., Hugunin, J., Kersten, M., Palm, J., Griswold, W.G.: An overview of Aspectj. In: European Conference on Object-Oriented Programming, pp. 327–354. Springer, Berlin (2001)
8. Kiczales, G., Lamping, J., Mendhekar, A., Maeda, C., Lopes, C., Loingtier, J.M., Irwin, J.: Aspect-oriented programming. In: European Conference on Object-Oriented Programming, pp. 220–242. Springer, Berlin (1997)
9. Lin, D., Shi, C., Ishida, T.: Dynamic service selection based on context-aware QoS. In: 2012 IEEE Ninth International Conference on Services Computing, pp. 641–648 (2012)
10. McDermott, D.: Estimated-regression planning for interactions with web services. In: Proceedings of the Sixth International Conference on Artificial Intelligence Planning Systems, pp. 204–211 (2002)
11. McIlraith, S., Son, T.C.: Adapting golog for composition of semantic web services. In: Proceedings of the 8th International Conference on Knowledge Representation and Reasoning, pp. 482–493 (2002)
12. Murakami, Y., Lin, D., Ishida, T.: Service-oriented architecture for interoperability of multilanguage services. In: Buitelaar, P., Cimiano, P. (eds.) Towards the Multilingual Semantic Web, pp. 313–328. Springer, Berlin (2014)
13. Murakami, Y., Lin, D., Tanaka, M., Nakaguchi, T., Ishida, T.: Service grid architecture. In: Ishida, T. (ed.) The Language Grid: Service-Oriented Collective Intelligence for Language Resource Interoperability, pp. 19–34. Springer, Berlin (2011)

14. Schumm, D., Dentsas, D., Hahn, M., Karastoyanova, D., Leymann, F., Sonntag, M.: Web service composition reuse through shared process fragment libraries. In: International Conference on Web Engineering, pp. 498–501. Springer, Berlin (2012)
15. Wolstencroft, K., Haines, R., Fellows, D., Williams, A., Withers, D., Owen, S., Soiland-Reyes, S., Dunlop, I., Nenadic, A., Fisher, P., Bhagat, J., Belhajjame, K., Bacall, F., Hardisty, A., Nieva de la Hidalga, A., Balcazar Vargas, M.P., Sufi, S., Goble, C.: The Taverna workflow suite: designing and executing workflows of web services on the desktop, web or in the cloud. Nucleic Acids Res. **41**(W1), W557–W561 (2013)

Policy-Aware Language Service Composition

Trang Mai Xuan, Yohei Murakami and Toru Ishida

Abstract Many language resources are being shared as web services to process data on the Internet. As dataset size keeps growing, language services are experiencing more big data problems, such as the storage and processing overheads caused by the huge amounts of multilingual texts. Parallel execution and cloud technologies are the keys to making service invocation practical. In the Service-Oriented Architecture approach, service providers typically employ policies to limit parallel execution of the services based on arbitrary decisions. In order to attain optimal performance, users need to adapt to the services policies. A composite service is a combination of several atomic services provided by various providers. To use parallel execution for greater composite service efficiency, the degree of parallelism (DOP) of the composite services need to be optimized by considering the policies of all atomic services. We propose a model that embeds service policies into formulae and permits composite service performance to be calculated. From the calculation results, we can predict the optimal DOP for the composite service that allows the best performance to be attained. Extensive experiments are conducted on real-world translation services. The analysis results show that our proposed model has good prediction accuracy in identifying optimal DOPs for composite services.

Keywords Parallel execution policy · Performance prediction · Degree of parallelism

T. Mai Xuan (✉) · T. Ishida
Department of Social Informatics, Kyoto University,
Kyoto 606-8501, Japan
e-mail: trangmx@ai.soc.i.kyoto-u.ac.jp

T. Ishida
e-mail: ishida@i.kyoto-u.ac.jp

Y. Murakami
Unit of Design, Kyoto University, 91 Chudoji Awata-cho,
Kyoto 600-8815, Japan
e-mail: yohei@i.kyoto-u.ac.jp

© Springer Nature Singapore Pte Ltd. 2018
Y. Murakami et al. (eds.), *Services Computing for Language Resources*,
Cognitive Technologies, https://doi.org/10.1007/978-981-10-7793-7_4

1   Introduction

The Service-oriented architecture (SOA) is a widely accepted and engaged paradigm for the realization of business processes that incorporate several distributed, loosely coupled partners. It allows users to combine existing services to define composite services that meet users' requirements. With the increasing volume of data on the Internet, the services need to deal with extremely large-scale datasets and thus the emergence of data-intensive services. As in natural language processing area, many language resources (e.g. machine translator, morphological analysis, etc.) have been provided as language services. Some problems in language processing such as translation of a large document often require long processing times. This type of data-intensive service requires parallel execution to improve performance.

Using the cloud environment to host web services offers numerous benefits. With cloud-based infrastructures, service providers are able to provide scalability for their services through parallel execution. However, there are several factors that potentially limit the efficiency of parallel execution such as serial fractions in a task as pointed out in Amdahl's law [1], and parallel overhead [2]. These factors consider the limitation of the program or computing resources from the viewpoint of service providers. Providers can control the limitation to enhance parallel execution efficiency.

In SOA, however, from the perspective of service users, the service providers' policies on parallel execution are an important factor that impacts the parallel execution efficiency. Service users cannot change the policies as they want when invoking the services. Since service providers have different preferences, their policies may also be different. For instance, only if a provider is rich in computing resources may he readily allow large numbers of concurrent requests. Service providers may have different policies that will trigger a degradation in service performance; e.g. the number of concurrent requests exceeds the limit set by the service provider. Therefore, when invoking a service with parallel execution, users should consider the service policy in order to attain the optimal performance improvement.

Composing and optimizing a composite service, or a workflow of atomic services, has gained increasing attention in SOA. Technologies such as data-intensive and many-task computing [3], and scientific workflows [4] have the potential to enable rapid data analysis. Many studies have proposed parallel and pipelined execution technique to speedup workflows [5], as well as adaptive parallel execution approach for workflows in cloud environments regarding the availability of resources [6]. Most of the approaches proposed to date do not consider the policies of the atomic services in optimizing the composite services. Different from current approaches, this chapter focuses on optimizing the Degree of Parallelism (DOP) of a composite service by considering the service policies of all participating providers. To tackle this problem, this chapter proposes a model that embeds parallel execution policies of atomic services into formulae to calculate composite service performance under parallel execution. To this end, we set the following goals:

- *Parallel execution policy model*: We propose a model to capture the policies of atomic services observed when using parallel execution. The model makes it easy to embed service policies into the calculation of composite service performance.
- *Predict optimal parallel execution of composite services*: We define formulae to calculate performance of a composite service with different structures. From the calculation, we predict the optimal DOP for the composite service.
- *Validate the model*: We validate our model by evaluating the accuracy of our model when predicting the optimal DOP of composite services. Extensive experiments are made on the real-world language services.

The remainder of the chapter is organized as follows. Section 2 presents a motivating example. Section 3 describes parallel execution model of atomic and composite services. The prediction model is proposed in Sect. 4. We evaluate our model in Sect. 5. We show some related work in Sect. 6. Finally, Sect. 7 concludes the chapter.

2 Motivating Example

The Language Grid is a service oriented infrastructure for sharing and combining language services [7, 8]. Service providers can share their tools (e.g. translator, dictionary, etc.) as atomic web services on this platform. Different providers are permitted to set different policies to maintain the QoS of their provided services. To build complex applications, users can combine different exiting atomic services to define new composite services that meet their requirements. For composite services dealing with large-scale data, using parallel execution can reduce the execution time. However, to raise the efficiency of parallel execution, we need to consider the different policies, especially parallel execution policies, of different atomic services when configuring the composite services.

To illustrate our approach, we show the parallel execution of a composite service in Fig. 1. This simple workflow shows a two-hop translation service consisting of two different translation services: the first service translates a document from Japanese to English, and then the second service translates the result from English to Vietnamese. The abstract atomic services in the composite service can be bound to different concrete translation services provided by different providers such as Google translation service, Bing translator, J-Server, and Baidu translation service. To reduce execution time, the client invokes the composite service with concurrent execution. The input data is split into independent portions, and several portions are processed in parallel. If the client sets the DOP of the composite service to n, each translation service in the composite service is executed concurrently as n processes.

Now, let us consider a scenario where the first and second atomic services are bound to J-Server translation service and Google translation service, respectively. J-Server and Google set different parallel execution policies for their translation services. Google limits the number of concurrent requests sent to its translation service from a registered user to 8. If more than 8 concurrent requests are received, the

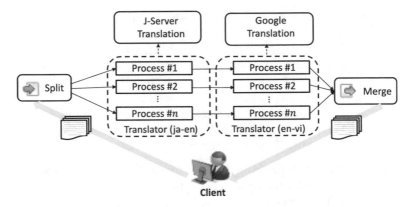

Fig. 1 Parallel execution of a composite service

performance becomes worse. J-Server limits its translation service to 16 concurrent requests per user, if more than 16 requests are sent to the service, the performance does not improve. In this scenario, when configuring parallel execution of the composite service we need to specify a suitable DOP of the composite service. This configuration should match the policies of all atomic services in order to optimize the composite service's performance. Several questions to be asked here are (1) How can we model parallel execution policies of web services? and (2) How the performance of a composite service can be predicted from the atomic services' policies? These issues are addressed in the next sections.

3   Parallel Execution Policy Model

In this section we propose a model to capture parallel execution policies of services based on our observation of executing different atomic services.

3.1   Parallel Execution of a Language Service

Language services are designed to process huge datasets. These services can benefit from the use of parallel execution to improve performance. We use *Data Parallelism* to set the parallel invocation of a language service as follows. Assume that a client wants to process a large dataset. At the client-side, the input data is split in to M partitions and n threads of the client are created to send n partitions to the service in parallel as shown in Fig. 2. At server-side the service needs to serve n requests in parallel. Execution time required for processing the input data depends on the number of concurrent requests, denoted by $f(n)$.

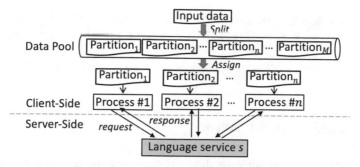

Fig. 2 Parallel execution of a language service

We use *Speedup* as a measure of the reduction in execution time taken to execute a fixed workload when increasing number of concurrent threads. Speedup is calculated by the following equation: $S(n) = f(1)/f(n)$, where $f(1)$ is the execution time required to perform the work with a single thread and $f(n)$ is the time required to perform the same task with n concurrent threads.

Several models have been proposed to describe those speedup curves for parallel algorithms and architectures [9]. The most cited model is Amdahl's law [1], which models the effect of the serial fraction of the task (F) to the speedup of the task. F is the fraction of the task's computation (algorithm) that is serial and cannot be parallelized. F ranges from 0 to 1 depending on algorithm of the task.

Amdahl's Law, however, does not include parameters that account for the impact of a service's policy on the execution speed. SOA allows service providers to make arbitrary decisions in setting policies to control parallel execution of their services. These policies limit the performance speedup achievable with their services. In some cases, if number of concurrent processes exceeds a certain number, service performance may actually be throttled. Figure 3 shows speed enhancements possible with an atomic service with the parallel execution under different conditions. The dashed line shows an ideal case of the service performance speedup $(F = 0)$. The dotted and

Fig. 3 Parallel execution speedup of a task

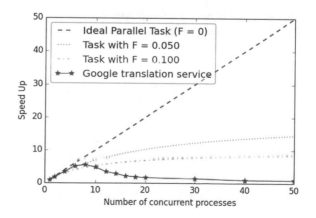

dash-dot lines show the performance speedup of the service follow the Amdahl's law with serial faction (F) values of 0.05 and 0.1, respectively. The solid line shows a real case of Google translation service. With this policy, when the number of concurrent processes exceeds 8, service user experiences a drop in the service performance.

3.2   Parallel Execution Policies

Our assumption is, for each service there exists a certain number of concurrent processes specified by the service provider, beyond which the performance improvement trend is changed. We defined our policy model [10] as following:

Definition (*Parallel Execution Policy*) The parallel execution policy of a web service is defined by the change of the performance improvement trend of the service under parallel execution. This performance improvement trend is determined by the tuple of parameters (α, $\alpha^\star$, α', P), each parameter is defined as follows:

- Suppose that the service processes M data partitions using parallel execution. Execution time of the service depends on number of concurrent processes (n) of the service, denoted by $f(n)$.
- α is execution time of the service when the M partitions are serially executed, i.e., $n = 1$: $f(1) = \alpha$.
- P is the upper bound of concurrent processes specified by the service provider, beyond which the performance improvement trend changes.
- $\alpha^\star$ is time taken by the service to process M partitions with P concurrent processes: $f(P) = \alpha^\star$.
- α' is time taken by the service to process M partitions with N ($P < N \leq M$) concurrent processes: $f(N) = \alpha'$.

Parallel execution policies of language services normally are not explicitly described by the service providers. We tested and observed parallel execution effect of many services registered on the Language Grid [8], and many other external services such as Google translation service, Baidu translation service, Amazon S3 service, etc. We found there were three main patterns in the performance improvement. We described these patterns by using the above parameters and define three types of parallel execution policy as follows: *Slow-down policy*, *restriction policy*, and *penalty policy*.

Slow-down Policy.   This policy reduces the performance improvement when the number of concurrent processes exceeds specified number (P_s). This means that execution time of the service decreases as the number concurrent processes increases. When number of concurrent processes exceeds P_s the execution time decreases but at a lower rate. This policy may due to the parallel execution limitation of the services' implementation. The performance pattern, given by this policy, is depicted in Fig. 4a. The execution time of the service to process M partitions can be calculated by the following equation:

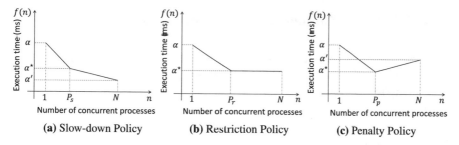

Fig. 4 Performance patterns of parallel execution policies

$$f(n) = \begin{cases} \alpha - \frac{\alpha - \alpha^\star}{P_s - 1}(n - 1), & \text{if } 1 \leq n < P_s \\ \alpha^\star - \frac{\alpha^\star - \alpha'}{N - P_s}(n - P_s), & \text{if } P_s \leq n \leq N \end{cases}$$

$$\text{with: } \alpha > \alpha^\star > \alpha', \text{ and } \frac{\alpha - \alpha^\star}{P_s - 1} > \frac{\alpha^\star - \alpha'}{N - P_s}$$

Restriction Policy. With this policy, service providers limit the maximum number of concurrent requests to their service. Service performance shows no improvement when the number of concurrent processes exceeds specified number (P_r). This may due to limitation of the service providers' computing resources. This policy creates the service performance pattern shown in Fig. 4b. Execution time of the service to process M partitions can be calculated by the following equation:

$$f(n) = \begin{cases} \alpha - \frac{\alpha - \alpha^\star}{P_r - 1}(n - 1), & \text{if } 1 \leq n < P_r \\ \alpha^\star = \alpha', & \text{if } P_r \leq n \leq N \end{cases}$$

$$\text{with: } \alpha^\star < \alpha, \text{ and } \alpha' = \alpha^\star$$

Penalty Policy. In some cases, due to some commercial strategies or security concerns, the service provider may penalize concurrent requests if the number of them exceeds specified number (P_p), service performance is actually reduced. The performance pattern of this policy is shown in Fig. 4c. The execution time of the service is calculated by the following equation:

$$f(n) = \begin{cases} \alpha - \frac{\alpha - \alpha^\star}{P_p - 1}(n - 1), & \text{if } 1 \leq n < P_p \\ \alpha^\star + \frac{\alpha' - \alpha^\star}{N - P_p}(n - P_p), & \text{if } P_p \leq n \leq N \end{cases}$$

$$\text{with: } \alpha > \alpha^\star, \text{ and } \alpha' > \alpha^\star$$

For simplicity, this work assumes each service provider uses a static value of P. Since, the value of P is normally not explicit stated, in order to choose P we invoke the service with different parallel execution configuration using a test data set. We analyze execution time, and determine P.

4   Prediction of Composite Service Performance

In this section we propose a model that can predict composite service performance when using parallel execution. The prediction changes with the workflow structures of the composite services.

4.1   Parallel Execution of Composite Language Service

To build an advanced language application, developers combine several atomic language services in a workflow. A service described by a workflow is called *composite service*. In order to improve the composite service performance when processing huge amounts of data, a promising approach is to use parallel execution. In this work, we focus on two parallelism techniques described as following: data parallelism and workflow pipeline execution.

Data parallelism. Similar to Data Parallelism in atomic service, when a composite service processes huge amount of data sets, the data sets are split into independent portions, and several computing tasks of the composite service are instantiated to process several portions in parallel.

Workflow pipeline execution. When a single workflow is operated in parallel on many data partitions, *Workflow pipeline execution* denotes that the processing of several independent partitions by several instances of an atomic service are independent. This parallelism enables pipeline processing of a workflow. That is, when n concurrent requests are sent to a composite service, multiple instances of each atomic service are created and processed in parallel. A pooling technique is used such that when processing M data sets, n out of M data sets are streamed to the composite service in parallel without waiting for responses. The execution of the composite service is done in pipeline manner. Consider an example of a sequential composition of two services. This example yields the pipeline processing time-line shown in Fig. 5, where $L = \lceil M/n \rceil$ is number of time-steps needed to send M data sets. At the beginning of time period, n data set are sent in parallel. t_{ij}^{n} is the time that n concurrent processes of service s_i take to finish processing n data sets at time step j.

Fig. 5 Pipeline processing time-line of a composite service

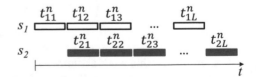

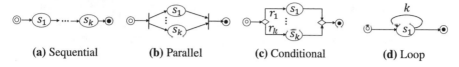

(a) Sequential   (b) Parallel   (c) Conditional   (d) Loop

Fig. 6 Four types of composite structures [11]

4.2 Prediction Model

A composite service can be seen as a set of atomic services that cooperate to execute
a process that defines the interaction workflow. There are four basic composite structure: *Sequential, Parallel, Conditional* and *Loop*, see Fig. 6, where circles represent
atomic services and arrows represent the transfer of data between services. QoS of a
composite service is aggregate QoS of all atomic services. Existing QoS calculation
methods can be classified into two categories: Reduction method with single QoS
for service composition [11], and direct aggregation method with multiple QoSs for
the service composition [12]. We adapt the formulae proposed in [11] to calculate
execution time of composite services in different structures under parallel execution.

4.2.1 Prediction of Sequential Structure

Consider a *Sequential* combination of two services s_1 and s_2. These two services
have different parallel execution policies as specified in Sect. 3. $f_1(n)$ and $f_2(n)$
are predicted execution time of s_1 and s_2 when processing M partitions, respectively.
Assume that $f_1(n) > f_2(n)$, processing time-line of the composite service is depicted
in Fig. 7a. From this time-line, we can easily see that execution time of the composite
service ($f_c(n)$) is calculated as follows:

$$f_c(n) = f_1(n) + t_{2L}^n \tag{1}$$

t_{2L}^n is the time taken by service s_2 to finish processing last n partitions in parallel.
Given that the execution time of s_2 to process each partition is approximate equal:

$$t_{2L}^n \approx f_2(n)/\lceil M/n \rceil \tag{2}$$

From Eqs. (1) and (2) we have:

$$f_c(n) \approx f_1(n) + f_2(n)/\lceil M/n \rceil \tag{3}$$

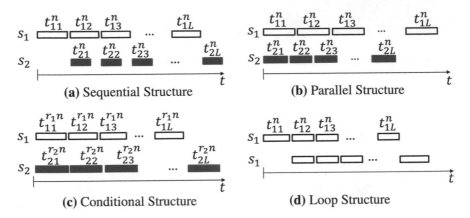

Fig. 7 Processing time-line of different structures

In general, execution time of a composite service that is a sequential combination of k services $(s_1, s_2, \ldots, s_k)$ can be predicted as follows:

$$f_c(n) \cong \max_{i=1}^{k} f_i(n) + (\sum_{i=1}^{k} f_i(n) - \max_{i=1}^{k} f_i(n))/\lceil M/n \rceil \qquad (4)$$

where $f_1(n)$, $f_2(n)$, ..., $f_k(n)$ are execution time of each services using parallel execution with with n concurrent instances.

4.2.2 Prediction of Parallel Structure

Consider a composite service with service s_1 and s_2 in the parallel structure. In this case the two services process data in parallel. The original dataset is separated into M partitions, n of which are sent to the composite service concurrently. Suppose $f_1(n)$ and $f_2(n)$ are execution time of s_1 and s_2 predicted using the policy model. The processing time-line of the composite service is illustrated in Fig. 7b. From this processing time-line, we can easily predict the execution time of the composite service $(f_c(n))$ is the maximum value of $f_1(n)$ and $f_2(n)$:

$$f_c(n) \cong \max(f_1(n), f_2(n)) \qquad (5)$$

To generalize, consider a parallel combination of k services $(s_1, s_2, \ldots, s_k)$. Using policy model, $f_i(n)$ is predicted execution time of service s_i with n concurrent processes. The execution time of the composite service is predicted with the following generalized equation:

$$f_c(n) \cong \max_{i=1}^{k} f_i(n) \qquad (6)$$

4.2.3 Prediction of Conditional Structure

Consider a *Conditional* combination of two service s_1 and s_2. The *Conditional* structure states that a portion of n partitions will be sent to service s_1, the remainder is sent to service s_2. Suppose that the ratios are r_1 and r_2 ($r_1 + r_2 = 1$). This means that $r_1 n$ partitions are processed by s_1 in parallel, while the remaining $r_2 n$ partitions are processed by s_2 concurrently. In total, $r_1 M$ partitions are processed by s_1, and $r_2 M$ partitions are processed by s_2. Using the policy model we can calculate execution time of s_1 and s_2 are $f_1(r_1 n)$ and $f_2(r_2 n)$ respectively.

When $n = 1$, partitions are sent to the composite service one at a time, one partition is processed by s_1 or s_2 at a time. The execution time the composite service to process M partitions is execution time of s_1 to process $r_1 M$ partitions adds execution time of s_2 to process $r_2 M$ partitions. When $n > 1$, since there are $r_1 n$ concurrent processes of s_1 and $r_2 n$ concurrent processes of s_2, the execution of the conditional structure is similar with parallel structure where s_1 processes $r M$ partitions and s_2 processes $r_2 M$ partitions concurrently. In this case, processing time-line of the conditional structure is as illustrated in Fig. 7c; the number of time-steps, $L = \lceil M/n \rceil$. The execution time of the conditional structure $f_c(n)$ is predicted as follows:

$$f_c(n) \approx \begin{cases} f_1(1) + f_2(1), & \text{if } n = 1 \\ \max(f_1(r_1 n), f_2(r_2 n)), & \text{if } n > 1 \end{cases} \tag{7}$$

To generalize, consider a *Conditional* structure of k services $(s_1, s_2, \ldots, s_k)$. Suppose that $r_1, r_2, \ldots, r_k$ are the ratios of requests sent to each service. We have:

- $\sum_{i=1}^{k} r_i = 1$
- $r_i M$ partitions are processed by s_i
- With n partitions sent to the composite service in parallel, $r_i n$ instances of service s_i will be initiated and processed concurrently.
- Execution time of service s_i when processing $r_i M$ partitions with $r_i n$ concurrent instances can be calculated with $f_i(r_i n)$, where the parallel execution policy of s_i is $(\alpha_i, \alpha_i^\star, \alpha_i', P_i)$.

The execution time of the composite service ($f_c(n)$) is predicted by the following equation:

$$f_c(n) \approx \begin{cases} \sum_{1}^{k} f_i(1), & \text{if } n = 1 \\ \max_{i=1}^{k} f_i(r_i n), & \text{if } n > 1 \end{cases} \tag{8}$$

4.2.4 Prediction of Loop Structure

Consider a loop of service s_1 with the iteration number of 2. This loop can be converted to a *Sequential* structure of two services s_1. Execution time of service s_1 is $f_1(n)$ can be predicted by using the policy model. The processing time-line of the composite service is illustrated in Fig. 7d; the number of time-steps is $L = \lceil M/n \rceil$. At the first time step, n requests are sent to s_1 in parallel, t_{11}^n is the time taken by n instances of s_1 to process the first n partitions. From the second time step to $(\lceil M/n \rceil - 1)$ time step, $2n$ requests are sent to service s_1 concurrently, so the time to process n partitions is maximum value of $f_1(n)$ and $f_1(2n)$. Let ΔT is duration from second time step to $(\lceil M/n \rceil - 1)$ time step, ΔT is calculated as follows:

$$\Delta T \approx (\lceil M/n \rceil - 1) \frac{\max(f_1(n), f_1(2n))}{\lceil M/n \rceil}$$

At the last time step, n last partitions are processed in parallel by n concurrent instances of s_1. The execution time of the composite service $(f_c(n))$ is predicted by the equation below:

$$f_c(n) \approx 2 \frac{f_1(n)}{\lceil M/n \rceil} + \Delta T$$
$$\approx 2 \frac{f_1(n)}{\lceil M/n \rceil} + (\lceil M/n \rceil - 1) \frac{\max(f_1(n), f_1(2n))}{\lceil M/n \rceil} \tag{9}$$

In general case where a service s is looped k time. The execution time of the composite service can be calculated by following general equation:

$$f_c(n) \approx \frac{2 \sum_{j=1}^{k-1} \max_{i=1}^{j} f(in)}{\lceil M/n \rceil} + (\lceil M/n \rceil - k + 1) \frac{\max_{i=1}^{k} f(in)}{\lceil M/n \rceil} \tag{10}$$

In the case a composite service that contains different control structures. To calculate execution time of this type of composite service, we first reduce the complex workflow to a simple one which contains only sequential structure. We use the reduction methodology proposed in [11] for converting the complex service to a sequential combination of components, each component is a composite service with a control structure. Using equation for each structure defined above we calculate execution time of each component. Finally, applying equation of sequential structure we can calculate execution of the whole complex composite service.

5   Evaluation

In this section we describe the results of testing the performance impact of parallel execution of web services offered by different providers. We also evaluate the accuracy of our prediction model by comparing its output to actual results.

5.1 Evaluation of the Parallel Execution Policy Model

We focus on analysing real world translation services. We use the integration engine of the Language Grid and UIMA [13] to configure and invoke services with parallel execution. In our experiments, a document with 500 paragraphs is translated from Japanese to English. The document is separated into one paragraph partitions, and several partitions are translated in parallel. The results demonstrate there are two group of parallel execution policies: Combination of *Slow-down Policy* and *Restriction Policy*, and combination of *Slow-down Policy* and *Penalty Policy* as shown in Fig. 8. For example, Mecab morphological analysis service employs slow-down and restriction policies with $P_{smecab} = 4$ and $P_{rmecab} = 14$, whereas the Tree Tagger service employs slow-down and penalty policies with $P_{stree} = 4$ and $P_{ptree} = 8$.

We evaluate our parallel execution policy model by using regression analysis. Our model is compared with two regression models: a linear fitting model and a curve fitting model with a quartic regression (curve fitting function: $y = ax^4 + bx^3 + cx^2 + dx + e$). Figure 9 shows comparison of our policy model and regression models of two different services: J-Server translation service and Google translation service.

We use standard error (S), and R-squared (R^2) to compare the models. S gives some idea of how much the model's prediction differs from the actual results. R^2 provides an index of the closeness of the actual results to the prediction. We also calculate P-value for evaluating statistical significance of our policy model. Table 1 shows comparison of the policy model with other two regression models. The results show that in all cases, the policy model has the lower standard error and higher R-Squared than either the linear regression model or the quartic regression model. The P-value of the policy model is significantly low (much less than 0.05). This indicates that our policy model is highly statistically significant and can faithfully estimate the parallel execution effects of web services.

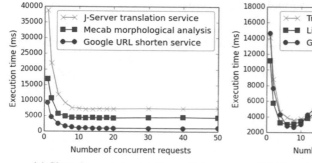
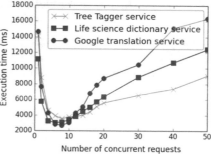
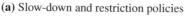

(a) Slow-down and restriction policies   (b) Slow-down and restriction policies

Fig. 8 Parallel execution policies of atomic services

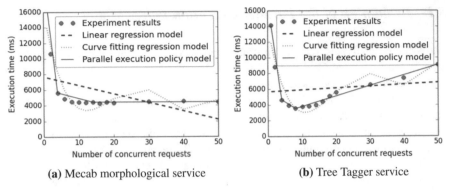

(a) Mecab morphological service   **(b)** Tree Tagger service

Fig. 9 Regression analysis

Table 1 Comparison of the proposed model with regression models

	S (milliseconds)			R-Squared (%)			P-value
	Linear model	Quartic model	Policy Model	Linear model	Quartic model	Policy model	Policy model
J-Server Tran.	3287.94	1583.47	1049.75	21.3	86.3	92.0	1.23e-09
Mecab	3310.78	1634.90	764.73	19.9	85.3	95.7	3.71e-11
Google URL	2080.93	1014.05	698.97	23.2	86.3	91.3	4.06e-09
Tree Tagger	3078.94	1297.93	659.91	1.2	86.8	95.5	5.82e-11
LSD	2521.01	1267.16	885.72	4.5	89.5	93.2	1.56e-09
Google Tran.	3415.02	1680.13	1075.34	4.9	82.73	90.6	2.55e-09

5.2   Evaluation of the Prediction Model

We analyse a realistic composite service which is a two-hop translation combining two translation service as shown in Fig. 10a. This composite service is combination of three translation services with two structures, i.e. *Sequential* structure and *Conditional* structure. We use this composite service to translate a mixed document containing information about rice and fertilizer. First, the document is translated into English using J-Server translation service. Then, that part of translated document, containing information about rice, is translated into Vietnamese by Google translation service. The other part, containing information about fertilizers, is translated into French by Bing translation service. J-server, Bing translation service, and Google translation service have different parallel execution policies as specified in previous section. Figure 10b shows a performance prediction when the composite service translates a

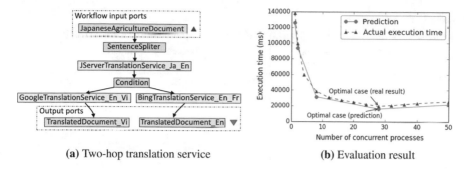

(a) Two-hop translation service   (b) Evaluation result

Fig. 10 Evaluating a composite service

document of 500 paragraphs. We can see that, in this case our model correctly predict the best DOP (28) where the composite service attains the best performance.

In order to evaluate the accuracy of the proposed model we invoked the above composite service with 15 different agriculture documents with different sizes ranging from 100 paragraphs to 1500 paragraphs. We use several measures as follows: Mean Prediction Error (*MPE*) to evaluate prediction bias, Mean Absolute Error (*MAD*) to show absolute size of prediction errors, and Tracking Signal (*TS*) to check whether there is some bias or not.

Table 2 shows evaluation of the model in two aspects:

- Predicting the optimal number of concurrent processes: $MPE = 0$ and $MAD = 1.07$ mean that the model yields good predictions; the average absolute error is 1.07 units.
- Prediction of the optimal execution time: $TS = 15$ indicates that the model is not so accurate in predicting the optimal execution time.

The proposed prediction model is not so accurate and always under-predict the optimal execution time. One reason for this is that our current model omits some parallel overhead such as time for creating and terminating threads. The accuracy of the model would be improved by adding the parallel overhead time to calculate execution time of an atomic service under parallel execution. We will consider this issue in our future works.

6   Related Work

Scientific workflows have emerged as an useful instrument to comprehensively design and share the best practices and create reproducible scientific experiments. Many Scientific Workflow Management Systems (SWMSs) have been developed, such as Taverna [14], or Kepler [15] to enable graphical design, execution and monitoring of local or distributed scientific workflows. In the era of big data, workflow optimization has become an important issue. One of the common optimization targets

Table 2 Evaluation result

Input data	Optimal degree of parallelism (DOP)			Optimal execution time (millisecond)		
	Prediction	Actual result		Prediction	Actual result	
100 paragraphs	28	24	MPE = 0 MAD = 1.07 TS = 0	2596	3531	MPE = 1204.33 MAD = 1204.33 TS = 15
200 paragraphs	24	24		5373	6550	
300 paragraphs	24	24		8390	9360	
400 paragraphs	24	24		11386	12670	
500 paragraphs	24	28		13984	15287	
600 paragraphs	28	28		17580	18574	
700 paragraphs	24	24		23177	24696	
800 paragraphs	24	24		25273	26344	
900 paragraphs	24	28		30170	31146	
1000 paragraphs	28	28		35567	36627	
1100 paragraphs	24	24		42164	43238	
1200 paragraphs	28	28		43960	45789	
1300 paragraphs	24	24		46757	48043	
1400 paragraphs	28	24		54229	55631	
1500 paragraphs	28	28		57951	59136	

is to improve the scientific workflow runtime performance. As the typical scientific workflow is executed in e-Science infrastructures, several different approaches exist to intelligently schedule workflows or tasks on the Grid and Cloud [16]. There also some recent works on scheduling workflows based on resource/task allocation [17]. These solutions are usually implemented for a specific SWMS and aim at the acceleration of workflow through scheduling.

There are also some existing studies proposing different factors to compute QoS in order to optimize service composition. In [18], to deal with context-aware QoS, where the QoS of a service may vary in different context, authors proposed a dynamic service selection approach based on context-aware QoS. A method that involved human to analyze QoS for service composition was also proposed in [19].

To the best of our knowledge, there is no existing works that consider service providers' decision on parallel execution of atomic services in service composition. In this regard, we conclude that our contribution is novel.

7 Conclusion

This chapter proposed a prediction model that considers the policies of atomic service providers in predicting the performance of a composite service under parallel execution. To the best of our knowledge, this is the first attempt to incorporate service providers' policies on parallel computing into service composition. We found that the parallel execution policies of atomic services fell into three different categories: Slow-down policy, Restriction policy, and Penalty policy. Based on these policies, our prediction model can calculate the execution times of composite services when using parallel execution and estimate the optimal degree of parallelism for the composite services. Our model is helpful in building a mechanism that can control the parallel execution of workflows; a Workflow Management System that uses this mechanism can execute a workflow with optimal DOP.

We conducted experiments on real-world translation services to evaluate the accuracy of our model. The analysis results show that our model offers good prediction accuracy with regard to identifying the optimal degree of parallelism for composite services. Our model is, however, not so accurate in predicting the execution time. Our future work includes improving the model to increase prediction accuracy and extending the model for other QoS metrics such as cost and reputation.

In designing the proposed model, we assumed that parallel execution policy of one service is static. That is, the limit set by the service provider on the number of concurrent process does not change regardless of input data size. However, in cloud environment, it seems highly likely that service providers will dynamically change their policy for requests of different sizes. In our future work, we will enhance our model to consider dynamic service policies.

Acknowledgements This research was partly supported by a Grant-in-Aid for Scientific Research (S) (24220002, 2012-2016) and a Grant-in-Aid for Young Scientists (A) (17H04706, 2017-2020) from Japan Society for the Promotion of Science (JSPS).

References

1. Amdahl, G.M.: Validity of the single processor approach to achieving large scale computing capabilities. In: Proceedings of the April 18–20, 1967, Spring Joint Computer Conference, AFIPS '67 (Spring), pp. 483–485. ACM, New York, NY, USA (1967)
2. Tallent, N.R., Mellor-Crummey, J.M.: Effective performance measurement and analysis of multithreaded applications. SIGPLAN Not. **44**(4), 229–240 (2009)
3. Raicu, I., Foster, I., Zhao, Y., Szalay, A., Little, P., Moretti, C.M., Chaudhary, A., Thain, D.: Towards data intensive many-task computing. In: Data Intensive Distributed Computing: Challenges and Solutions for Largescale Information Management, vol. 13, no. 3, pp. 28–73 (2012)
4. Taylor, I.J., Deelman, E., Gannon, D.B., Shields, M.: Workflows for e-Science: scientific workflows for grids. Springer Publishing Company, Incorporated (2014)
5. Pautasso, C., Alonso, G.: Parallel computing patterns for grid workflows. In: 2006 Workshop on Workflows in Support of Large-Scale Science, pp. 1–10 (2006)
6. de Oliveira, D., Ogasawara, E., Ocaa, K., Baio, F., Mattoso, M.: An adaptive parallel execution strategy for cloud-based scientific workflows. Concurrency Comput. Pract. Experience **24**(13), 1531–1550 (2012)
7. Ishida, T. (ed.): The Language Grid: Service-Oriented Collective Intelligence for Language Resource Interoperability. Springer Science & Business Media (2011)
8. Murakami, Y., Lin, D., Ishida, T.: Service-Oriented Architecture for Interoperability of Multilanguage Services, pp. 313–328. Springer, Berlin (2014)
9. Sun, X.H., Chen, Y.: Reevaluating Amdahl' s law in the multicore era. J. Parallel Distrib. Comput. **70**(2), 183–188 (2010)
10. Trang, M., Murakami, Y., Ishida, T.: Policy-aware optimization of parallel execution of composite services. IEEE Trans. Serv. Comput. **PP**(99), 109–113 (2017)
11. Cardoso, J., Sheth, A., Miller, J., Arnold, J., Kochut, K.: Quality of service for workflows and web service processes. Web Semant. Sci. Serv. Agents World Wide Web **1**(3), 281–308 (2004)
12. Yu, Q., Bouguettaya, A.: Framework for web service query algebra and optimization. ACM Trans. Web **2**(1), 6:1–6:35 (2008)
13. Xuan, T.M., Murakami, Y., Lin, D., Ishida, T.: Integration of workflow and pipeline for language service composition. In: Chair, N.C.C., Choukri, K., Declerck, T., Loftsson, H., Maegaard, B., Mariani, J., Moreno, A., Odijk, J., Piperidis, S. (eds.) Proceedings of the Ninth International Conference on Language Resources and Evaluation (LREC'14), pp. 3829–3836. European Language Resources Association (ELRA), Reykjavik, Iceland (2014)
14. Oinn, T., Addis, M., Ferris, J., Marvin, D., Senger, M., Greenwood, M., Carver, T., Glover, K., Pocock, M.R., Wipat, A., Li, P.: Taverna: a tool for the composition and enactment of bioinformatics workflows. Bioinformatics **20**(17), 3045–3054 (2004)
15. Ludscher, B., Altintas, I., Berkley, C., Higgins, D., Jaeger, E., Jones, M., Lee, E.A., Tao, J., Zhao, Y.: Scientific workflow management and the kepler system. Concurrency Computat. Pract. Experience **18**(10), 1039–1065 (2006)
16. Yu, J., Buyya, R., Ramamohanarao, K.: Workflow Scheduling Algorithms for Grid Computing, pp. 173–214. Springer, Berlin (2008)
17. Szabo, C., Sheng, Q.Z., Kroeger, T., Zhang, Y., Yu, J.: Science in the cloud: Allocation and execution of data-intensive scientific workflows. J. Grid Comput. **12**(2), 245–264 (2014)
18. Lin, D., Shi, C., Ishida, T.: Dynamic service selection based on context-aware QoS. In: 2012 IEEE Ninth International Conference on Services Computing, pp. 641–648 (2012)
19. Lin, D., Ishida, T., Murakami, Y., Tanaka, M.: Qos analysis for service composition by human and web services. IEICE Trans. Inf. Syst. **97**(4), 762–769 (2014)

Optimizing Crowdsourcing Workflow for Language Services

Shinsuke Goto, Toru Ishida and Donghui Lin

Abstract Recently, attempts have been to request translation services from anonymous crowds. Compared with platform-based language services, services performed by humans have the advantages of flexibility and quality. However, due to the nature of human services the results are not consistent and quality is not assured. This research tries to solve this problem by creating workflows that make collaboration among crowdsourcing workers far more effective and efficient. We model workers and tasks, and calculate the optimal workflow. To confirm the feasibility of this model, we conduct a computational experiment to calculate the best workflow under various parameters. The results are consistent with existing research so the model is useful in understanding crowdsourcing workflows. In addition, a system is developed for realizing crowdsourcing workflows for translation services. Finally, we develop a translation interface that demonstrates the feasibility of the proposed method.

Keywords Crowdsourcing · Human services · Workflow modeling · Workflow optimization

1 Introduction

Today, as the amount of multilingual communication on the Internet continues to increase, truly effective language services are becoming more and more important. The Language Grid enables users to create and utilize composite services [7]. A parallel study strand is the service platform [19]. Underlying all the work to date to the acknowledgment that high-quality translation is required when handling contracts

S. Goto (✉) · T. Ishida · D. Lin
Department of Social Informatics, Kyoto University,
Kyoto 606-8501, Japan
e-mail: s-goto@ai.soc.i.kyoto-u.ac.jp

T. Ishida
e-mail: ishida@i.kyoto-u.ac.jp

D. Lin
e-mail: lindh@i.kyoto-u.ac.jp

or purchases. In such cases, composite services on multi-language service platforms may fail to offer the quality demanded.

Human services performed through crowdsourcing are an attractive source of language services [14]. Crowdsourcing is being used for a variety of open-ended tasks such as writing, design and translation. Crowdsourcing has the advantages of flexibility against machine services. However, when performing the open-ended tasks like translation, the quality of the result from a single worker is not guaranteed because of the various abilities of crowdsourcing workers. To ensure the quality, requesters create a workflow, in which the result of one crowd worker is incrementally refined by other workers. Although the importance of crowdsourcing workflow has already been addressed [10], the general characteristics of such workflows are not yet well comprehended.

Until recently, the crowdsourcing workflow for collaboration among workers mainly lies on two processes: the iterative process and the parallel process. In an iterative process, the result of a task conducted by one worker is iteratively improved by other workers [10]. Crowdsourcing is an inherently parallel process, where the same task is executed by multiple workers and the final result is selected by voting or some other means [11, 17]. Analyses of iterative and parallel processes in crowdsourcing workflows have yielded two main findings: (1) the variety of crowd workers is important [17], and (2) prior results can have a negative effect on quality by leading subsequent workers down the wrong path if the tasks are iterative and very difficult [15]. Previous research mainly focused on workflow analysis for special tasks, and did not provide a comprehensive understanding of crowdsourcing workflows. Even though there exist several studies on workflow optimization, these works focused on optimizing fixed workflow structures such as the number of iterations or degree of parallelism.

To make better use of crowdsourcing, we should solve two key problems. One is how task requesters can get an accurate estimation of crowdsourcing utility. The estimated utility can help them decide whether they use crowdsourcing or not prior to the actual request. The other is an interface that enables users to request tasks easily.

Let us consider the scenario wherein a requester wants to use crowdsourcing to execute a translation task. There are numerous workers available on the crowdsourcing platform. However, the suitability of a worker remains unknown until the task is executed by that worker. Since translation quality cannot be ensured if only one worker is involved, it is necessary to consider a translation workflow that consists of several improvement tasks performed by multiple workers. In each iteration, a worker improves the best result from among those output in the previous iteration. However, the requester wants to obtain the best result while balancing cost off against quality. In addition, the requester has to decide whether to request a task or not in advance according to the predicted cost and quality before actually posting a task. Therefore, it is necessary to model crowd workers, tasks and requester utility towards a better understanding of general crowdsourcing performance.

2 Modeling Iterative and Parallel Processes

To understand the crowdsourcing workflow, we first develop the model to estimate the utility from the workflow composed of iterative and parallel processes. The model is characterized by the ability distribution of crowdsourcing workers, the difficulty of the task, and the preference of the requester. We first explain the scenario where the model is used, then define the workflow, and detail the method that can estimate the utility for a given workflow.

2.1 Workers

High worker ability should yield high quality results. To simplify our model, we assume that the quality of a task execution result is determined uniquely by the ability of the worker who executed the task. Since the ability is unknown before the task is undertaken, we use a beta distribution to model the distribution of worker ability. Probability density function $f(x|a, v)$ is given by Eq. (1).

$$f(x|a, v) = \text{Beta}(\frac{a}{\min(a, 1-a)v}, \frac{(1-a)}{\min(a, 1-a)v}) \tag{1}$$

Here $a \in (0, 1)$ is the normalized value of the average ability of the workers in the crowdsourcing platform. $v \in (0, 1)$ is a parameter that determines the variance in worker ability. If v is near 0, then the variance approaches 0. If v is near 1, then the variance is approaches the highest variance with average a. The above model extends the previous work [5] by modifying a parameter that describes the variance of worker ability.

2.2 Workflows

An open-ended task consists of iterations of improvement tasks, and so is called an iterative process; high-quality results are achieved by iteratively improving the prior work by a new worker. However, there is also the situation where multiple workers improve the same task in parallel, i.e. a parallel process. Examples of improvement tasks implemented as iterative and parallel processes are reported by Little et. al [15].

We formally define a workflow as $w = (p_1, \ldots, p_n)$, where n is the number of improvement tasks in the iterative process and $p_i (1 \leq i \leq n)$ is the number of workers that execute the ith improvement task in parallel. As a result, the total number of workers in the workflow is given by $m = \sum_{i=1}^{n} p_i$.

After each iteration, the best result will be automatically selected. If none of the results have better quality than the input of the improvement task, the input will be selected as the best result.

2.3 *Improvement Task*

Different types of tasks have different difficulties. For each task, we set parameter $d \in [0, 1]$ to denote its improvement difficulty. If the improvement difficulty, d, is 0, then the improvement task is extremely easy. In contrast, the quality of a task with $d = 1$ is extremely difficult to improve. For example, if the task is to provide a missing illustration caption, then d is near 0 since it is easy for a new worker to improve the quality by adding information. If the task is to improve the illustration, then d might approach 1 since it is always extremely difficult to improve the output of another designer. For most of other types of tasks like translation improvement, the value of d lies between 0 and 1. Given the improvement difficulty d of a task, we use function $q'(a, q)$ to define the quality of the result after executing the improvement task once, where a is worker ability and q is the quality of the input result of the current improvement task.

$$q'(a, q) = q + (1 - q)a - q(1 - a)d \tag{2}$$

The above equation is the sum of three parts. The first part denotes the original quality q of the input result for the current improvement task. The second part means the increase in quality after execution of the improvement task. The third part shows the penalty in quality if the improvement fails. Let us explain the second part and the third part in more detail. If the original quality of the input result is q, then the room left for quality improvement is $1 - q$. The second part, $(1 - q)a$, means that the improvement is proportional to the worker's ability a. On the other hand, $q(1 - a)$ denotes the possibility of improvement failure. When the original quality is high or the worker's ability is low, the possibility of improvement failure is high. The reason why the improvement difficulty d is multiplied in the third part is that it is more probable that quality decreases if d is larger, i.e., the task has higher improvement difficulty. In the situation that the improvement task is executed by just one worker, the expected value of the quality after executing the improvement task is $q'(a, q)$ since the expected value of the worker's ability is a.

Next, we explain the quality improvement with the addition of parallel processing. If two or more workers perform the improvement task simultaneously, the result with maximum quality will be selected as assumed. Therefore, the quality of result is equal to that performed by the worker with maximum ability in the iteration. Here, we note p as the number of workers participating in the improvement task in the current iteration. The maximum ability among p workers ($a_p^{\max}$) is estimated the average of the maximum distribution (Eq. (4)). Here, $F(x|a, v)$ is the cumulative density function for $f(x|a, v)$. Also, $I_x(y, z)$ is the regularized beta function calculated by Eq. (3).

$$I_x(y, z) = \frac{\int_0^x t^{y-1}(1-t)^{z-1}dt}{\text{Beta}(y, z)} \tag{3}$$

$$a_p^{\max} = \int_0^1 xF(x|a, v)^p dx \tag{4}$$

$$= [xF(x|a, v)]_0^1 - \int_0^1 F(x|a, v)^p dx$$

$$= 1 - \int_0^1 I_x(\frac{a}{\min(a, 1-a)v}, \frac{(1-a)}{\min(a, 1-a)v})^p dx$$

Taking $a_p^{\max}$ as a, the quality obtained by parallel processing with p workers will be $q'(a_p^{\max}, q)$.

2.4 Utility

The utility of the requester in executing workflow U is used as the objective function of workflow optimization. In previous research, the utility of a workflow is calculated based on the quality of the task and the cost of the execution [5, 8]. We define utility as the weighted sum of quality Q and cost C [21]. The preference of the requester is denoted by the weight of quality, β, which is used for calculating the utility. Thus, the weight of cost is $1 - \beta$.

$$U = \beta Q + (1 - \beta)C \tag{5}$$

$Q \in [0, 1]$ can be acquired from the predicted quality of workflow w. The cost, $C \in [0, 1]$, is the normalized value given by Eq. (6), where m is the number of workers and M is the predefined maximum number of workers. Here we count only the number of workers to perform improvement tasks. Therefore, iterative and parallel processes do not affect the total cost.

$$C = \frac{M - m}{M} \tag{6}$$

3   Workflow Optimization

3.1   *The Search Algorithm*

Based on the process model introduced in the previous section, we can predict the utility of a given workflow. Since the number of possible workflows is large (if the number of workers is n, there are 2^n possible workflows), it is necessary to consider an efficient search approach for workflow optimization. We propose a search algorithm that extracts the maximum expected value of utility from a limited search space.

We assume that the cost increases in proportional to the number of crowd workers. Therefore, utility will monotonically decrease as worker number increases when the quality is fixed. On the other hand, the quality will monotonically increase with worker number. Although there might be occasional failures in the improvement tasks, it is assumed that the result with better quality is selected when comparing the input and output of an improvement task. Therefore, increasing worker number does not lead to a drop in quality. From the above assumptions, we can see that the utility will become low if the number of workers is increased excessively since quality always has an upper bound. That is why there always exists an optimal workflow that can maximize the utility.

Algorithm 1 Searching Optimal Workflow *search*

1: w /* workflow */
2: $utility(w)$ /* utility function for workflow w */
3: s /* current best workflow */
4: u /* utility value of the current best workflow */
5: $Closed$ /* set of workflows already expanded */
6: $Open$ /* set of workflows to be expanded */
7: $s \leftarrow (1)$
8: $u \leftarrow utility(s)$
9: $Open \leftarrow \{s\}$
10: $Closed \leftarrow \{\}$
11: **while** Open $\neq null$ **do**
12:      Select $w \in Open$
13:      $Open \leftarrow Open - \{w\}$
14:      $Closed \leftarrow Closed \cup \{w\}$
15:      **for all** $w' \in expand(w)$ **do**
16:          **if** $w' \notin Closed$ and $utility(w') \geq utility(w)$ **then**
17:              $Open \leftarrow Open \cup \{w'\}$
18:              **if** $utility(w') \geq u$ **then**
19:                  $s \leftarrow w'$
20:                  $u \leftarrow utility(w')$
21:              **end if**
22:          **end if**
23:      **end for**
24: **end while**
25: **return** s

Algorithm 2 Expanding Workflow *expand*

Input: w

1: p_i /* number of workers that execute the ith improvement task in parallel */
2: n /* number of iteration */
3: $w = (p_1, \ldots, p_n)$ /* workflow */
4: $W = \{w_1, \ldots, w_m\}$ /* the set of created workflows by expansion of w */
5: m /* number of workflows created by expansion of w */
6: $W \leftarrow \{\}$
7: $W \leftarrow W \cup \{(1, p_1, \ldots, p_n)\}$
8: **for** $i = 1$ to n **do**
9:   $W \leftarrow W \cup \{(p_1, \ldots, (p_i + 1), \ldots, p_n)\}$
10:   $W \leftarrow W \cup \{(p_1, \ldots, p_i, 1, \ldots, p_n)\}$
11: **end for**
12: **return** W

3.2 Optimality

The optimality of the workflow search algorithm (Algorithm 1) for crowdsourcing tasks is described below: In a crowdsourcing workflow that consists of iterative and parallel processes, let the search algorithm start from an initial workflow state that consists of just one crowd worker and search the state space that is expanded gradually by adding one crowd worker at each epoch. The search algorithm stops when the workflow state with maximum utility has reached the optimal workflow under the given assumptions.

To prove the termination of our search algorithm, we show that the increase in utility created by adding a worker monotonically decreases with higher utility. Let the expected values of the quality and cost of workflow w with m crowd workers be q and c, respectively. Assume that one crowd worker is added and the value of utility changes by the following quality and cost.

First, we show that incremental quality monotonically decreases if one crowd worker is added with either iteration or parallelism. Assume that the additional crowd worker is used to increase the iteration number, the incremental quality satisfies $\Delta q = a(1 - q) - (1 - a)qd$. Here a and d are constants assuming the additional worker always has expected quality a. In each iteration, q monotonically increases. Therefore, $a(1 - q)$ monotonically decreases and $(1 - a)qd$ monotonically increases. As a result, incremental quality Δq monotonically decreases.

On the other hand, when an additional crowd worker is used to increase the parallelism, quality increment Δq depends on the increment of the maximum ability of worker Δa. Since the maximum expected ability is calculated from the regularized beta function which satisfies $I_x(y, z) \leq 1$, Δa monotonically decreases with the increase of parallelism. Therefore, strengthening parallelism, triggers a monotonic decrease in Δq. The increment of the maximum value of a beta distribution monotonically decreases as it approaches 1, so quality increment Δq monotonically decreases with the addition of a worker. Second, cost increment Δc is always constant if one crowd worker is added. This means normalized cost C monotonically decreases. As utility is calculated by the weighted summation of quality and cost, the increase in the amount of utility decreases and turns negative.

To summarize, the incremental utility will monotonically decrease and finally become a negative value at a certain point. Therefore, the search algorithm will stop under the given assumptions. Moreover, since the expansion of the workflow state space will stop when the incremental utility becomes a negative value, the workflow state with the maximum utility is obtained when the search algorithm stops.

The above discussion does not ensure an optimal solution when increasing crowd workers in real crowdsourcing tasks. Rather, given set values, the model can calculate the optimal workflow. However, we can understand the characteristics of crowdsourcing workflows and use the knowledge in real crowdsourcing task design if the optimal solution search can be conducted efficiently.

3.3 Analysis of Optimal Workflows

Based on the model and its optimization algorithm, we can estimate the utility for every workflow on each parameter setting. We conducted two experiments to verify the proposed model. The first analyzes the structure of optimal workflow for various parameters, while the other compares iterative and parallel processing.

We use the proposed search algorithm to obtain optimal workflow w for various parameter combinations. In addition, we calculate the utility for each w. The parameters are set as follows.

Average ability of workers $a \in (0, 1)$:   varied from 0.1 to 0.9 in steps of 0.2.
Variance of worker ability $v \in (0, 1)$:   varied from 0.1 to 0.9 in steps of 0.2.
Improvement difficulty $d \in [0,1]$:   0 (low), 0.5 (middle) and 1 (high).
Preference of the requester over quality β: 0.1, 0.5 and 0.9.

We first analyze the optimal workflows obtained by the search algorithm.

Tables 1 and 2 list the results of optimal workflows and their utilities with different values of the variance of worker ability and improvement difficulty of tasks. The

Table 1 Optimal workflows in different variations of v and d

v	$d = 1$	$d = 0.5$	$d = 0$
0.9	(2)	(2)	(1,1,1)
0.7	(2)	(2)	(1,1,1)
0.5	(2)	(2)	(1,1,1)
0.3	(2)	(1,1)	(1,1,1)
0.1	(1)	(1,1)	(1,1,1)

Table 2 Utilities of the optimal workflow in different variations of v and d

v	$d = 1$	$d = 0.5$	$d = 0$
0.9	0.7313	0.7257	0.7875
0.7	0.7229	0.7225	0.7875
0.5	0.7144	0.7129	0.7875
0.3	0.7024	0.7125	0.7875
0.1	0.7	0.7125	0.7875

results in Tables 1 and 2 show that optimal workflows are more parallel as the variance of worker ability increases. Moreover, the parallelism of optimal workflows also increases with the improvement difficulty. The utility of optimal workflows increases as the improvement difficulty decreases. However, the utility of optimal workflows can also increase as the variance in worker ability increases even when the improvement difficulty is high. This is because the workflow with high degree of parallelism is apt to be an optimal solution and worker ability is more significant when the variance of worker ability is high.

Tables 3 and 4 list the results of optimal workflows and their utilities with different variations of the average worker ability and quality preference of the requester. The results in Tables 3 and 4 show that the optimal workflows are most parallel when the average worker ability occupies the middle level (i.e., $a = 0.5$). Moreover, the degree of parallelism of optimal workflows falls and iterative improvement becomes more effective when the average worker ability trends away from the middle level (higher or lower). Not surprisingly, an optimal workflow has greater worker number

Table 3 Optimal workflows in different variations of a and β

a	$\beta = 0.9$	$\beta = 0.5$	$\beta = 0.1$
0.9	(1,2)	(1)	(1)
0.7	(1,4)	(1,1)	(1)
0.5	(8)	(2)	(1)
0.3	(3,6)	(1,1)	(1)
0.1	(2,5)	(1)	(1)

Table 4 Utilities of the optimal workflow in different variations of a and β

a	$\beta = 0.9$	$\beta = 0.5$	$\beta = 0.1$
0.9	0.9378	0.9	0.9
0.7	0.8683	0.8025	0.88
0.5	0.7517	0.717	0.86
0.3	0.5819	0.6025	0.84
0.1	0.2452	0.5	0.82

when the quality preference of the requester is high, i.e., cost has low importance. The utility of optimal workflows is more affected by average worker ability when the requester emphasizes quality.

The above analysis can also explain previous research results. For example, [11] indicated that the variety of crowd workers is important in a parallel process. Reference [8] suggested that it is effective to increase the number of crowd workers when the cost is low. Further, [15] showed that prior work with poor quality can have a negative effect on the overall quality of the workflow if the crowdsourcing task is difficult.

4 Crowdsourcing Translation System

Based on the model and optimization method of crowdsourcing workflow explained above, we propose a system that facilitates the use of workflows for both the task requester and task interface developer.

4.1 System Overview

Figure 1 shows our approach to designing a complete system that separates workflow optimization from task interface creation. This system consists of two modules. One is the workflow management module. This module calculates the optimal workflow

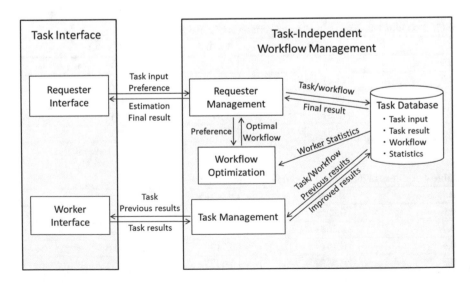

Fig. 1 Structure of proposed system

based on the average and variance of the ability of workers accumulated from past execution results and an estimation of task difficulty. Requesters select a workflow that they consider reasonable based on the predicted values of quality and cost. The other module is a task interface for requesters and workers. Implementation of this module varies depending on the task, but communication among them is common to all tasks. The system receives input data through the task interface and communicates with the workflow management module.

4.2 Example of Use Case

In order to test the proposed system in an actual crowdsourcing environment, we implemented the interface for typical translation tasks. The implementation separated the workflow optimization module and the interface module. Crowdsourcing is expected to be effective for translations as a machine translation can be used as the initial result to be improved. In translation, the material to be improved is called the down translation, and the higher the quality of the down translation, the better the quality of the crowdsourcing translation will be. This has been verified by previous studies [15] and is supported by a series of studies on post-editing in translating tasks [2, 6, 14].

This interface is implemented in PHP and JavaScript using the Language Grid Toolbox.[1] Here we explain the process of the crowdsourcing translation interface based on the proposed system.

First, we explain the process using the interface for requesters (Fig. 2). The requester first enters the importance of quality by entering a number in some range. This range varies with the situation, and natural expressions are possible. An example of such an expression is "Quality is very important (importance of quality is near 1)", "Cost is very important (importance of quality is near 0)", or in between. After the preference is input, the system presents a prediction of quality and cost. In the example shown in the figure, the predicted value of quality is 0.86, and the estimated cost is 200 yen, which is the sum of the costs of five workers. For this example, the cost of one improvement task was set at 40 yen, but this value can be changed arbitrarily by the task designer side. When requester is satisfied with the prediction result presented by the system, the sentences are posted in the form of a text file. In addition, the language of the input sentence and the language to be translated are selected. In the screenshot, the requester sees predicted values of cost and quality together with the importance of quality. The optimal workflow is automatically configured by the system for the task request, and the input text is displayed. The input text is divided into sentences so that crowdsourcing can be completed in a short time. Each sentence is processed using the same workflow.

After the system posts the task, the workers carry out the translation task through the workers' interface. The workers' interface is shown in Fig. 3. This presents a

---

[1]http://langrid.org/tools/toolbox/.

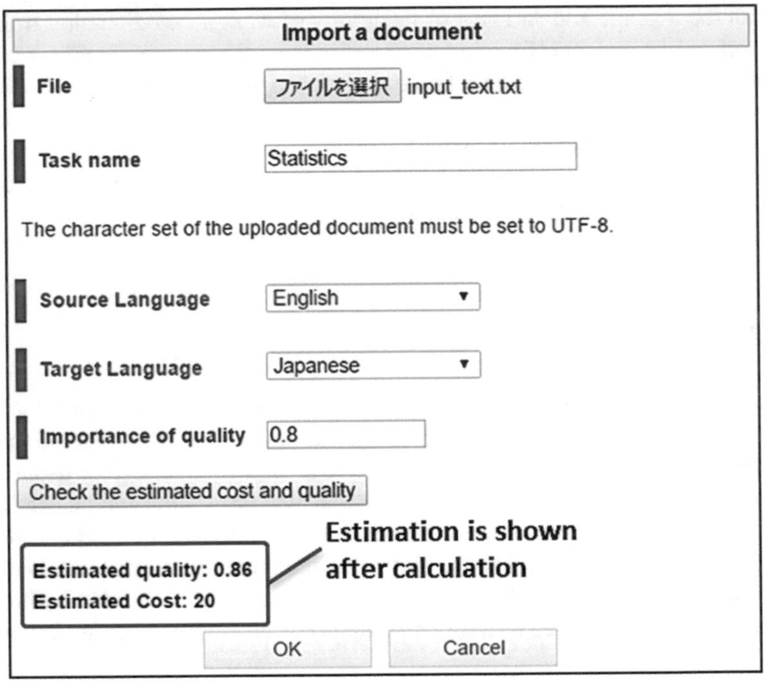

Fig. 2 Requesters' view of task interface

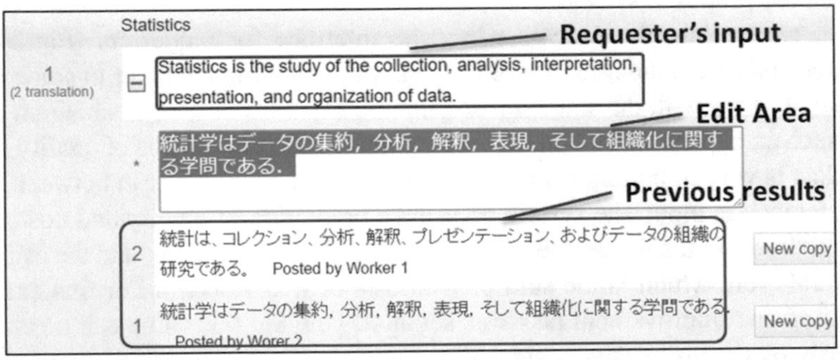

Fig. 3 Workers' view of task interface

screenshot of the situation where a third person is improving the translation while referring to the results of the two previous workers. As for the presentation of the past translation, this system is designed to be able to select a translation sentence from the execution result of improvement task by click the "New copy" button. The worker who performs the translation task first checks past translation results. Here, presented translations are decided by the workflow management module. For example, in the iterative process, after one person performs an improvement task, his/her results will be displayed. After deciding the translation to be used, the translation worker clicks the copy button to perform the improvement task. This process is repeated until the end of the workflow, and the finally translation result is displayed to the requester.

5 Related Work

Crowdsourcing workflows are widely used for enhancing the quality of difficult tasks. They were originally proposed to complete the tasks whose quality cannot be guaranteed by a single worker. Quality control of the classification or voting task by multiple workers can be regarded as the workflow of parallel processing [20]. On the other hand, the iterative process of improvement is proposed to deal with open-ended tasks.

Several workflow processes for special tasks have been proposed considering the issue of quality control. Soylent uses the Find-Fix-Verify crowd programming pattern to improve worker quality; it splits word processing tasks into a series of generation and review stages [4]. Zaidan and Callison-Burch propose a crowdsourcing translation workflow that attains high quality translations by aggregating multiple translations, redundantly editing them, and then selecting the best of the results based on machine learning [22].

Various workflow support tools have been proposed for managing the crowdsourcing of complex tasks. For example, TurKit is a toolkit for prototyping and exploring algorithmic human computation [16]. CrowdForge decomposes and recomposes complex crowdsourcing tasks based on the MapReduce algorithm [11]. Turkomatic was developed for supporting task decomposition by crowd workers [12]. Crowd-Weaver is a system to visually manage complex tasks and revise task decomposition during execution [9]. Tool development for modeling and managing workflows is of interest as it actually shares our objective of enhancing the understanding of crowdsourcing workflows. Our research can be regarded as a theoretical basis for workflow design in crowdsourcing.

Some crowdsourcing studies have also addressed translation. Zaidan et al. showed the feasibility of crowdsourcing translation using a sequence of tasks [22]. Workers create translation drafts, edit the translated sentences, and then vote to select the best translation. Ambati et al. proposed a combination of active learning and crowdsourcing translation in order to improve the quality of statistical machine translation [1]. In addition, Aziz, et al. developed and investigated a crowdsourcing based tool that enables post-editing of machine translations and evaluation of machine translations [3]. In a discussion of nonprofessional cost, Lin et al. suggest that low-cost language resource creation can be easily realized by utilizing non-experts [14]. Morita et al. introduced a protocol to create translations by a machine translation system and two monolingual non-experts [18]. Green et al. analyzed the effects of post-editing [6].

Finally, there is a study on the design process of translation services; it considered the balance between cost and translation quality [13]. Their method makes use of the iterative improvement of service composition, while our goal is to predict quality before posting translation task to the crowds.

6 Conclusion

There are opportunities to apply the power of crowds to translation for language services. We tried to solve the problem of the unpredictable nature of crowdsourcing workers by modeling and optimizing the crowdsourcing workflow. Experiments that examined various situations yielded results consistent with existing works, and confirmed that the concepts provided herein are useful in more fully understanding crowdsourcing workflows. In addition, we have proposed a system to realize cooperation in the workflow processing of multiple workers and to optimize the trade-off between cost and quality. For the proposed structure, we proposed a mechanism that automatically maximizes the quality attained by crowdsourcing without requiring the requester's active involvement. We also designed a task interface that enables the proposed crowdsourcing workflow.

Acknowledgements This work was partially supported by a Grant-in-Aid for Scientific Research (S) (24220002, 2012-2016) from Japan Society for the Promotion of Science (JSPS), Scientific Research (A) (17H00759, 2017-2020) from Japan Society for the Promotion of Science (JSPS), and Service Science, Solutions and Foundation Integrated Research Program from JST RISTEX.

References

1. Ambati, V., Vogel, S., Carbonell, J.G.: Active learning and crowd-sourcing for machine translation. In: Proceedings of the Seventh Conference on International Language Resources and Evaluation (LREC'10), vol. 11, pp. 2169–2174 (2010)
2. Aziz, W., Castilho, S., Specia, L.: Pet: a tool for post-editing and assessing machine translation. In: LREC, pp. 3982–3987 (2012)
3. Aziz, W., Castilho, S., Specia, L.: Pet: a tool for post-editing and assessing machine translation. In: Proceedings of the Eighth International Conference on Language Resources and Evaluation (LREC'12), pp. 3982–3987 (2012)
4. Bernstein, M.S., Little, G., Miller, R.C., Hartmann, B., Ackerman, M.S., Karger, D.R., Crowell, D., Panovich, K.: Soylent: a word processor with a crowd inside. In: Proceedings of the 23rd Annual ACM symposium on User interface software and technology, pp. 313–322. ACM (2010)
5. Dai, P., Lin, C.H., Weld, D.S.: Pomdp-based control of workflows for crowdsourcing. Artif. Intell. **202**, 52–85 (2013)
6. Green, S., Heer, J., Manning, C.D.: The efficacy of human post-editing for language translation. In: Proceedings of the SIGCHI Conference on Human Factors in Computing Systems, pp. 439–448. ACM (2013)
7. Ishida, T. (ed.): The Language Grid: Service-Oriented Collective Intelligence for Language Resource Interoperability. Springer Science & Business Media (2011)

8. Kamar, E., Hacker, S., Horvitz, E.: Combining human and machine intelligence in large-scale crowdsourcing. In: Proceedings of the 11th International Conference on Autonomous Agents and Multiagent Systems—Volume 1, AAMAS '12, pp. 467–474. International Foundation for Autonomous Agents and Multiagent Systems, Richland, SC (2012)

9. Kittur, A., Khamkar, S., André, P., Kraut, R.: Crowdweaver: Visually managing complex crowd work. In: Proceedings of the ACM 2012 Conference on Computer Supported Cooperative Work, CSCW '12, pp. 1033–1036. ACM, New York, NY, USA (2012)

10. Kittur, A., Nickerson, J.V., Bernstein, M., Gerber, E., Shaw, A., Zimmerman, J., Lease, M., Horton, J.: The future of crowd work. In: Proceedings of the 2013 Conference on Computer Supported Cooperative Work, CSCW '13, pp. 1301–1318. ACM, New York, NY, USA (2013)

11. Kittur, A., Smus, B., Khamkar, S., Kraut, R.E.: Crowdforge: crowdsourcing complex work. In: Proceedings of the 24th Annual ACM Symposium on User Interface Software and Technology, pp. 43–52. ACM (2011)

12. Kulkarni, A., Can, M., Hartmann, B.: Collaboratively crowdsourcing workflows with turkomatic. In: Proceedings of the ACM 2012 Conference on Computer Supported Cooperative Work, CSCW '12, pp. 1003–1012. ACM, New York, NY, USA (2012)

13. Lin, D., Ishida, T.: Participatory service design based on user-centered QoS. In: 2013 IEEE/WIC/ACM International Joint Conferences on Web Intelligence (WI) and Intelligent Agent Technologies (IAT), vol. 1, pp. 465–472 (2013)

14. Lin, D., Murakami, Y., Ishida, T., Murakami, Y., Tanaka, M.: Composing human and machine translation services: language grid for improving localization processes. In: Proceedings of the Seventh Conference on International Language Resources and Evaluation (LREC'10), vol. 10, pp. 500–506 (2010)

15. Little, G., Chilton, L.B., Goldman, M., Miller, R.C.: Exploring iterative and parallel human computation processes. In: Proceedings of the ACM SIGKDD Workshop on Human Computation, HCOMP '10, pp. 68–76. ACM, New York, NY, USA (2010)

16. Little, G., Chilton, L.B., Goldman, M., Miller, R.C.: Turkit: human computation algorithms on mechanical turk. In: Proceedings of the 23rd Annual ACM Symposium on User Interface Software and Technology, UIST '10, pp. 57–66. ACM, New York, NY, USA (2010)

17. Luther, K., Hahn, N., Dow, S.P., Kittur, A.: Crowdlines: supporting synthesis of diverse information sources through crowdsourced outlines. In: Third AAAI Conference on Human Computation and Crowdsourcing, pp. 110–119 (2015)

18. Morita, D., Ishida, T.: Designing protocols for collaborative translation. In: Proceedings of the 12th International Conference on Principles of Practice in Multi-Agent Systems (PRIMA'09), pp. 17–32. Springer (2009)

19. Murakami, Y., Lin, D., Ishida, T.: Service-Oriented Architecture for Interoperability of Multilanguage Services, pp. 313–328. Springer, Berlin (2014)

20. Sheng, V.S., Provost, F., Ipeirotis, P.G.: Get another label? Improving data quality and data mining using multiple, noisy labelers. In: Proceedings of the 14th ACM SIGKDD International Conference on Knowledge Discovery and Data Mining, pp. 614–622. ACM (2008)

21. Yoon, K.P., Hwang, C.L.: Multiple Attribute Decision Making: An Introduction, vol. 104. Sage Publications (1995)

22. Zaidan, O., Callison-Burch, C.: Crowdsourcing translation: professional quality from nonprofessionals. In: ACL, pp. 1220–1229 (2011)

Cascading-Failure Tolerance for Language Service Networks

Kemas M. Lhaksmana, Toru Ishida and Yohei Murakami

Abstract One of the main features of The Language Grid is its support for service composition, i.e. creating new language services that meet user requirements by combining the existing ones. Despite the potential of service composition, such a service-oriented computing (SOC) application may experience cascading failure when a disruption on one or more component services is propagated to the composite services that combine them. As the number of language services grows, composite language services will become more common, and thus understanding cascading failure among language services becomes more important. This chapter investigates how failure may propagate among language services and how to improve language service tolerance to cascading failure. To this end, the dependency between language services is modeled as service network on which cascading failure is simulated and analyzed. We also generated service networks in scale-free, exponential, and random topology to analyze how cascading failure occurs in different topology. The simulation reveals that service networks with scale-free topology have better cascading-failure tolerance compares to that of other topology.

Keywords Cascading failure · Service network · Scale-free network

K. M. Lhaksmana (✉)
School of Computing, Telkom University, Jl. Telekomunikasi No. 1,
Bandung 40257, Indonesia
e-mail: kemasmuslim@telkomuniversity.ac.id

T. Ishida
Department of Social Informatics, Kyoto University,
Kyoto 606-8501, Japan
e-mail: ishida@i.kyoto-u.ac.jp

Y. Murakami
Unit of Design, Kyoto University, 91 Chudoji Awata-cho,
Kyoto 600-8815, Japan
e-mail: yohei@i.kyoto-u.ac.jp

© Springer Nature Singapore Pte Ltd. 2018
Y. Murakami et al. (eds.), *Services Computing for Language Resources*,
Cognitive Technologies, https://doi.org/10.1007/978-981-10-7793-7_6

1   Introduction

The Language Grid was designed as service-oriented infrastructure for sharing language resources as services and combining the language services to create new services by using service composition [10]. Despite the advantages of service composition, bindings between composite services and their component services introduce dependency that may cause cascading failure issue.

To address cascading failure in The Language Grid, Fig. 1 illustrates an example of service composition. Suppose The Language Grid provides a composite service type "Translation Combined with Bilingual Dictionary" that combines "Morphological Analyzer", "Bilingual Dictionary", and "Translation" service types. Each service type can be realized by one or more service instances (hereafter "services" for brevity). For example, Mecab and TreeTagger are services of "Morphological Analyzer" service type. We call these two services as substitutable services since each of them can perform generally the same functions, and thus can substitute each other.

In the composite service "Translation Combined with Bilingual Dictionary", cascading failure may occur when one of the component services fails and no substitutable service is available. Therefore, language service infrastructure, such as The Language Grid, should maintain sufficient number of substitutable services such that cascading failure can be minimized. Since The Language Grid currently has sufficient substitutable services for each service type, i.e. roughly 11 substitutable services for each component service in average, cascading failure is less likely to

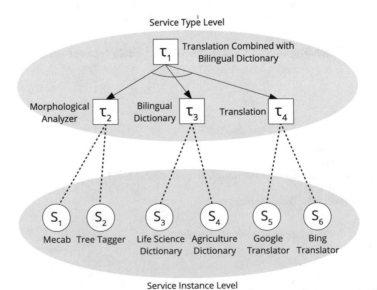

Fig. 1 Service composition in The Language Grid is modeled into two abstraction level

occur. However, in the near future The Language Grid is expected to be populated with more services and service types due to the Open Language Grid initiative that was designed to allow user groups to establish their own Language Grid servers. In addition, users may create composite services out of their own services or combining the services from other servers [11]. Therefore, investigating cascading failure among language services is still of importance.

To investigate cascading failure among language services, the dependency between the services is modeled as service network whose nodes represent services and links represent the dependency between them. On these service networks, cascading failure is simulated by randomly selecting a node to experience failure which then may trigger subsequent failures on the other dependent nodes. We observe the failure propagation in service networks of different topology. The simulation reveals that the number of failed nodes decay exponentially over the number of substitutable services. This result suggests that the existence of several substitutable services significantly improves the tolerance to cascading failure. As for the effect of network topology to cascading-failure tolerance, the simulation result shows service networks with scale-free topology have better tolerance compared to the other topologies. This is contrast to cascading failure in power networks, where scale-free topology shows poor tolerance [5].

2 Cascading Failure

Cascading failure possibly occurs in interdependent systems where failure of one system component disrupts the other dependent components. One of the well-known cascading failure in the Internet industry is Amazon EC2 outage that caused disorder to some major Internet companies which used their services [1]. In the study of critical infrastructure, cascading failure is defined as a disruption in one infrastructure that causes disruption in another [19]. Cascading failure has gained more interest since major cascading failure events [16] and power grid failures affecting large areas occurred in the past, such as those in Italy [20], North America [13], Australia, and New Zealand [2]. Major cascading failure events have also occurred in the past, such as fires in the aftermath of earthquake in San Francisco (1906) and Kobe (1995), and the disruption on some public services after a communication satellite orbital shift (May 1998) [16].

Even though much cascading failure research has been done in power network and critical infrastructure domains, it has not been much analyzed in SOC. In service networks, cascading failure happens when there is a failure in a node (link) and it is spreading into one or more than one nodes (links). Cascading failure is classified into two types: vertical and horizontal cascading failure [14]. The former happens when the failure follows a path along the links to either direction or to both direction, which is determined by the dependency among the neighboring cascades. As for the latter, the failure spreads to the other nodes (links) which are not necessary adjacent, such as that of in power network where the failure cascades due to load redistribution [5].

3 Language Service Network Model

We present the model of language service network (hereafter "service network" for brevity) as a directed network where a node represents a language service and a link represents dependency of one language service on the other. Next, we address the properties of a service network that are relevant to its tolerance against cascading failure. Finally, we address The Language Grid service network to support our analysis on cascading failure propagation and tolerance. The formal definition of a service network is given as follows:

- A service network is defined as $N = (S, E)$.
- $S = A \cup C$ is a set of services that consists of atomic services A and composite services C.
- $E = L \cup R$ is a set of links.
- L is the set of dependency links in the service network. L_i is the set of dependency links of a composite service s_i.
- R is the set of alternate links in the service network. $R_{i,j}$ is the set of alternate links of a dependency link $l_{i,j} \in L_i$ (see Fig. 2).

In addition to the definition above, to quantify the degree of interdependency between the services, the following measures are provided:

- Let service degree of dependency $dep_i = |L_i|$ be the number of services that may be executed at runtime by a composite service s_i.
- Let dependency link degree of alternative $alt_{i,j} = |R_{i,j}| - 1$ be the number of substitutable services that can substitute a failed service that associated to the same dependency link $l_{i,j}$.

An example of a service network is illustrated in Fig. 2, where a service is represented as a circle, and the dependency of a composite service on a component service

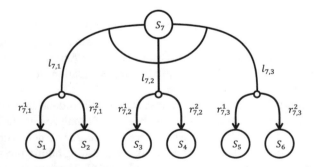

Fig. 2 The service network representation of the composite service "Translation Combined with Bilingual Dictionary" (Fig. 1). Each service is represented as a circle, while the dependency between two services is illustrated by an arrow. An arc connecting two or more links indicates that the service depends on all of the services pointed by the links, whereas a small circle indicates that the service requires either service connected by the links

is represented as an outgoing link originated from the composite service. The figure represents the dependency of the composite service "Translation Combined with Bilingual Dictionary" on its component services. In the service network, the composite service "Translation Combined with Bilingual Dictionary" is represented by the node s_7. The set of dependency links of s_7 is $L_7 = \{l_{7,1}, l_{7,2}, l_{7,3}\}$. Therefore, the degree of dependency of s_7 is $dep_7 = |L_7| = 3$.

The existence of a substitutable service is illustrated by splitting a dependency link into two or more alternate links. For example, the set of alternate links on $l_{7,1}$ is $R_{7,1} = \{r_{7,1}^1, r_{7,1}^2\}$. The degree of alternative of $l_{7,1}$ is $alt_{7,1} = |R_{7,1}| - 1 = 1$. Likewise, $l_{7,2}$ and $l_{7,3}$ degree of alternative is also 1. The existence of substitutable services, as well as alternate links, is useful to prevent cascading failure. Suppose service s_3 (Life Science Dictionary) is unexecutable, then the composite service s_7 is still able to perform its functions because there is another service, which is s_4 (Agriculture Dictionary), that can be invoked to perform the same functions.

3.1 Network Topology

We present some relevant properties that contribute to cascading-failure tolerance, which are network topology, the degree of interdependency between services, the depth of composite services, and the proportion of composite services in the network.

Some related work has proved that network topology influences tolerance to cascading failure [5]. For complex and large-scale networks, their topology is classified to their degree distribution [6]. Directed networks have in-degree distribution and out-degree distribution, which can be acquired by calculating the distribution of incoming and outgoing links. In service network, the out-degree of a service represents the number of component services that the service depends to, while the in-degree is the number of composite services that require this service as one of its components.

In this work, cascading failure is observed in service networks of three kinds of network topology: scale-free, exponential, and random network topology. The first two are the topology of growing networks, i.e. the type of networks on which the number of nodes and links increases over time. Scale-free network gains interests from researchers because of its high tolerance against random failure [3]. This network grows due to preferential attachment. Every time a node is added to the network, new connections are made from the newly added node to the existing ones. However, existing nodes with higher in-degree is always preferable to be chosen than those with lower in-degree. Scale-free networks are indicated with degree distribution that follows power-law as follows

$$P(k) \sim k^{-\gamma} \tag{1}$$

In Eq. 1, $P(k)$ is the probability to find a node having k connections, while γ is a constant within $2 < \gamma < 3$. Unlike scale-free networks on which the nodes are

Fig. 3 In-degree distribution
of scale-free, exponential,
and random service network
topology. The in-degree
distribution of these
topologies follow power-law,
exponential, and Poisson
distribution,
respectively [15]

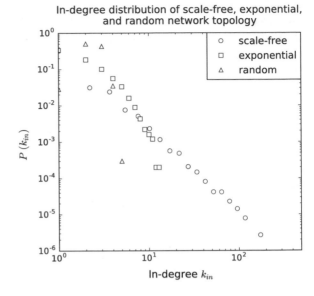

connected by preferential attachment, new nodes in exponential networks randomly
choose existing nodes to connect. Due to this random connections, the network will
exhibit exponential degree distribution [3].

Another network topology that has been long studied is random network. The
number of nodes in a random network is considered to be fixed, while the connections
are made in random manner between these existing nodes [7]. In this way, the network
will exhibit Poisson degree distribution.

Scale-free and exponential networks are discussed since most real networks are
growing networks where the number of nodes increases over time. Random network
is also observed in this chapter since this type of network has been widely studied and
represents the kind of service networks with fixed number of nodes. The in-degree
distribution of scale-free, exponential, and random service network is illustrated in
Fig. 3.

3.2 Degree of Interdependency Between Services

To measure the level of service interdependency in a service network, we provide
several metrics. First, the *network degree of dependency* ⟨*dep*⟩ measures the number
of required services for all composite services in the network. This is a global variable,
whereas the *composite service degree of dependency* dep_i, which has been addressed
earlier, applies only to a particular service $s_i \in C$. The formal definition of this
measure is as follows [14].

$$\langle dep \rangle = \frac{1}{|C|} \sum_i dep_i \tag{2}$$

Second, we also define the network degree of alternative $\langle alt \rangle$ to quantify the number of substitutable services in the network. Likewise, $\langle alt \rangle$ is also a global variable, whereas $alt_{i,j}$ represents the degree of alternative for the particular dependency link $l_{i,j}$. This measure is defined as [14]

$$\langle alt \rangle = \frac{1}{|L|} \sum_{i,j} alt_{i,j} \tag{3}$$

In addition to the aforementioned measures, another metric is also considered since it affects a service network tolerance to cascading failure [15]. The measure is the depth of service composition, which is considered because service composition can be nested. The deeper the composition, the more possible a composite service to experience cascading failure after random failure of one of its component services. The depth of a service s_i is defined as [14]

$$depth_i = \begin{cases} \frac{1}{|S_i|} \sum_{j=0}^{|S_i|-1} [depth_j + 1], & s_i \text{ is a composite service} \\ 0, & \text{otherwise} \end{cases} \tag{4}$$

while the depth of service composition for the whole network is defined as [15]

$$\langle depth \rangle = \frac{1}{|C|} \sum_i depth_i \tag{5}$$

In this chapter, we only consider the first two measures: $\langle dep \rangle$ and $\langle alt \rangle$. Even though the other measure also affects service network tolerance to cascading failure, it can be ignored in the current service network of The Language Grid. We found that The Language Grid service composition is shallow at $\langle depth \rangle = 1.29$ [15]. This shows that most composite services in The Language Grid are not nested.

4 The Language Grid Service Network

The Language Grid is a typical example of a service network, where users can add new services and combine existing services by means of service composition [10]. In The Language Grid, service types classify services based on their functionalities. Services belong to the same service type if they share the same functionalities A composite service type is a combination of different service types. An example of a composite service type has been illustrated in Fig. 1.

Fig. 4 In-degree distribution of The Language Grid service networks

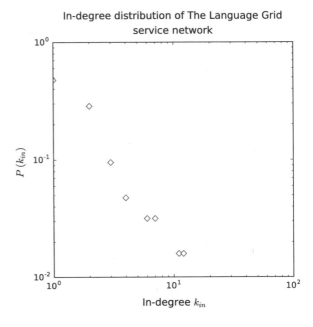

The Language Grid operation centers have been established in several countries, including Japan (Kyoto), Thailand (Bangkok), Indonesia (Jakarta), and China (Urumqi), which in total provide 188 services as of October 2014 when the experiment was conducted. The architecture of The Language Grid allows one to combine services across different operation centers [17]. Here, we limit our analysis on 117 atomic services and 21 composite services provided by Kyoto Language Grid operation center. Even though the proportion of composite services in The Language Grid (15%) is much less than the proportion of atomic service, they are frequently invoked, which is 47% of all invocations. This indicates that the composite services are vital for The Language Grid users. These composite services mostly consist of 2–3 atomic services at $\langle dep \rangle = 2.81$. The Language Grid has many substitutable services at $\langle alt \rangle = 10.92$ [14]. The high $\langle alt \rangle$ gives The Language Grid high tolerance to cascading failure, as it will be explained in Sect. 5.2.1.

Even though the number of services in The Language Grid is expected to grow, the current size of the network is rather small. Therefore, the network topology of The Language Grid still cannot be classified by its in-degree distribution as it shows neither power-law nor exponential distribution (Fig. 4). However, larger service networks generally exhibit scale-free topology [8, 9, 12, 18]. As the other scale-free networks on which the connections are made in preferential manner [3], composite services in the Language Grid also tend to combine widely used and popular services, and thus would become scale-free [15].

5 Cascading Failure Simulation

To perform cascading failure simulation, some service networks are generated with different topology and different degree of interdependency. The first part provides the algorithms to generate these networks, while the second part addresses the way to simulate cascading failure and the analysis of the simulation result.

5.1 Generating Service Networks

In this Section, we generate artificial service networks, i.e. the networks that are computationally created from scratch instead of generated from existing service networks. We generate some service networks with different degree of interdependency and different topologies, which are scale-free, exponential, and random networks. Analyzing these three topologies help us to understand which one has better tolerance towards cascading failure.

5.1.1 Scale-Free, Exponential, and Random Service Network

Both scale-free network and exponential network are a part of growing network, which is why the same algorithm is used to generate them. What make these two are different is the way they choose existing nodes for making connections. Scale-free networks use preferential attachment to choose the service to connect to, while exponential networks choose randomly.

Our algorithm uses the preferential attachment probability function as follows [4]

$$\Pi(k_i^{in}, \alpha) = \frac{k_i^{in} + \alpha}{\Sigma_j (k_j^{in} + \alpha)} \tag{6}$$

where k_i^{in} is the service s_i in-degree, j is the index for all services, and α is the initial attractiveness parameter. According to this function, the higher the in-degree of a service, the more possible it is to be chosen. The initial attractiveness α gives value to the services with zero in-degree, such as those which are newly added to the network.

The algorithm to generate scale-free and exponential service networks uses the following parameters [15]:

- n_0 is the number of isolated services at the beginning of the simulation t_0
- $\Delta t \geq 0$ is the duration of the network generation
- $c \in [0, 1]$ is the expected proportion of composite services in the network
- δ is the expected degree of dependency (dep) such that $\delta \sim \langle dep \rangle$
- λ is the expected degree of alternative $\langle alt \rangle$ such that $\lambda \approx \langle alt \rangle$
- α is the initial attractiveness parameter

The algorithm begins at t_0 when n_0 service nodes are added to the network without making connections between them. The next steps are to add some more nodes and to make connections from the newly added nodes to the existing ones. The following steps will be performed iteratively at each timestep from $t = t_1$ until $t = t_0 + \Delta t$ [15]:

1. Create a service s_i.
2. Under probability c, generate dep_i, a random number within $[1, \delta \times 2 - 1]$.
3. If dep_i is generated in step (2)
   a. Create the set of dependency links $L_i = \{l_{i,0}, ..., l_{i,dep_i-1}\}$.
   b. For each dependency link $l_{i,j} \in L_i$, generate a random number $alt_{i,j}$ within $[0, \lambda \times 2]$.
   c. If $alt_{i,j} = 0$
      i. Choose a service $s_p \in S \mid s_p \neq s_i$.
      ii. Connect the dependency link $l_{i,j}$ from s_i to s_p.
   d. Else
      i. Choose $alt_{i,j} + 1$ services.
      ii. Split the dependency link $l_{i,j}$ into $alt_{i,j} + 1$ alternate links.
      iii. Connect these alternate links to the chosen services.

The connections will only be made between services that are currently not connected and will not be connected to themselves, i.e. the network restricts multiple links and self links. In the algorithm, the first step is to initialize a service network with some number of atomic services, and then add one service at a time. The number of composite services is determined by the probability c (step 2). A newly added service becomes an atomic service if no dependency link created for the service, but it will become composite service if one or more dependency links are added to the service. In making connections (step 3.c and 3.d) the way to choose the existing nodes depends on the network topology to be created. If the network is expected to be scale-free, then preferential attachment (Eq. 6) is applied. Otherwise, the nodes are chosen randomly such that the network will grow as exponential network.

The same algorithm to generate exponential service network is used when we want to generate random service network, but it does not need node addition. Thus, random service network algorithm uses all the parameters except the number of duration of the network generation Δt and the number of nodes is fixed so that $n_0 = |S|$. The algorithm to generate random service network is as follows [15]:

1. Populate the network with n_0, which is also the expected size of the network.
2. For each $s_i \in S$, do the steps 2 and 3 in the algorithm as generating exponential service networks.

5.1.2 The Language Grid Service Network

Apart from generating service networks with different topology, we also generate The Language Grid service network to observe cascading failure in a real language service network. As illustrated in Fig. 1, The Language Grid services are classified into service types according to the functionalities they provide. The Language Grid service network is generated by representing service instances as atomic service nodes, and service types as composite service nodes. The links from composite service nodes to their component service nodes are created based on the service types they combined. If a combined service type is realized by only one service instance, a dependency link is created connecting the composite service node to the atomic service node. If there are more than one service instance that can provide the functionality for the service type, alternate links are created to connect the composite service node to these atomic service nodes. Nested composition is created when a composite service types combines one or more composite service types. The service network representation of a composite service in The Language Grid, including its component services, has been illustrated in Fig. 2.

5.2 Simulation Result and Analysis

In this simulation, we use different types of topology to create service networks, each of which has different $\langle dep \rangle$ and $\langle alt \rangle$, using the algorithm explained in Sect. 5.1. Therefore, according to their topology, the simulation generate three typical types of service network (scale-free, exponential, and random) and The Language Grid service network that is simulated from real world service network.

Scale-free and exponential service networks are created with a few initial services, i.e. $n_0 = 10$. Then, for the duration of $\Delta t = 10,000$, adding one service at a time to make the network grows until it reaches the size of 10,010 nodes. The scale-free networks are generated with the initial attractiveness parameter α is set at 1. For random service networks, it is initialized with fixed number of services $n_0 = 10,010$. For all these three kinds of topology, the composite service proportion parameter is $c = 0.4$ so that 40% of the nodes are composite services, whereas 60% are atomic services. Different $\langle dep \rangle$ and $\langle alt \rangle$ are also implemented to these networks by setting different values for δ and γ parameters. As for The Language Grid service network, as we have explained in Sect. 5.1.2, it is generated based on its existing composite services.

Briefly, the simulation works as follow. First, a service network is generated for the expected network topology, $\langle dep \rangle$, and $\langle alt \rangle$ according to the algorithm in Sect. 5.1. After the service network is created, the following algorithm is executed.

While there is an active service in the network, do the following:

1. An active service is chosen randomly to be deactivated to simulate random failure. This service is called random failed service.
2. If the random failed service is a component service, i.e. it participates in one or more service compositions, deactivate the composite services when there is no substitutable service. The deactivation is performed recursively all the way to the outermost composite services.

To analyze how cascading failure occurs in service networks, we observe the number of cascade failed services n_c over the number of random failed services n_r. The value n_c is acquired by counting the failed composite services in step 2. For each iteration above, one active service is chosen randomly to experience random failure (step 1). Therefore, n_r is actually the number of iteration. The last iteration is performed when the network is collapse, which is when $n_r + n_c = |S|$. The analysis of the simulation results are addressed next.

5.2.1 Network Topology and Cascading-Failure Tolerance

To analyze the effect of network topology on the cascading failure, we observe the number of cascade failed services over the number of random failed services (Fig. 5). The value $\langle dep \rangle$ is set at its lowest possible value 1, while the value $\langle alt \rangle$ varies at 0, 0.5, and 1 on Fig. 5a, b, c, respectively. From the figures, networks with scale-free topology have a better tolerance compared to exponential networks because

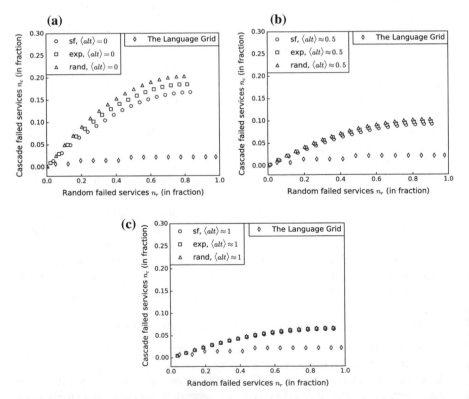

Fig. 5 The number of cascade failed services over the number of random failed services on different topology and different degree of interdependency

the fraction of high in-degree nodes in scale-free network is much less than that in an exponential network. This is similar to when we compare exponential network to random network, in that exponential network has better tolerance than random network because the fraction of high-degree nodes in exponential network is much less than the ones in random network. In addition, the graphs also show that the effect of network topology on the tolerance to cascading failure getting less significant as $\langle alt \rangle$ increases, because the more substitutable services in the network, the higher tolerance to cascading failure. The existence of substitutable services also explains the high tolerance of The Language Grid on cascading failure. With $\langle alt \rangle = 10.92$, the number of cascade failed services in The Language Grid is very low.

5.2.2 Degree of Dependency and Cascading-Failure Tolerance

To analyze the effect of $\langle dep \rangle$ on cascading failure, Fig. 6a provides the number of cascade failed services over $\langle dep \rangle$ for service networks at $\langle alt \rangle = 0$ and $n_r = 0.2$. Cascade failed services are frequent in service networks with higher $\langle dep \rangle$. This is because the interdependency between the services is stronger.

The graph also shows linear relationship between the number of cascade failed services and $\langle dep \rangle$. The shallow depth of service composition in the network is the one which is responsible for this linear relationship. So from the result above, we can decrease the number of required component services from each composite service in order to increase the cascading-failure tolerance. Unfortunately, $\langle dep \rangle$ cannot always be predefined since the number of component services in service composition is usually determined by the problem domain. Therefore, it is important to consider improving $\langle alt \rangle$ to achieve an expected degree of tolerance instead of restricting the number component services.

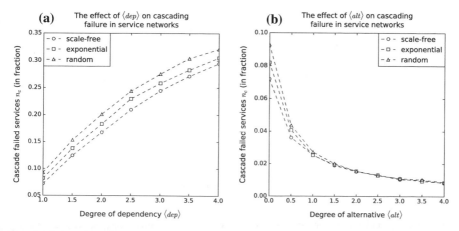

Fig. 6 The number of cascade failed services over the degree of dependency (**a**) and the degree of alternative (**b**) [15]

5.2.3 Degree of Alternative and Cascading-Failure Tolerance

To observe the effect of $\langle alt \rangle$ to service network tolerance on cascading failure, Fig. 6b illustrates the graphs of the number of cascade failed services over $\langle alt \rangle$. In these service networks, $\langle dep \rangle$ is set to 1, which is the lowest possible value to vary $\langle alt \rangle$. From the result, we can increase the network tolerance towards cascading failure by increasing $\langle alt \rangle$. However, the improvement of the tolerance to cascading failure will be significant only when the $\langle alt \rangle$ is currently low at $\langle alt \rangle < 2$. On higher $\langle alt \rangle$, the improvement of the tolerance becomes less significant. When having many substitutable services is considered costly, the simulation result suggests that having several substitutable services (e.g. 2 or 3) would be sufficient to have a good tolerance.

6   Conclusion

The purpose of this study is to analyze the effect of interdependency between services and network topology to cascading failure tolerance in language service networks. To this end, we executed a random failure simulation on scale-free, exponential, and random service networks with different degree of interdependency to observe cascading failure tolerance. In addition, the simulation was also performed on The Language Grid service networks.

We conclude some important findings in this chapter as follows [15]:

1. The effect of network topology on tolerance is more significant on lower degree of alternative, i.e. where the average number of substitutable services for each required component service is low.
2. The number of cascade failed services, i.e. the nodes experiencing cascading failure, is inversely proportional to the degree of alternative.
3. The number of cascade failed services is somewhat linear to the degree of dependency, i.e. the average number of component services.
4. Scale-free topology has better tolerance to cascading failure, followed by exponential and random topology. This statement is in contradiction with the load-based cascading failure tolerance in power networks which stated that random topology has better tolerance than scale-free [5].

Acknowledgements This research was supported by the Grant-in-Aid for Scientific Research (S) (24220002, 2012–2016) from Japan Society for the Promotion of Science (JSPS).

References

1. Armbrust, M., Fox, O., Griffith, R., Joseph, A.D., Katz, Y., Konwinski, A., Lee, G., Patterson, D., Rabkin, A., Stoica, I., Zaharia, M.: Above the Clouds: A Berkeley View of Cloud Computing. Technical Report, University of California at Berkeley (2009)

2. Ash, J., Newth, D.: Optimizing complex networks for resilience against cascading failure. Phys. A Stat. Mech. Appl. **380**, 673–683 (2007)
3. Barabási, A.L., Albert, R., Jeong, H.: Mean-field theory for scale-free random networks. Phys. A Stat. Mech. Appl. **272**(1), 173–187 (1999)
4. Chen, Q., Shi, D.: The modeling of scale-free networks. Phys. A Stat. Mech. Appl. **335**(1), 240–248 (2004)
5. Crucitti, P., Latora, V., Marchiori, M.: Model for cascading failures in complex networks. Phys. Rev. E **69**(4), 045104 (2004)
6. Dorogovtsev, S.N., Mendes, J.F.: Evolution of networks. Adv. Phys. **51**(4), 1079–1187 (2002)
7. Erdős, P., Rényi, A.: On the evolution of random graphs. Magyar Tud. Akad. Mat. Kutató Int. Közl **5**, 17–61 (1960)
8. Feng, Z., Lan, B., Zhang, Z., Chen, S.: A study of semantic web services network. Comput. J. **58**, 1293–1305 (2014)
9. Huang, K., Fan, Y., Tan, W.: An empirical study of programmable web: a network analysis on a service-mashup system. In: 2012 IEEE 19th International Conference on Web Services (ICWS), pp. 552–559 (2012)
10. Ishida, T. (ed.): The Language Grid: Service-Oriented Collective Intelligence for Language Resource Interoperability. Springer Science & Business Media (2011)
11. Ishida, T., Murakami, Y., Lin, D., Nakaguchi, T., Otani, M.: Open Language Grid: towards a global language service infrastructure. In: The Third ASE International Conference on Social Informatics (SocialInformatics 2014), Cambridge, Massachusetts, USA (2014)
12. Kil, H., Oh, S.C., Elmacioglu, E., Nam, W., Lee, D.: Graph theoretic topological analysis of web service networks. World Wide Web **12**(3), 321–343 (2009)
13. Kinney, R., Crucitti, P., Albert, R., Latora, V.: Modeling cascading failures in the North American power grid. Eur. Phys. J. B Condens. Matter Complex Syst. **46**(1), 101–107 (2005)
14. Lhaksmana, K.M., Murakami, Y., Ishida, T.: Cascading failure tolerance in large-scale service networks. In: 2015 IEEE International Conference on Services Computing (SCC), pp. 1–8 (2015)
15. Lhaksmana, K.M., Murakami, Y., Ishida, T.: Analysis of large-scale service network tolerance to cascading failure. IEEE Internet Things J. **3**(6), 1159–1170 (2016)
16. Little, R.G.: Controlling cascading failure: understanding the vulnerabilities of interconnected infrastructures. J. Urban Technol. **9**(1), 109–123 (2002)
17. Murakami, Y., Tanaka, M., Lin, D., Ishida, T.: Service grid federation architecture for heterogeneous domains. In: 2012 IEEE Ninth International Conference on Services Computing (SCC), pp. 539–546 (2012)
18. Oh, S.C., Lee, D., Kumara, S.R.: Effective web service composition in diverse and large-scale service networks. IEEE Trans. Serv. Comput. **1**(1), 15–32 (2008)
19. Rinaldi, S., Peerenboom, J., Kelly, T.: Identifying, understanding, and analyzing critical infrastructure interdependencies. IEEE Control Syst. **21**(6), 11–25 (2001)
20. Rosato, V., Issacharoff, L., Tiriticco, F., Meloni, S., Porcellinis, S., Setola, R.: Modelling interdependent infrastructures using interacting dynamical models. Int. J. Crit. Infrastruct. **4**(1), 63–79 (2008)

Part III
Language Resources and Services Creation

A Constraint Approach to Lexicon Induction for Low-Resource Languages

Mairidan Wushouer, Donghui Lin, Toru Ishida and Yohei Murakami

Abstract Bilingual lexicon is a useful language resource, but such data rarely available for lower-density language pairs, especially for those that are closely related. The lack or absence of parallel and comparable corpora makes bilingual lexicon extraction becomes a difficult task. Using a third language to link two other languages is a well-known solution in low-resource situation, which usually requires only two input bilingual lexicons to automatically induce the new one. This approach, however, is weak in measuring semantic distance between bilingual word pairs because it has never been demonstrated to utilize the complete structures of the input bilingual lexicons as dropped meanings negatively influence the result. This research discuss a constraint approach to pivot-based lexicon induction in case the target language pair are closely related. We create constraints from language similarity and model the structures of the input dictionaries as an optimization problem whose solution produces optimally correct target bilingual lexicon. In addition, we enable created bilingual lexicons of low-resource languages accessible through service grid federation.

Keywords Low-resource languages · Bilingual dictionary induction · Pivot language · Weighted partial max-SAT · Constraint satisfaction problem

M. Wushouer (✉)
Department of Computer Science, Xinjiang University,
666 Shengli Road, Urumqi, Xinjiang Uyghur Autonomous Region,
People's Republic of China
e-mail: mardan@xju.edu.cn

D. Lin · T. Ishida
Department of Social Informatics, Kyoto University,
Kyoto 606-8501, Japan
e-mail: lindh@i.kyoto-u.ac.jp

T. Ishida
e-mail: ishida@i.kyoto-u.ac.jp

Y. Murakami
Unit of Design, Kyoto University,
91 Chudoji Awata-cho, Kyoto 600-8815, Japan
e-mail: yohei@i.kyoto-u.ac.jp

© Springer Nature Singapore Pte Ltd. 2018
Y. Murakami et al. (eds.), *Services Computing for Language Resources*,
Cognitive Technologies, https://doi.org/10.1007/978-981-10-7793-7_7

1 Introduction

Machine readable bilingual lexicon is very useful in information retrieval and natural language processing researches, yet usually unavailable for low resource language pairs. Hence researchers have investigated the issue of automatic creation of bilingual lexicon. For example, a bilingual lexicon has been induced from large scale parallel corpus [1]. More recently, the use of comparable corpora has drawn increasing attention [2, 22] since the Internet era has made monolingual data readily available while parallel corpus remain scarce.

From the viewpoint of the etymological closeness of languages, some studies directly tackled the creation of dictionaries for closely related language pairs such as Spanish and Portuguese [13], by using specific heuristics such as spelling. These studies, however, describe techniques that are not language transparent. Another well-known approach, pivot-based induction, uses a widespread language as a bridge between less-resourced language pairs. In other word, it induces a new bilingual lexicon A-C from two existing dictionaries A-B and B-C. Due to the polysemic and ambiguous words in the pivot language this approach easily produce incorrect translation pairs as lexicons are generally intransitive. To cope with the issue of divergence, previous studies attempted to select correct translation pairs by using semantic distances from the structures of the input dictionaries [18] or by using additional resources [4, 14, 15]. Although the technique of adding resources to pivot-based induction is promising for improving performance [14], a basic method that uses the structures of the input dictionaries must be developed because: (1) It is essential for inadequately-resourced languages; (2) It is compatible with other approaches and so can be combined [11]; (3) There is potential for improving quality by considering the missing meanings [12].

In this research, inspired by [5], we investigate a constraint-based method for pivot-based lexicon induction to promote the quality of output bilingual lexicon A-C, where A and C are closely related languages while pivot language B is distant [21]. More precisely, we try to obtain semantic distance by constraining the types of connection in the structures of the input dictionaries based on a one-to-one assumption of intra-family language lexicons, which assumes that lexicons of closely related languages offer one-to-one mapping and share a significant number of cognates (words with similar spelling and meaning which originated from the same root language). Furthermore, instances of pivot-based lexicon induction are represented by graphs, to which weighted edges are added to represent missing meanings. In this context, Weighted Partial Max-SAT framework (WPMax-SAT), an optimization extension of Boolean Satisfiability is used to encode the graphs that will generate the optimal output bilingual lexicon. The reasons for using the WPMax-SAT framework as a primary formalization are that (1) the hidden facts such as whether a word pair is a correct translation, whether a meaning of pivot word is missing from the dictionaries have binary states when they are unknown to machine, (2) automatic detection of correct translation pairs and missing meanings whose states are bounded by certain weights can be seen as an optimization problem, which is to find the most reliably correct translation pairs, and while adding the most probable missing meaning(s), and (3) the constraints inferred from language similarity can easily be transformed into propositional expressions. Meanwhile, we explore a possible extensions to our framework: using an additional input bilingual lexicon to obtain more complete information for calculating the semantic distance between word senses which is key to suppressing wrong sense matches [20]. Automatically created bilingual lexicons of low-resource languages are accessible through service grid federation [3, 6, 7].

2   Pivot-Based Bilingual Lexicon Induction

Let $D_{l_1-l_2}$ denote the bilingual lexicon of l_1 and l_2 languages. It is a relation linking any word in one language to one or more words in the other language. Using a pivot language is well known in research on machine translation, and service computing since a large number of language resources are being accumulated as web services, and the recent service computing technologies allow us to utilize existing services to create new composite services [19]. However, in this context, the pivot-based induction is used to induce new bilingual lexicon D_{A-C} from existing D_{A-B} and D_{B-C}, where a pair of words in languages A and C is added to D_{A-C} if they have same translation in B. Such a D_{A-C} may include both correct and incorrect translation pairs. More precisely, if pivot word w^B is a translation of w^A with respect to a sense s and w^C is a translation of w^B with respect to the same sense s we can say that w^C is a translation of w^A. Assume that we are seeking translations of words in language A to those in language C using D_{A-B} and D_{B-C}. If pivot word w^B is a translation of w^A in D_{A-B} and w^C is a translation of w^B in D_{B-C}, we could say that w^C is hence a translation of w^A. Note that this deduction is not correct because it does not take account the word sense: in Fig. 1, w^C (in case of w_2^C) can be the translation of w^B (w_1^B) for sense s (s_3) different from the sense for which w^B (w_1^B) is the equivalent of w^A (w_1^A). This can happen when pivot word w^B is polysemous or ambiguous.

The structures of D_{A-B} and D_{B-C} forms a graph in which vertex represents a word and an edge indicates shared meanings. Each connected component in this graph is called a *transgraph* which is defined as follows.

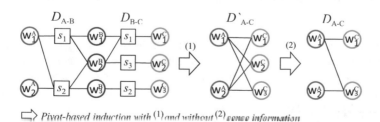

⇨ Pivot-based induction with $^{(1)}$ and without $^{(2)}$ sense information

Fig. 1 Pivot-based bilingual lexicon induction and ambiguity problem

Definition 1 a transgraph is defined as undirected graph $G = \{V, E\}$, in which a vertex $w_i^l \in V$ is a word in language $l \in \{A, B, C\}$, and an edge $e(w_i^A, w_j^B) \in E$ or $e(w_h^C, w_j^B) \in E$ represents the belief that the word w_i^A and w_h^C shares at least one meaning with pivot word w_j^B, while $\neg e(w_i^A, w_j^B)$ and $\neg e(w_h^C, w_j^B)$ expresses the belief that there is no meaning in common.

We also use V^A, V^B and V^C to denote all the words (in terms of a *transgraph*) in language A, B and C, respectively. For the further use, $V_{w_i^{l_1}}^{l_2}$ denotes a set of meanings of $w_i^{l_1}$ in language l_2.

3 Constraint-Based Approach

3.1 Semantic Constraint Assumption

Historical linguistics is the scientific study of language change over time in term of sound, analogical, lexical, morphological, syntactic, and semantic information. Comparative linguistics is a branch of historical linguistics that is concerned with language comparison to determine their historical relatedness and to construct language families. There are many methods, techniques, and procedures utilized in the investigation of the potential distant genetic relationship of languages, including lexical comparison, sound correspondences, grammatical evidence, borrowing, semantic constraints, chance similarities, sound-meaning isomorphism, etc. The genetic relationship of languages is used to classify languages into language family. Closely related languages are those that have the same origin or proto-language, and usually belong to the same language family. Glottochronology, one of lexical comparison method as formulated by Swadesh [16], is a method for estimating the amount of time elapsed since related languages diverged from a common ancestral language. Glottochronology depends on basic, relatively culture-free vocabulary, which is known as Swadesh list.

The key characteristic of intra-family languages is that their lexicons are similar, and share a significant number of cognates – words that are derived from same origin and are similar in both spelling and meaning. Most cognate pairs have direct translations, meaning that they correspond one-to-one. A classical lexicostatistical study of 15 Turkic languages,[1] mostly used in central Asia, indicated that cognate pairs shared among members of Turkic language family scales from 44% to 94% of their lexicons, and majority of non-cognates tend to be noun. Although, there are some studies on constructing bilingual lexicon for intra-family languages by recognizing these cognate pairs, they often turned out to be language-pair-dependent since subsequent separate phonetic development of languages has made many cognates not identical in spelling (Table 1).

---

[1] http://turkic-languages.scienceontheweb.net.

Table 1 The lexicostatistical matrix of turkic languages

(%)	Kyrgyz	Kazakh	Uzbek	Uyghur	Tatar	Turkmen	Azeri
Kazakh	92						
Uzbek	82.9	82.8					
Uyghur	83.8	81.9	86.3				
Tatar	83.9	82.1	78	79.6			
Turkmen	71.2	71.9	75.9	71.7	69.8		
Azeri	66.9	67.8	70	68.8	68.4	78.2	
Turkish	64.9	64.8	67.2	66.7	65.6	73.6	86

Taking account of such facts, we make the following semantic assumption: *lexicons of intra-family languages offer one-to-one relation.* That is, if A and C are intra-family, for any w_i^A there exists a unique w_j^C, such that they have exactly same meaning. Such a pair is called one-to-one pair, and denoted by $\mathbb{O}(w_i^A, w_j^C)$. Accordingly, $\neg\mathbb{O}(w_i^A, w_j^C)$ denies, logically, the state of one-to-one relation.

3.2 Semantic Constraints

As the initial step of pivot-based techniques, the possible translation pairs are selected to generate a noisy $D_{A\text{-}C}$ based on the structures of the input dictionaries. In this research, we also take such step, so that whether word pair (w_i^A, w_j^C) can be a one-to-one pair candidate is decided by the following constraint.

Constraint 1 *A pair of words, w_i^A and w_j^C, in a transgraph, can be one-to-one pair candidate if they are connected via at least one pivot word.*

That is, a word pair is taken to be a candidate and subjected to further evaluation only if they share at least one word in the pivot language. This constraint can be expressed by the following propositional expression, which states that if two sets, $V_{w_i^A}^B$ and $V_{w_j^C}^B$, do not overlap, then w_i^A and w_j^C never be translation pair candidate.

$$(V_{w_i^A}^B \cap V_{w_j^C}^B = \emptyset) \rightarrow \neg\mathbb{O}(w_i^A, w_j^C) \tag{1}$$

Constraint 2 *Given a pair of words, w_i^A and w_j^C, in a transgraph, if they are a one-to-one pair, then they should be symmetrically connected through pivot word(s).*

In other words, a one-to-one pair must share the same words in pivot language; the number of edges between w_i^A and pivot words should equal to the number of edges between w_j^C and pivot words. This constraint is written in the following propositional expression:

$$\mathbb{O}(w_i^A, w_j^C) \rightarrow \bigwedge_{w_h^B \in V_{w_i^A w_j^C}^B} \left[e(w_i^A, w_h^B) \wedge e(w_j^C, w_h^B) \right] \tag{2}$$

where $V_{w_i^A}^B$ and $V_{w_j^C}^B$ are the sets of meanings of w_i^A and w_j^C in language B, and $V_{w_i^A w_j^C}^B = V_{w_i^A}^B \cup V_{w_j^C}^B$.

The one-to-one assumption restricts that a translation pair of intra-family languages should be unique, meaning any w_i^A must have single one-to-one equivalent in language C, and vice versa. This needs a constrain which can be stated as follows.

Constraint 3 *Given a pair of words, w_i^A and w_j^C, in a transgraph, if they are a one-to-one pair, then they should be unique, such that all other candidates involving w_i^A or w_j^C are not one-to-one pairs. This constraint is written as the following propositional expression.*

$$\mathbb{O}(w_i^A, w_j^C) \rightarrow \left[\bigwedge_{h \neq j} \neg \mathbb{O}(w_i^A, w_h^C) \right] \wedge \left[\bigwedge_{p \neq i} \neg \mathbb{O}(w_p^A, w_j^C) \right] \tag{3}$$

where the first AND operation iterates over the words w_h^C (excluding the given w_j^C) that are one-to-one candidates of w_i^A, and, likewise, the last AND operation iterates over the words w_p^A (excluding the given w_i^A) that are one-to-one candidates of w_j^C.

3.3 Weight Estimation

The completeness of input dictionaries is seldom guaranteed. Due to data incompleteness there could be missed meanings that would lead to asymmetry in the word pair w_i^A and w_j^C in a transgraph, which could harm the quality of induction. To satisfy the symmetry assumption, new edges can be added. However, to travel a new edge, a cost must be paid as it is uncertain if a edge is really missed. We calculate the cost based on the possibility of the translation pair candidate being wrongly selected according to the structure of the transgraph, which we define as the weight of a translation pair candidate. The weight of a new edge from a non-pivot word w_i^A to a pivot word w_j^B is defined as $\omega(w_i^A, w_j^B)$ and the weight of a new edge from pivot word w_j^B to non-pivot word w_k^C is defined as $\omega(w_j^B, w_k^C)$. Both of their values equal the weight of the translation pair candidate (w_i^A, w_k^C). The weight of adding the new edges is $1 - P(w_i^A, w_k^C)$. The higher the possibility of the translation pair candidate being selected correctly is (determined by the structure of the transgraph), the lower is the cost to be paid of adding any new edge to it. For sake of simplicity, following [8], to calculate the possibility of translation pair candidate $P(w_i^A, w_k^C)$, we calculate the conditional translation probabilities $P(w_i^A | w_k^C)$ and $P(w_k^C | w_i^A)$. We further calculate the product of the probabilities using $P(w_i^A | w_k^C) \times P(w_k^C | w_i^A)$. The algorithm to calculate probability of the translation pair candidates is shown in Algorithm 1.

Algorithm 1 Weight Estimation

Input: G – a transgraph
Output: C – set of translation pair candidates
1: **for** *each* w_i^A *in* G **do**
2:     **for** *each* w_j^B *that share edge with* w_i^A **do**
3:         **for** *each* w_k^C *that share edge with* w_j^B **do**
4:             $P(w_i^A|w_k^C) = 0; P(w_k^C|w_i^A) = 0;$
5:             **for** *each path from* w_i^A *to* w_k^C **do**
6:                 $P(w_i^A|w_j^B) = 1/\text{indegree toward } w_j^B;$
7:                 $P(w_j^B|w_k^C) = 1/\text{indegree toward } w_k^C;$
8:                 $P(w_k^C|w_j^B) = 1/\text{outegree from } w_j^B;$
9:                 $P(w_j^B|w_i^A) = 1/\text{outegree from } w_i^A;$
10:              $P(w_i^A|w_k^C)+ = P(w_i^A|w_j^B) \times P(w_j^B|w_k^C);$
11:              $P(w_k^C|w_i^A)+ = P(w_k^C|w_j^B) \times P(w_j^B|w_i^A);$
12:             **end for**
13:         **end for**
14:         $P(w_i^A, w_k^C) = P(w_i^A|w_k^C) \times P(w_k^C|w_i^A);$
15:         $C \leftarrow C \cup t(w_i^A, w_k^C)$
16:     **end for**
17: **end for**
18: **return** C;

---

4 Framework Generalization

4.1 Preliminaries

Boolean Satisfiability (SAT) is the problem of finding, if it exists, an assignment to the set of Boolean variables $\mathbb{V}$ that satisfies the Boolean formula expressed in CNF (Conjunctive Normal Form). A *literal* is a Boolean variable υ or its negation $\neg\upsilon$; a *clause* is a disjunction (logical OR) of literals (e.g., $\upsilon_1 \vee \neg\upsilon_2 \vee \neg\upsilon_3$). Each clause consists of ORed literals. A CNF φ is the conjunction (logical AND) of m clauses $c_1, \dots, c_m$, where c_i is a disjunction of k_i literals. φ is *satisfied* if it evaluates to 1 (TRUE), such that all $c_i \in \varphi$ evaluate to 1.

There are several extensions to the SAT problem. One such extension of interest is Weighted partial Max-SAT (WPMax-SAT), which aims to satisfy a partial set of clauses. In a WPMax-SAT problem, clauses are assigned weights (natural number in most cases, though real numbers is also widely used), and are separated into hard and soft types. Hard clauses have maximum weights (represented by infinity ∞) and all must be satisfied, while soft clauses need to be satisfied such that the sum of the weights of the satisfied soft clauses is maximized or sum of the weights of the unsatisfied (falsified) is minimized.

Formally, $\varphi = \{(c_1, \omega_1), \dots, (c_m, \omega_m), (c_{m+1}, \infty), (c_{m+m'}, \infty)\}$ is the representation of WPMax-SAT, where the first m clauses (φ^+) are soft and last m' clauses

(φ^∞) are hard. WCNF formula (weighted extension of CNF) φ is the problem of finding an assignment to the set of Boolean variables $\mathbb{V}$ that minimizes the cost of the assignment on φ. If the cost is infinity, it means that we must falsify a hard clause, and say that the multiset is unsatisfiable.

4.2 Encoding

As a first step of casting the problem in WPMax-SAT form, we apparently need a variable to denote whether a given word pair is a one-to-one pair. Moreover, another variable is also needed to represent whether an edge is missing, since the identification of a one-to-one pair requires the existence of particular edges. Overall, we use x and y to denote one-to-one pair candidates and edges in the transgraph, respectively:

- $x_{i,j}$, representing a pair (w_i^A, w_j^C), turns TRUE if it is one-to-one pair; turns FALSE otherwise. (It is easily estimated that number of x variables of a transgraph never exceeds $|V^A| \times |V^C|$). X denotes a set of x variables in given problem instance.
- $y_{i,j}^A$, representing an edge $e(w_i^A, w_j^B)$, turns TRUE if it exist; turns FALSE otherwise.
- $y_{h,j}^C$, represents an edge $e(w_h^C, w_j^B)$, turns TRUE if it exist; turns FALSE otherwise.

Note that $Y_{existing}^l$ and $Y_{missing}^l$, $l \in \{A, C\}$, denote the set of existing and missing edges, respectively.

Before evaluating a WPMax-SAT problem by using a solver, it must be encoded to CNF. We use hard clauses to encode all the constraints that must be satisfied, and an apparent constraint: *an existing edge cannot be deleted*. Meanwhile, the missing edges are encoded with soft clauses since adding an edge is not mandatory. In the following clause formulations, φ^∞ indicates hard, while φ^+ indicates soft.

Hard clauses in encoding to prevent edge deletion

$$\varphi_1^\infty = [\bigwedge (y_{i,j}^A, \infty)] \wedge [\bigwedge (y_{h,j}^C, \infty)] \tag{4}$$

where $y_{i,j}^A \in Y_{existing}^A$, $y_{h,j}^C \in Y_{existing}^C$

Soft clauses in encoding for addition of missing edges

$$\varphi^+ = [\bigwedge (\neg y_{i,j}^A, 1 - \omega_{i,j}^A)] \wedge [\bigwedge (\neg y_{h,j}^C, 1 - \omega_{h,j}^C)] \tag{5}$$

where $y_{i,j}^A \in Y_{missing}^A$, $y_{h,j}^C \in Y_{missing}^C$; ω is the weight.

Hard clauses encoding Symmetry Constraint

$$\varphi_2^\infty = [\bigwedge (\neg x_{i,j} \vee y_{i,h}^A, \infty)] \wedge [\bigwedge (\neg x_{i,j} \vee y_{j,h}^C, \infty)] \tag{6}$$

Hard clauses encoding Uniqueness Constraint

$$\varphi_3^\infty = [\bigwedge_{j \neq h} (\neg x_{i,j} \vee \neg x_{i,h}, \infty)] \wedge [\bigwedge_{i \neq p} (\neg x_{i,j} \vee \neg x_{p,j}, \infty)] \tag{7}$$

4.3 Finding Solution

CNF formula $\varphi = \varphi^+ \wedge \varphi_1^\infty \wedge \varphi_2^\infty \wedge \varphi_3^\infty$ can be evaluated by a Max-SAT solver to output an optimal variable assignment (solution). However, any satisfiable assignment on φ ends up with minimum cost, equally zero, because no hard clause in φ requires x variables to evaluate to TRUE (doing so may need edge addition that eventually increases the cost of assignment). However, we resolve this by adding a new hard clause whose constraint is that at least one x variable must evaluate to TRUE. This clause is simply the disjunction of all the x variables.

Constraint 4 *In a transgraph, at least one one-to-one pair should be extracted.* It is encoded as follows.

$$\varphi_4^\infty = \bigvee (x_{i,j}, \infty) \tag{8}$$

Therefore, the complete CNF becomes $\varphi = \varphi^+ \wedge \varphi_1^\infty \wedge \varphi_2^\infty \wedge \varphi_3^\infty \wedge \varphi_4^\infty$; solving it returns an optimal assignment with minimum cost,[2] which equals 0 when no edge is added, or exceeds 0 when the most probable missing edge(s) is added.

An optimal assignment can have a single variable $x_{m,k} \in X$ evaluated to TRUE, while all others, if available, are falsified. In this case, the corresponding pair (w_m^A, w_k^C) is considered to be the most reliably correct one-to-one pair. We add it into output bilingual lexicon $D_{A\text{-}C}$, and regenerate φ by reflecting the awareness of $\mathbb{O}(w_m^A, w_k^C)$, which can be encoded by a new hard clause $(x_{m,k}, \infty)$. The regenerated φ is again evaluated by the solver to identify one more one-to-to pair. The same process is iterated until φ becomes unsatisfiable, at which point the extraction of the output bilingual lexicon completes (as in Algorithm 2).

4.4 Framework Extension

When there is a third bilingual lexicon $D_{B\text{-}D}$ available in addition to $D_{A\text{-}B}$ and $D_{B\text{-}C}$, where A, B and C are closely related languages, adding it to existing transgraphs may introduce more complete semantic information that could ultimately boost the accuracy of induction result. This is because the number of meanings of a given pivot word in each input bilingual lexicon might be depending on its completeness.

---

[2]Notice that the optimal assignment may not be unique, since more than one assignments may have equally minimum cost. If it is the case, solver selects one randomly based on its designated behavior.

Algorithm 2 Extracting one-to-one pairs from a transgraph

Input: G – a transgraph
Output: R – Set of one-to-one pairs
1: $(\varphi, map) \leftarrow$ encode G to CNF /* $\varphi = \varphi^{+} \wedge \varphi_1^{\infty} \wedge \varphi_2^{\infty} \wedge \varphi_3^{\infty} \wedge \varphi_4^{\infty}$
    where $\varphi_4^{\infty} = (\bigvee x_{i,j}, \infty)$*/
2: $X \leftarrow \emptyset$
3: **while** φ is *satisfied* **do**
4:     $\mathscr{A} \leftarrow$ take an optimal assignment on φ
5:     $x_{m,k} \leftarrow$ take $x_{i,j} \in \mathscr{A}$,where $x_{i,j} \notin X$, and $x_{i,j} = 1$
6:     $X \leftarrow X \cup \{x_{m,k}\}$
7:     $\varphi_4^{\infty} \leftarrow \varphi_4^{\infty} - x_{m,k}$ /*exclude $x_{m,k}$ from $\bigvee x_{i,j}$*/
8:     $\varphi \leftarrow \varphi \wedge (x_{m,k}, \infty)$ /* create a new hard clause and insert it into φ */
9: **end while**
10: **return** $R \leftarrow map(X)$

Therefore, taking advantage of the most compete part of each bilingual lexicon is reasonable. In this work, we conclude the effect of an additional bilingual lexicon to the induction with only two input dictionaries as follows:

1. A more accurate weight of a possibly missing edge can be obtained by taking the maximum weight from each from each combination of input dictionaries. For example, in transgraph-a in Fig. 2, edges $e(w_1^B, w_2^C)$ and $e(w_2^B, w_1^C)$ have the same weight (=0.50), so that it is impossible to select one of the (w_1^A, w_1^C) and (w_1^A, w_2^C) as a one-to-one pair with higher confidence. But when transgraph-b is formed due to the additional input bilingual lexicon D_{B-D}, the weights of the two edges can be recalculated for each pairwise combination of the three input dictionaries. In this example, (w_1^A, w_1^C) secures a higher value (=0.66), which is then propagated to the transgraph-a.

2. A new constraint, one-to-one pairs among intra-family language pairs must be consistent, needs to be imposed, which might contribute to the accuracy of the output dictionaries. For example, given three words of three intrafamily languages: w_i^A, w_j^C and w_k^D, which can form three word pairs. If any two of these three pairs are one-to-one pairs, then the third must also be one-to-one pair. This can prevent the false associations during the optimization process to some extent.

Fig. 2 Difference weights can be obtained for an edge from different combinations of input dictionaries; for the same edge $e(w_1^B, w_2^C)$ two different weights are obtained

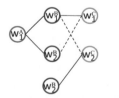 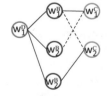

(a) Link D_{A-B} and D_{B-C} (b) Link D_{A-D} and D_{B-C}

Table 2 Details of source dictionaries

Bilingual lexicon	zh words	ug, kk or kg words	Pairs
D_{zh-ug}	28,806	44,400	76,501
D_{zh-kk}	28,806	61,000	143,515
D_{zh-kg}	28,806	27,351	40,381

5 Experiment

We designed a tool to implement the proposal using Sat4j[3] as the default solver due to its flexibility in integration with third-party software. ith this tool, we evaluated our approach by creating new dictionaries from D_{zh-ug}, D_{zh-kk} and D_{zh-kg}, where ug (Uyghur), kk (Kazakh) and kg (Kyrgyz) are Turkic languages, while zh (Chinese) belongs to the Sino-Tibetan language family. Table 2 details these three input directions. Notice that zh words whose translation are not available in all three languages have been excluded from the experiment because the proposal does not apply to such cases. Moreover, the number of available ug, kk and kg words are different which indicates that the output dictionaries could have different size. However, we assume that they will have similar precision and recall in evaluating the performance of our proposal.

1. Evaluating the performance of induction in the case of two input dictionaries with comparison to a baseline method: Three input dictionaries were paired into three groups, and each group independently processed to extract a new bilingual lexicon. In this phase, we compared our proposal to a baseline method, IC (Inverse Consultation) [17]. Let's denote the output dictionaries produced in this phase as $D_1 = D_{ug-kk}, D_{ug-kg}, D_{kk-kg}$.
2. Evaluating the proposal of using more than two input dictionaries: In this phase, we created a new set of dictionaries $D_2 = D_{ug-kk}, D_{ug-kg}, D_{kk-kg}$ by processing the same input dictionaries as a single optimization problem. By doing this, we observed what effect the use of an additional input bilingual lexicon has on the quality of the output dictionaries.

5.1 Result and Analysis

In the first phase of evaluation, we randomly selected 3×100 sample pairs from newly created $D_{ug-kk} \in D_1$ and asked a bilingual human to judge whether they are indeed correctly mapped as one-to-one. As a result, 80% of precision and 69% of recall are achieved when we assume that the size of the one-to-one space is equal to the maximum of numbers of unique ug and kk words. However, it is not reasonable

---

[3]Library of SAT and Boolean Optimization solver: http://www.sat4j.org.

to directly compare these numbers with one in related works and reach a conclusion on the efficiency of the proposal, since the experimental language pairs and resources chosen in each similar research are not quite the same. In response, we processed the same dataset with the IC method, because it is a well-known approach to creating new bilingual lexicon from only two input dictionaries without additional resources and heuristics, hence often used as a baseline method [14]. IC examines the two pivot word sets: set of pivot translations of word w_i^A, and the set of pivot translations of each w_j^C word that is a candidate for being a translation to w_i^A. The more closely they match, the better the candidate is. Since the IC has no one-to-one constraint on translation pairs, it allows multiple translations for a word through induction setting. However, in our implementation of IC, we only leave a top ranked translation candidate in language C for each word in language A to make the two methods are consistent. This does not harm the performance of IC as long as the top ranked candidate is selected. As a result, the proposal yields about 10% higher precision with similar recall 72% of IC.

In the second phase, we conducted a human evaluation on samples from six output dictionaries in D_1 and D_2. As the details show in Fig. 3 and Table 3, both precision and recall were slightly improved when three input dictionaries were processed as a whole. Although the degree of the improvements varies from one language pair to another, an improvement was achieved in every case. On average, 4%, 2.6% and 4% gains in precision, recall and F_1-measure.

Recall that in this research we did not allow one-to-many translations in output bilingual lexicon in accordance with one-to-one assumption, because relaxing

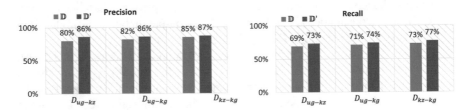

Fig. 3 Precision and recall comparison for the cases of two and three input dictionaries

Table 3 Details of results for the case of two and three input dictionaries

Input Lexicon	# of 1-to-1 pairs		Precision			Recall			F_1-measure		
	D_1	D_2	D_1(%)	D_2 (%)	+(%)	D_1 (%)	D_2 (%)	+(%)	D_1(%)	D_2 (%)	D_2 over D_1 (%)
D_{ug-kk}	1973	1954	80	86	6	69	73	4	76	80	6
D_{ug-kg}	1415	1414	82	86	4	71	74	3	76	80	4
D_{kk-kg}	1465	1457	85	87	2	76	77	1	80	82	2

one-to-one constraint resulted in relatively higher recall but the lost in precision was remarkable. We consider such an output bilingual lexicon is less useful than a higher accurate bilingual lexicon with lower coverage. However, we acknowledge that being high in recall has potential to overcome the precision problem if further processing is made, such as using parallel or comparable corpora to eliminate wrong translations [10], and considering spelling similarity [13]. Moreover, imposing the one-to-one restriction well controlled runtime addition of possibly missing edges into the transgraphs while relaxing it gives the solver to add more edges, which indeed further escalates the reduction in precision. However, we consider allowing one-to-many translation by disabling Uniqueness constraint is a worth try for controlling a balance between recall and precision of automatically created bilingual lexicon.

6 Conclusion

Bilingual lexicons have yet to be created for many languages. Such work is challenging because many language pairs lack useful language resources like a parallel corpus, and even comparable corpora. To provide an efficient, robust and accurate bilingual lexicon creation method for poorly resourced language pairs, we presented a constraint approach to pivot-based lexicon induction, where a new bilingual lexicon of closely related language pair is induced from two exiting dictionaries using a distant language as a pivot. In our approach, the lexical intransitivity divergence is tackled by modeling instance of induction as an optimization problem, where the new bilingual lexicon is produced as the solution of the problem. We also considered data incompleteness to some extent. An experiment showed the feasibility of our approach. However, we note following points: (1) The problem may also be tackled by maximum weighted bipartite matching, and it is important to explore more efficient modeling approaches and algorithms for bilingual lexicon induction; (2) There is the potential of including spelling as additional information; (3) More comparisons are expected to find whether the method can indeed rely purely on the structure and still outperform the methods that utilize cheap external resources such as monolingual data; (4) The one-to-one assumption may be too strong for the general case, but we consider it is reasonable for the case of intra-family languages as it greatly reduce the complexity of the problem; (5) Extending the proposal to language pairs which have one-to-many characteristics is also promising [9].

Acknowledgements This research was partially supported by Service Science, Solutions and Foundation Integrated Research Program from JST RISTEX, and a Grant-in-Aid for Scientific Research (S) (24220002) from Japan Society for the Promotion of Science.

References

1. Finch, A., Harada, T., Tanaka-Ishii, K., Sumita, E.: Inducing a bilingual lexicon from short parallel multiword sequences. ACM Trans. Asian Low-Resour. Lang. Inf. Process. 16(3), 15:1–15:20 (2017)
2. Haghighi, A., Liang, P., Berg-Kirkpatrick, T., Klein, D.: Learning bilingual lexicons from monolingual corpora. Proc. ACL-08: HLT, 771–779 (2008)
3. Ishida, T. (ed.): The Language Grid: Service-Oriented Collective Intelligence for Language Resource Interoperability. Springer Science & Business Media, Berlin (2011)
4. István, V., Shoichi, Y.: Bilingual dictionary generation for low-resourced language pairs. In: Proceedings of the 2009 Conference on Empirical Methods in Natural Language Processing, vol. 2, pp. 862–870. Association for Computational Linguistics, Stroudsburg (2009)
5. Matsuno, J., Ishida, T.: Constraint optimization approach to context based word selection. In: Proceedings of the Twenty-Second international joint conference on Artificial Intelligence, vol. 3, pp. 1846–1851. AAAI Press (2011)
6. Murakami, Y., Lin, D., Ishida, T.: Service-Oriented Architecture for Interoperability of Multi-language Services. Springer, Berlin (2014)
7. Murakami, Y., Tanaka, M., Lin, D., Ishida, T.: Service grid federation architecture for heterogeneous domains. In: IEEE Ninth International Conference on Services Computing, pp. 539–546 (2012)
8. Nakov, P., Ng, H.T.: Improving statistical machine translation for a resource-poor language using related resource-rich languages. J. Artif. Intell. Res. 44(1), 179–222 (2012)
9. Nasution, A.H., Murakami, Y., Ishida, T.: Constraint-based bilingual lexicon induction for closely related languages. In: Proceedings of the Tenth International Conference on Language Resources and Evaluation (LREC 2016), pp. 3291–3298. Paris, France (2016)
10. Otero, P.G., Campos, J.R.P.: Automatic generation of bilingual dictionaries using intermediary languages and comparable corpora. In: Computational Linguistics and Intelligent Text Processing, pp. 473–483. Springer, Berlin (2010)
11. Saralegi, X., Manterola, I., San Vicente, I.N.: Building a Basque-Chinese dictionary by using English as pivot. In: LREC, pp. 1443–1447 (2012)
12. Saralegi, X., Manterola, I., Vicente, I.S.: Analyzing methods for improving precision of pivot based bilingual dictionaries. In: Proceedings of the Conference on Empirical Methods in Natural Language Processing, pp. 846–856. Association for Computational Linguistics, Stroudsburg (2011)
13. Schulz, S., Markó, K., Sbrissia, E., Nohama, P., Hahn, U.: Cognate mapping: a heuristic strategy for the semi-supervised acquisition of a Spanish lexicon from a Portuguese seed lexicon. In: Proceedings of the 20th International Conference on Computational Linguistics, COLING '04, pp. 813:1–813:7. Association for Computational Linguistics, Stroudsburg (2004)
14. Shezaf, D., Rappoport, A.: Bilingual lexicon generation using non-aligned signatures. In: Proceedings of the 48th Annual Meeting of the Association for Computational Linguistics, pp. 98–107. Association for Computational Linguistics, Stroudsburg (2010)
15. Sjobergh, J.: Creating a free digital Japanese-Swedish lexicon. In: Proceedings of PACLING, pp. 296–300. Citeseer (2005)
16. Swadesh, M.: Towards greater accuracy in lexicostatistic dating. Int. J. Am. Linguist. 21(2), 121–137 (1955)
17. Tanaka, K., Iwasaki, H.: Extraction of lexical translations from non-aligned corpora. In: Proceedings of the 16th conference on Computational linguistics, vol. 2, pp. 580–585. Association for Computational Linguistics, Stroudsburg (1996)
18. Tanaka, K., Umemura, K.: Construction of a bilingual dictionary intermediated by a third language. In: Proceedings of the 15th Conference on Computational Linguistics, COLING '94, vol. 1, pp. 297–303. Association for Computational Linguistics, Stroudsburg (1994)
19. Tanaka, R., Murakami, Y., Ishida, T.: Context-based approach for pivot translation services. In: IJCAI 2009, Proceedings of the International Joint Conference on Artificial Intelligence, Pasadena, CA, USA, pp. 1555–1561 (2009)

20. Wushouer, M., Lin, D., Ishida, T., Hirayama, K.: Pivot-Based Bilingual Dictionary Extraction from Multiple Dictionary Resources. Springer, Berlin (2014)
21. Wushouer, M., Lin, D., Ishida, T., Hirayama, K.: A constraint approach to pivot-based bilingual dictionary induction. ACM Trans. Asian Low-Res. Lang. Inform. Process. **15**(1), 1–26 (2015)
22. Zhang, M., Peng, H., Liu, Y., Luan, H.B., Sun, M.: Bilingual lexicon induction from non-parallel data with minimal supervision, pp. 3379–3385. AAAI Press (2017)

Language Service Design Based on User-Centered QoS

Donghui Lin, Toru Ishida and Yohei Murakami

Abstract To design complicated language services for intercultural collaboration, it is important to consider how to compose different atomic language services so as to satisfy the requirements raised by the users. In the research area of services computing, many approaches to QoS-aware service composition have been proposed, where the assumption is that the QoS of a composite service can be calculated by aggregating the individual QoS values of atomic services. However, the QoS of a composite service is difficult to predict due to the QoS uncertainty of services in the real world. In this chapter, we address the above concerns by proposing a service design approach based on user-centered QoS and then confirming it in a case study of language service design for multi-language communication. To achieve this goal, we first introduce a QoS model to address the issues of user requirements and QoS uncertainty. We then propose a service design process that consists of composite service generation, participatory simulation, QoS evaluation and QoS data update. Finally, we introduce a field study of multi-language service design for agricultural knowledge communication to elucidate the benefits of our proposal approach.

Keywords Language service design · User-centered approach · Multi-language communication

D. Lin (✉) · T. Ishida
Department of Social Informatics, Kyoto University,
Kyoto 606-8501, Japan
e-mail: lindh@i.kyoto-u.ac.jp

T. Ishida
e-mail: ishida@i.kyoto-u.ac.jp

Y. Murakami
Unit of Design, Kyoto University
91 Chudoji Awata-cho, Kyoto 600-8815, Japan
e-mail: yohei@i.kyoto-u.ac.jp

© Springer Nature Singapore Pte Ltd. 2018
Y. Murakami et al. (eds.), *Services Computing for Language Resources*,
Cognitive Technologies, https://doi.org/10.1007/978-981-10-7793-7_8

1   Introduction

With the development of services computing technologies, service-oriented environments have become more and more popular as they enable users to create, share and combine Web services for various purposes. The Language Grid [11, 12], a typical example of a service-oriented environment for language services, allows multi-language communication services by combining various atomic language services including machine translation services, dictionary services, and so on. Language service design can be regarded as a typical problem of QoS-aware service composition, where the set of atomic services that generate maximum overall QoS value while satisfying some constraints is selected as the optimized solution [1, 7, 31]. In such problems, there is always the assumption that composite services are given beforehand, which might not be reasonable in the real world. Therefore, we focus on designing composite services for real world use, rather than assuming the provision of a composite service for which we then select atomic services.

To design composite services in the real world, we need to deal with the two issues when applying traditional QoS-aware service composition approaches. First, service performance may fluctuate due to dynamic change of service environments in the real world [20] so QoS is inherently uncertain [30], which makes it difficult to design composite service based on historical QoS data. This is especially true if human services are combined with Web services as occurs often in the real world [14, 15, 18], which makes the problem of QoS uncertainty even more complicated. Second, when there are multiple QoS attributes for evaluating services, it is difficult to maximize all the QoS attributes because there might always be counteractive relations between them [2]. For example, improving the translation quality in multi-language communication service might trigger an unacceptable increase in cost. Therefore, it is necessary to design composite service based on user requirements.

As shown in Fig. 1, there are two QoS attributes (Attribute 1 and Attribute 2) that counter each other. Users have their own requirements on the attributes and there are several candidate composite services. However, only an approximate QoS range can be obtained from the QoS data for each composite service due to QoS fluctuations. It might not be appropriate to utilize average QoS values when designing the composite services due to uncertainty in the distribution of the QoS values. This is exactly what happens when designing a multi-language communication service in the real world. Therefore, we try to design composite services while being aware of the above issues. A previous study noted that the user-centered approach is important in creating interactive systems [13]. In this chapter, we aim at a service design approach based on user-centered QoS, where users' satisfaction is evaluated throughout the whole design process. To achieve this goal, we first describe a QoS model for service design that takes into consideration the user requirements by extending existing QoS models for service composition. Then, we propose a participatory service design process that consists of composite service generation, participatory simulation, QoS evaluation and QoS data update. Finally, we use a field study of multi-language communication service design to validate our proposed design approach.

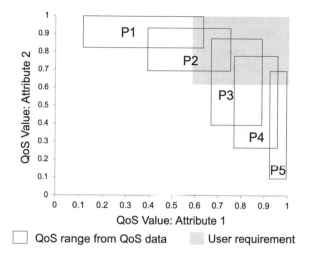

Fig. 1 Counteractive relations between two QoS attributes (P1-P5 are alternative composite services)

The rest of this chapter is organized as follows: In Sect. 2, we provide a motivating example of multi-language communication service design to show our research problem, and then introduce our QoS model that can handle multiple attributes for user-centered QoS evaluation in Sect. 3. Section 4 describes the service design approach. Section 5 uses a case study to show the effectiveness of our proposed approach in language service design. Section 6 introduces some related work to elucidate the benefits of this research. Finally, the conclusion is presented in the last section.

2 Motivating Example of Language Service Design

In this chapter, we introduce a motivating example of designing a multi-language communication service, the YMC (Youth Mediated Communication)-Viet project. This project helps Vietnamese farmers obtain agricultural knowledge provided by Japanese experts [16]. Since the literacy rate of farmers in the field area is low, youths (children of the farmers) with high literacy act as mediators between the Japanese experts and the Vietnamese farmers. This project was conducted over four seasons from 2011 to 2014 in Tra On District of Vinh Long Province, Vietnam with 15–30 family of farmers in each season.

Communication between Japanese experts and Vietnamese youths in the YMC-Viet project is supported by an online multi-language tool, the YMC system [26, 27]. Vietnamese youths send field data and questions via the YMC system. The Japanese experts get the data and questions from the youths and answer the questions in Japanese via the system, which translates the replies into Vietnamese and delivers them to the youths. Therefore, the most important issue here is how to design a multi-language communication service that would make the YMC system truly effective.

To design the multi-language communication service, we used the Language Grid as the language service composition platform [11]. Due to the increase in various language resources (machine translators, dictionaries, parallel texts, etc.) for multi-language communication on the Internet, it has become possible for people to design language services to suit their own requirements [19, 25]. However, difficulties arise due to the uncertain QoS of different language services. For example, the QoS of a machine translation service is always difficult to estimate. Therefore, it is necessary to provide an approach for designing the composite services like multi-language communication services that can well handle QoS uncertainty.

In this example, the following alternative services (processes) can be used to create a multi-language communication service between Japanese and Vietnamese: (1) composite machine translation service combined with Japanese-English machine translation service and English-Vietnamese machine translation service, (2) composite Japanese-Vietnamese machine translation service combined with agriculture dictionary, (3) composite translation service combined with Japanese-Vietnamese machine translation service and Vietnamese post-editing human service, and so on. However, it is difficult to decide which composite service should be used due to the uncertain QoS of translation services as described above. Therefore, it is necessary to consider how to design an appropriate composite service to satisfy users' requirements. Moreover, it seems likely that some combination of human services and Web services will be needed, which makes the service design problem even more complicated. In this chapter, we try to address these issues by proposing a participatory service design approach based on user-centered QoS [3].

3   QoS Model for Service Design

3.1   QoS Attributes

QoS models have been widely discussed in the area of services computing. Zeng et al. proposed a multidimensional QoS model for service composition, which considers several non-functional service attributes like cost, response time, availability, reputation and so on [31]. Some previous work also considered domain-specific QoS attributes [4, 23]. To design services for the real world, it is always necessary to consider both generic non-functional QoS attributes like response time and cost, and domain-specific QoS attributes like translation quality. To achieve our goal, this work introduces an extension of previous QoS models.

We start with the definition for QoS attributes as adopted by most previous studies, i.e., the ith QoS attribute of service s is written as $q_i(s)$. We use $Q(s) = (q_1(s), q_2(s), \ldots, q_n(s))$ to represent the vector of QoS values of service s.

To design complicated services in the real world like multi-language communication services, it is not appropriate to compute the average QoS values due to uncertainty in the QoS values. Therefore, we use quality ranges to describe the QoS attributes. Mohabbati et al. proposed the approach [24] of aggregating the quality range of a composite service from those of atomic services, and this is used in our research, i.e., the quality range of the ith QoS attribute of service s is defined as $q_i^R(s) = [q_i^{LB}(s), q_i^{UB}(s)]$, where $q_i^{LB}(s)$ and $q_i^{UB}(s)$ are lower and upper bound values of the QoS attributes, respectively. There is a disadvantage in using quality ranges to handle QoS uncertainty. When the volume of QoS data becomes huge, the quality range will become large. In that case, the quality range becomes ineffective as a basis for designing a composite service. This disadvantage can be addressed by analyzing the distribution of QoS data as well as the quality range.

Since different QoS attributes have different computation methods, it is necessary to normalize different QoS attributes when using quality ranges to aggregate multiple QoS attributes. We normalize QoS attributes by using the min-max Equation (1).

$$q_i'(s) = \begin{cases} \frac{q_i(s) - min(q_i(s))}{max(q_i(s)) - min(q_i(s))} & \text{if QoS attribute is positive} \\ \frac{max(q_i(s)) - q_i(s)}{max(q_i(s)) - min(q_i(s))} & \text{if QoS attribute is negative} \end{cases} \tag{1}$$

where $max(q_i(s))$ and $min(q_i(s))$ are the pre-defined maximum value and minimum value of QoS attribute $q_i(s)$, which are different from the lower and upper bound values of the QoS attributes obtained from the historical data. Positive QoS attributes represent valuable attributes that should be increased, e.g. translation quality. Negative attributes represent a type of penalty and should be reduced, e.g. the cost of invoking a service. The quality range of the ith QoS attribute of service s after normalization can be described as $q_i'^R(s) = [q_i'^{LB}(s), q_i'^{UB}(s)]$.

The min-max normalization approach may not be applicable to some QoS attributes with high variation with a skewed distribution; take as an example a Poisson distribution, it could have a large max value but the mean may be relatively small. Some previous work focuses on how to solve the normalization methods of QoS attributes [29], but this is not the focus of this chapter.

3.2 User-Centered QoS Evaluation

We define the QoS requirements over m ($m \leq n$) attributes from a user as $C(s) = (c_1(s), c_2(s), \ldots, c_m(s))$, where $c_i(s)$ is the ith constraint of the QoS attribute from the user over service s. Moreover, we use $P(s) = (p_1(s), p_2(s), \ldots, p_m(s))$ to define whether the QoS constraint is satisfied or not. For each QoS constraint $c_i(s)$, $p_i(s)$ is calculated using Eq. (2).

$$p_i(s) = \begin{cases} 1 & \text{if } c_i(s) \text{ is satisfied} \\ 0 & \text{if } c_i(s) \text{ is not satisfied} \end{cases} \tag{2}$$

We use $w_i(s) \in [0, 1]$ to define the weight of $c_i(s)$ that is decided by user priority of QoS constraints, where $\sum_{i=1}^{m} w_i(s) = 1$.

To evaluate user satisfaction, we use two utility functions: feasibility $Utility_F(s)$, and optimity $Utility_O(s)$, which was proposed in our previous work [21].

Utility of feasibility is used to evaluate whether the service composition is feasible based on user requirements, and is calculated by Eq. (3). $Utility_F(s) = 1$ means that all the QoS constraints from the user are satisfied. Otherwise, one or more constraints are not satisfied.

$$Utility_F(s) = \sum_{i=1}^{m} p_i(s) \cdot w_i(s) \tag{3}$$

Utility of optimity is used to evaluate whether the service composition is optimal based on user requirements, and is calculated by Eq. (4). $Utility_O(s)$ is calculated when $Utility_F(s) = 1$ and it is an aggregation of the QoS values of all attributes. $w_i'(s) \in [0, 1]$ is the weight of $q_i'(s)$ that is decided by user priority of QoS attributes, where $\sum_{i=1}^{n} w_i'(s) = 1$.

$$Utility_O(s) = \sum_{i=1}^{n} q_i'(s) \cdot w_i'(s) \tag{4}$$

In previous work, Alrifai et al. proposed several types of relations between QoS attributes: independent, correlated, and anti-correlated [2], which is also useful in our research. With the independent type, the values of two QoS attributes are independent of each other, e.g. the QoS attributes of availability and translation quality in a translation service. With the correlated type, a service that is good in one attribute is also good in the other attribute. In the anti-correlated type, there is a clear trade-off between the two attributes, e.g. the QoS attributes of translation quality and cost in a translation service. In the case of anti-correlated type, *Utility of optimity* is affected by the weights yielded by the users' various requirements.

4   Service Design Process

Considering QoS uncertainty, combination of human services and Web services, and users' various requirements, it is important to design composite services by using iterative evaluation and simulation of the QoS before the service is implemented and used in the real world. First, it is natural to evaluate users' satisfaction throughout the whole design process. Moreover, when designing hybrid composite services by combining Web services and human services, it is necessary to evaluate the quality of each hybrid service by simulation. Therefore, we propose a participatory service design approach for addressing these issues. Participatory design has been proposed for community informatics [6] and multiagent systems [13], which is new in service-oriented computing especially in the context of user-centered QoS for service composition. The process of service design includes four steps.

(1) *Composite service generation*: Composite service for participatory design is generated (created or refined) based on existing QoS data by applying the following process. First, predicted utility of feasibility $Utility_F^p(s_i)$ of each candidate composite service is computed based on the upper bound values of the QoS attributes and user requirements. If the candidate is feasible ($Utility_F^p(s_i) = 1$), predicted utility of optimity $Utility_O^p(s_i)$ is then computed. The candidate service with the largest utility of optimity is then subjected to a participatory simulation.

(2) *Participatory simulation*: In the participatory simulation, human services are simulated by human participants, whose features are selected or trained to be similar to the human services in the composite service. Participatory simulations are useful for controlled experiments because they make it easy to prepare the environment for testing [13]. To conduct the participatory simulation, the service designer does not have to create a real system. Instead, all interactions between the computer (services) and human are described using simple scenario description languages like Q Language [10]. We extended the Q Language to develop a participatory simulation tool for service design, on which the simulation scenario can be conducted.

(3) *QoS evaluation*: In the participatory simulation, the log data of the participants can be used for analysis and refinement of the service model. Therefore, the values of QoS attributes can be obtained from the execution logs of the simulation, and used for interactive service model refinement. In this step, if the evaluated QoS can satisfy users' requirements, real-world experiments (field application) can be conducted. Otherwise, composite service is refined.

(4) *QoS data update*: QoS data will be updated based on results of the participatory simulation for further user-centered service modeling and refinement. Participatory design is iterated until the simulation result satisfies user requirements.

5   Case Study

5.1   *Experiment, Result and Analysis*

To illustrate the effectiveness of our proposed approach for service design, especially in the hybrid service composition environments involving Web services and human services, we conducted a field experiment (YMC-Viet project) to design a multi-language communication service for supporting Vietnamese farmers as was mentioned in Sect. 2.

Services for composition. In realizing the multi-language communication service for the YMC-Viet project, many composite services were available, e.g. human translation, parallel text service, machine translation service combined with dictionary, and so on. All of these composite services can be created based on atomic services. Table 1 shows a part of the Web services provided by the Language Grid and human services as used in case study.

Table 1 List of web services and human services for multi-language communication service design in the YMC-Viet experiment

Service	Service type	Description
s_1	Composite web service	Composite Japanese-Vietnamese machine translation service combined with agriculture dictionary
s_2	Composite web service	Composite Japanese-English machine translation service combined with agriculture dictionary
s_3	Composite web service	Composite English-Vietnamese machine translation service combined with agriculture dictionary
s_4	Atomic web service	Japanese-Vietnamese parallel text service for agriculture
h_1	Human service	Japanese pre-editing service
h_2	Human service	English post-editing service
h_3	Human service	Vietnamese post-editing service
h_4	Human service	Japanese-English human translation service
h_5	Human service	Japanese-Vietnamese human translation service

QoS attributes and QoS data. QoS in the language service domain consists of non-functional QoS attributes (translation cost, execution time, etc.) and functional QoS attributes (translation quality). In our experiment, cost, execution time and translation quality are used as the dominant QoS attributes. Since there is no QoS data available before the field experiments, the QoS ranges of the different composite services were created based on the simulations using the same conditions as the YMC-Viet project.

User requirements. The user requirements for QoS attributes of the multi-language communication service are $q'_{translation\_quality}(s) > 0.7$ (weight is 0.2) and $q'_{cost}(s) > 0.5$ (weight is 0.8) after normalization. Since the QoS attributes of cost and execution time are related to each other, we do not take the attribute of execution time as one of the user requirements.

We use the participatory service design approach proposed in this chapter for designing the multi-language communication service in the first two seasons' experiments. Table 2 shows the iterative participatory design result (from process P1 to P5). Since the parallel text service is used from process P2 to P5, we omit it from the Table 2. Figure 2 shows details of the quality ranges and QoS values in each process described in Table 2. Moreover, the refinement process of composite service design is also shown. Four times of refinement were observed in the experiment: from P1 to P2, from P2 to P3, from P3 to P4, and from P4 to P5. Finally, composite service P5 satisfied the user requirements and was the best of all possible composite services. Accordingly, it was used as the composite service model for implementation of the multi-language communication tool (YMC system) for the field experiment after the second season in 2012. The refinement of composite services is described in detail in [17].

Table 2 Composite service processes for participatory simulation used in the YMC-Viet experiments and QoS evaluation result of different QoS attributes

Composite service	Service workflow	QoS value		
		Cost (USD)	Time (min)	Translation quality
P1	s_1	0.10	0.01	1.36/5.00
P2	$h_1 \rightarrow s_1$	1.33	10	2.14/5.00
P3	$h_1 \rightarrow s_1 \rightarrow h_3$	3.33	20	2.67/5.00
P4	$h_4 \rightarrow s_3 \rightarrow h_3$	25.18	102	4.40/5.00
P5	$h_1 \rightarrow s_2 \rightarrow h_2 \rightarrow s_3 \rightarrow h_3$	17.51	77	4.28/5.00
P6	h_5 (for comparison)	44.00	150	5.00/5.00

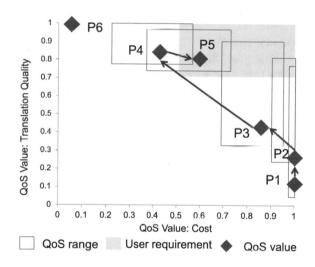

Fig. 2 Change of composite services and QoS values with participatory service design (P = Process)

5.2 Discussion

The final service model (Process P5) worked well in the field experiment. However, there are several issues that should be considered in the future.

First, it is effective but not efficient to use just quality range in refining service model because quality range is large when a lot of data are collected and cannot always reflect the prediction as described in Sect. 3. Note that four times of refinement were needed as all composite service candidates had the possibility (their upper bound) to satisfy the user requirements, see Fig. 2. A simple heuristic is to consider the distribution of QoS values within each range. For example, most of the QoS values of process P1 are quite low, so it seems reasonable to drop process P1 from further consideration.

Second, some participatory simulations yielded results that did not improve the user requirements. There are two possible reasons: one lies in the uncertainty of the QoS data, and the other is the human participants in the simulation did not provide an adequate view of reality. Therefore, it is also necessary to support virtual participatory simulations with real-world experiments.

Finally, the service design problem becomes more complicated as the number of anti-correlated QoS attributes increases, which makes it difficult to satisfy the user requirements. In that case, the service workflow optimization approach should be introduced, as we have shown it to be effective in designing crowdsourcing workflows for complicated tasks [8].

6 Related Work

Research into traditional QoS-aware service composition problems, always makes the assumption that composite services are given beforehand. The main research issue is then to select the most appropriate set of atomic services based on QoS optimization. Zeng et al. [31] proposed a multidimensional QoS model for Web service composition and several optimization approaches for service selection in both static and dynamic environments. Liu et al. described in detail the computation process for QoS selection, including normalization, and weighted aggregation [22]. Wang et al. described not only the processes of normalization and weighed aggregation, but also a QoS ontology description [28]. The process of filtering Web service according to user preference was described by Cao et al. [5]. Huang et al. described QoS aggregation for different workflow patterns in a composition service [9]. To deal with the dynamic service selection problem, QoS prediction has been studied including approaches that use historical data, user experience, and so on [32, 33].

The biggest difference between our research and previous research is that we deal with designing composite services in the real world rather than selecting atomic services for a given composite service. Moreover, most of the above work neglected the difficulties of handling QoS issues in real service composition environments. First, there are situations that some QoS attributes cannot be aggregated for composite services. For example, it is difficult to compute the translation quality of a composite translation service by simply aggregating its component atomic service (machine translation service, morphological analysis service, dictionary service, etc.). Second, when there are multiple QoS attributes for services, it is always difficult to maximize all the QoS attributes because some may have anti-correlated relations. Third, QoS values always vary with the context for different types of service invocation, which has been pointed out as QoS uncertainty [30]. Therefore, it is important to evaluate QoS uncertainty and consider user requirements when designing composite services, which is the focus of this chapter.

In recent years, combining human services with Web service has become a new important issue with the development of crowdsourcing and cloud computing environments. Kern et al. proposed a statistical quality control approach for human services and validated their approach using crowdsourcing experiments [14]. Efforts to deal with human services in crowdsourcing environments can be also found in some other works [15, 18]. To design multi-language communication (or translation) services, attempts have been to combine human services and Web services [18] for ensuring translation quality. However, most previous studies focused on the quality control of human services and the composition mechanisms of hybrid services. It is extremely important to test the service composition environments for human-computer interaction and study human behaviors. In this chapter we use the participatory service design approach to deal with the QoS uncertainty issues and human-computer interaction issues.

7 Conclusion

Language service design is a typical problem tackled by QoS-aware service composition since it deals with how to design composite services considering the uncertainty of services in the real world and how to meet the requirements of various users. In this chapter, we proposed a service design approach based on user-centered QoS using a case study of designing language services for a multi-language communication experiment. We first extended the QoS model proposed in previous work to address the uncertainty of language services and user requirements by defining two types of utilities to compute user-centered QoS. Then, we proposed the participatory service design process that consists of composite service generation, participatory simulation, QoS evaluation and QoS data update. Finally, we used a field study of multi-language communication service design to illustrate the effectiveness of our proposed design approach.

Acknowledgements This research was supported by a Grant-in-Aid for Scientific Research (A) (17H00759, 2017-2020) and a Grant-in-Aid for Young Scientists (A) (17H04706, 2017-2020) from Japan Society for the Promotion of Science (JSPS).

References

1. Alrifai, M., Risse, T.: Combining global optimization with local selection for efficient QoS-aware service composition. In: Proceedings of the 18th International Conference on World Wide Web, pp. 881–890. ACM (2009)
2. Alrifai, M., Skoutas, D., Risse, T.: Selecting skyline services for QoS-based web service composition. In: Proceedings of the 19th International Conference on World Wide Web, pp. 11–20. ACM (2010)
3. Bramantoro, A., Ishida, T.: User-centered QoS in combining web services for interactive domain. In: Fifth International Conference on Semantics, Knowledge and Grid, 2009. SKG 2009, pp. 41–48. IEEE (2009)

4. Canfora, G., Penta, M.D., Esposito, R., Perfetto, F., Villani, M.L.: Service composition (re)binding driven by application-specific QoS. In: Proceedings of the 4th ICSOC, pp. 141–152 (2006)
5. Cao, J., Huang, J., Wang, G., Gu, J.: QoS and preference based web service evaluation approach. In: Eighth International Conference on Grid and Cooperative Computing, (GCC 2009), pp. 420–426 (2009)
6. Carroll, J.M., Rosson, M.B.: Participatory design in community informatics. Des. Stud. 28(3), 243–261 (2007)
7. Cavallo, B., Di Penta, M., Canfora, G.: An empirical comparison of methods to support QoS-aware service selection. In: Proceedings of the 2nd International Workshop on Principles of Engineering Service-Oriented Systems, pp. 64–70. ACM (2010)
8. Goto, S., Ishida, T., Lin, D.: Understanding crowdsourcing workflow: modeling and optimizing iterative and parallel processes. In: Fourth AAAI Conference on Human Computation and Crowdsourcing, pp. 52–58 (2016)
9. Huang, A.F.M., Lan, C.W., Yang, S.J.H.: An optimal QoS-based web service selection scheme. Inf. Sci. 179, 3309–3322 (2009)
10. Ishida, T.: Q: A scenario description language for interactive agents. Computer 35(11), 42–47 (2002)
11. Ishida, T. (ed.): The Language Grid: Service-oriented Collective Intelligence for Language Resource Interoperability. Springer Science & Business Media, Berlin (2011)
12. Ishida, T.: Intercultural collaboration and support systems: a brief history. International Conference on Principle and Practices in Multi-Agent Systems (PRIMA 2016). Invited paper, pp. 3–19 (2016)
13. Ishida, T., Nakajima, Y., Murakami, Y., Nakanishi, H.: Augmented experiment: participatory design with multiagent simulation. In: Proceedings of the 20th international joint conference on Artifical intelligence, pp. 1341–1346. Morgan Kaufmann Publishers Inc., Burlington (2007)
14. Kern, R., Thies, H., Satzger, G.: Statistical quality control for human-based electronic services. Serv.-Oriented Comput. 243–257 (2010)
15. Khazankin, R., Psaier, H., Schall, D., Dustdar, S.: QoS-based task scheduling in crowdsourcing environments. Serv.-Oriented Comput. 297–311 (2011)
16. Lin, D., Ishida, T.: Participatory service design based on user-centered QoS. In: Proceedings of the 2013 IEEE/WIC/ACM International Joint Conferences on Web Intelligence (WI) and Intelligent Agent Technologies (IAT), vol. 01, pp. 465–472. IEEE Computer Society (2013)
17. Lin, D., Ishida, T.: User-centered service design for multi-language knowledge communication. In: Serviceology for Services, pp. 309–317. Springer, Berlin (2014)
18. Lin, D., Ishida, T., Murakami, Y., Tanaka, M.: Improving service processes with the crowds. In: Service-Oriented Computing-ICSOC 2011 Industry Track, pp. 295–306. Springer, Berlin (2012)
19. Lin, D., Murakami, Y., Ishida, T., Murakami, Y., Tanaka, M.: Composing human and machine translation services: language grid for improving localization processes. In: Proceedings of the Seventh International Conference on Language Resources and Evaluation, pp. 500–506 (2010)
20. Lin, D., Murakami, Y., Tanaka, M.: Designing dynamic control mechanisms for service invocation. J. Inform. Process. 19, 52–61 (2011)
21. Lin, D., Shi, C., Ishida, T.: Dynamic service selection based on context-aware QoS. In: 2012 IEEE Ninth International Conference on Services Computing (SCC), pp. 641–648. IEEE (2012)
22. Liu, Y., Ngu, A.H., Zeng, L.Z.: QoS computation and policing in dynamic web service selection. In: Proceedings of the 13th international WWW Alt, pp. 66–73. ACM, New York (2004)
23. Ma, Q., Wang, H., Li, Y., Xie, G., Liu, F.: A semantic QoS-aware discovery framework for web services. In: IEEE International Conference on Web Services (ICWS 2008), pp. 129–136 (2008)
24. Mohabbati, B., Gašević, D., Hatala, M., Asadi, M., Bagheri, E., Bošković, M.: A quality aggregation model for service-oriented software product lines based on variability and composition patterns. Serv.-Oriented Comput. pp. 436–451 (2011)

25. Murakami, Y., Lin, D., Ishida, T.: Service-oriented architecture for interoperability of multi-language services. In: Towards the Multilingual Semantic Web, pp. 313–328. Springer, Berlin (2014)
26. Takasaki, T., Mori, Y., Ishida, T., Otani, M.: Youth mediated communication: knowledge transfer as intercultural communication. Serv. Comput. Lang. Res. (2017)
27. Takasaki, T., Murakami, Y., Mori, Y., Ishida, T.: Intercultural communication environment for youth and experts in agriculture support. In: 2015 International Conference on Culture and Computing (Culture Computing), pp. 131–136. IEEE (2015)
28. Wang, X., Vitvar, T., Kerrigan, M., Toma, I.: A QoS-aware selection model for semantic web services. In: Proceedings of the 4th ICSOC, pp. 390–401. Springer, Berlin (2006)
29. Yau, S.S., Yin, Y.: QoS-based service ranking and selection for service-based systems. In: Proceedings of the 2011 IEEE International Conference on Services Computing (SCC 2011), pp. 56–63. Washington, D.C. (2011)
30. Yu, Q., Bouguettaya, A.: Computing service skyline from uncertain qows. IEEE Trans. Serv. Comput. 3(1), 16–29 (2010)
31. Zeng, L., Benatallah, B., Ngu, A.H., Dumas, M., Kalagnanam, J., Chang, H.: QoS-aware middleware for web services composition. IEEE Trans. Softw. Eng. 30(5), 311–327 (2004)
32. Zeng, L., Lingenfelder, C., Lei, H., Chang, H.: Event-driven quality of service prediction. Serv.-Oriented Comput.-ICSOC 2008, 147–161 (2008)
33. Zheng, Z., Ma, H., Lyu, M.R., King, I.: Qos-aware web service recommendation by collaborative filtering. IEEE Trans. Serv. Comput. 99, 140–152 (2011)

Part IV
Understanding and Designing Language Services

Consistency Analysis in Multi-language Knowledge Sharing System

Amit Pariyar, Yohei Murakami, Donghui Lin and Toru Ishida

Abstract Unprecedented growth in knowledge sharing among multi-language communities, both common and distinct languages, has raised the possibility of sharing inconsistent content. Though popular with traditional system, the approach to explicitly state consistency rules to avoid inconsistency is practically not suited for multi-language knowledge sharing system because of sheer complexity. Alternatively this chapter focuses on potential cause of inconsistency, cases such as *content omitted*, *content updates not propagated* and *content conflicts*. Ignoring such cases in knowledge sharing has undesirable consequences: *community bias*, *global and local inconsistency* and *regional discrepancies*. Consistency constraints from opposing knowledge sharing goals among communities is another issue. Due to which consistency policy ranges from rigid 'one to one consistency' to non-rigid 'consistency where needed'. This chapter contributes with (a) process-based approach for multi-lingual content synchronization to leverage knowledge equally and (b) propagation-based approach to analyze community preferences when sharing specific content categories/geographic regions, to customize knowledge sharing; a value add-on to designing language services adhering to knowledge sharing goals.

Keywords Inconsistency · Multi-language · Knowledge sharing · Content category · Geographic region

A. Pariyar (✉)
Institute of Social Informatics and Technological Innovations,
University Malaysia Sarawak, Sarawak, Malaysia
e-mail: amitpariyar@gmail.com; pamit@unimas.my

Y. Murakami
Unit of Design, Kyoto University,
91 Chudoji Awata-cho, Kyoto 600-8815, Japan
e-mail: yohei@i.kyoto-u.ac.jp

D. Lin · T. Ishida
Department of Social Informatics, Kyoto University,
Kyoto 606-8501, Japan
e-mail: lindh@i.kyoto-u.ac.jp

T. Ishida
e-mail: ishida@i.kyoto-u.ac.jp

© Springer Nature Singapore Pte Ltd. 2018
Y. Murakami et al. (eds.), *Services Computing for Language Resources*,
Cognitive Technologies, https://doi.org/10.1007/978-981-10-7793-7_9

1 Introduction

Recent advances in online community participation has accelerated knowledge sharing beyond human imagination. Wikipedia aptly represents such a prodigy in action serving as a storehouse for millions of articles contributed by 200+ language communities. Another evolving community are global brands publishing country-specific websites to represent 100+ countries exceeding 40 languages. The implication of such emergent multi-language knowledge sharing communities is the publication and sharing of massive content in several languages. The daunting and challenging task is to manage inconsistency in the shared content, both *common* as well as *distinct* languages. Logical and Factual inconsistency widely studied in database and knowledge-based system are also equally anticipated in multi-language knowledge sharing system (MLKSS). Though approaches to explicitly state consistency rules as *foreign key constraints* or *using logical formulae* are popular with past systems, it is not practically viable solution for MLKSS due to complexity with growing number of languages. The alternative approach adopted in this chapter is to highlight cases that are expected to cause inconsistency in logic and fact as community share content, analyze their consequences and design consistency rules.

Cases such as *content omitted*, *content updates not shared* and *content conflicts* are expected to occur during collaboration. The cases may seem trivial at first, nonetheless the complexity to handle inconsistency is raised when they are dispersed across several languages. Some consequences are (a) *community bias with one community preferred over another* (b) *inconsistency at scales leading to globally and locally shared inconsistent content* and (c) *regional discrepancies*. MLKSS should address such issues to enable consistent knowledge sharing. Another issue is the constraint in content consistency meaning *'opposing views to support consistency'*. Knowledge sharing goals of communities vary along the continuum, where one end puts emphasis on leveraging knowledge equally while other end supports customized knowledge sharing to cater to community preferences. For example, documents such as product manual, technical specification are usually produced with the intention to share same information in several language editions. A *'rigid consistency policy'* is a better match to enforce one-to-one correspondences in multiple languages. The growing cultural homogeneity among communities with 'one size fits all' notion or legislative rules could have demanded such a stern policy. On the contrary, the persistence of cultural difference among communities widely valued in past studies stresses on relevant knowledge shared to suit specific community preferences. Knowledge sharing is viewed as not uniform among communities and exact correspondences in the shared content is not always preferred. For example, the need to restrict publication and description of content in specific languages in country-specific websites makes *'non-rigid consistency policy'* a better choice. Such opposing views has to be supported in the design of MLKSS. Consistency analysis will give a context to design language services adhering to knowledge sharing goals.

To avoid *undesirable consequences of inconsistency* in knowledge sharing and to allow *consistency constraints* resulting from divergent knowledge sharing goals among communities, this chapter contributes in the design of MLKSS to support content consistency. Section 2 illustrates an example of inconsistency revealing its causes and consequences. Section 3 details approach to leverage knowledge equally. Section 4 illustrates underlying community preferences for customized knowledge sharing. Section 5 discusses and Sect. 6 concludes this chapter.

2 Illustrating Cause and Consequences

We refer to corporate related content '3M at a glance' of a global brand 3M, published in its country-specific websites for Switzerland, Canada, United States, France, India and Australia. Note that Switzerland and Canada have multiple official languages; '*French*' is a common language among France, Canada and Switzerland. Websites also represent geographic regions: North America, Europe and Asia Pacific. Following observations are compiled.

Cause. As shown in Fig. 1, the information about 'product donations' for the year '2013' is omitted in '*French*' version of websites for France, Switzerland and Canada. The latest information related to '2014' is not propagated to most of the websites except for India and United States. This also means that content updates are not available in languages '*French*', '*Deutsch*' and even '*English*'. The information about

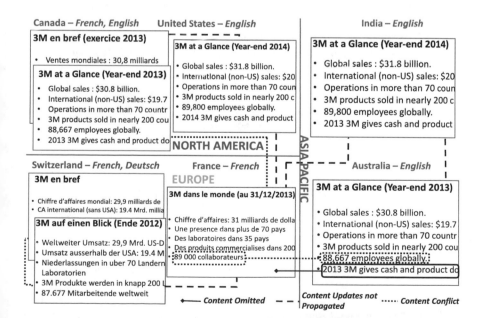

Fig. 1 Causes of inconsistency among country specific websites

'number of employees', 'global sales' also appears to conflict among France, Canada, Australia and Switzerland. This means conflict among languages. We compiled cases as *content omitted, content updates not propagated* and *content conflicts* as potential cause for inconsistency. Next we show consequences.

Consequences. The presence of cases *content omitted, content updates not propagated* and *content conflicts* in knowledge sharing have following consequences.

(a) **Community Bias.** The delay in the simultaneous release of content updates among communities creates bias, as one community or language is assumed to be prioritized over another community. In this example, *'English'* seems to be a language choice and India and United States seems to be country choice in sharing content. Within Canada, it seems more information is in *'English'* compared to *'French'* language, room for bias inside a country.

(b) **Global and Local Inconsistency.** Content updates for the year '2014' published by websites for India and United States is not shared with remaining countries in multiple languages *'French'* and *'Deutsch'*. Also not shared in common language *'English'* with Canada and Australia. Failing to propagate content updates either in common and distinct languages among countries gives rise to globally shared inconsistent content. Content conflict between languages *'Deutsch'* and *'French'* for information on 'statistics for the number of employees' within Switzerland gives rise to local inconsistency.

(c) **Intra and Inter Regional Discrepancies.** Intra-regional discrepancies occur among countries inside same geographic region such as Asia Pacific (India and Australia) and North America (United States and Canada) as updates for '2014' is not propagated. The statistics in 'global sales' and 'number of employees' offered are also conflicting in France, Canada and Australia leading to inter-regional discrepancies.

We are motivated to design MLKSS to address community bias, global and local inconsistencies and regional discrepancies. Next we will detail approaches to support consistency for specific knowledge sharing goals.

3   Leverage Knowledge Equally

Multilingual correspondences is achieved when content updates are allowed to propagate consistently across languages. Language neutral representation is used in [3] to automate generation of consistent multilingual instruction. Since technical skill is required to modify underlying knowledge representation to amend changes, its use is limited to domain experts. Cosyne [9] on the other hand uses language processing with state of art machine translation, concept network, cross-lingual entailment to pinpoint differences and overlapping among languages. Ziggurat [1] another automated system uses self-supervised learning to align info boxes in multilingual Wikipedia articles. Both systems support resource rich languages mostly to

European languages and replicating them to resource poor language is not practical due to limited linguistic resources. Restructuring multilingual correspondences with MLHTML [14] and alignment tools [2] suffers management overhead to manage central representation in order to ensure consistent updates propagation. The collaborative wiki style translation in [5] is also inadequate in highlighting specific inconsistent cases and keeping track of language from which the information originates. Referring to limits of past studies, particularly inadequate support for resource poor languages, the goal of this section is to leverage knowledge equally in variety of languages and communities. The approach to detect inconsistency in multilingual content is presented next.

3.1 Process-Based Approach

Our work is based on the concept of *synchronizing user editing activities* and detect inconsistency as it occurs in the process of creating a multilingual document. For this we extend multilingual correspondences structure in [2] by augmenting information about states of parallel aligned content, keep track of their modification and employ rules to detect inconsistency.

Notation. A Monolingual Document d^l is the document with the content available in language l. A sentence e_i^l in the document d^l is the ith sentence in language l. Content in monolingual document are organized into a collection of sentences $d^l = \{e_i^l \mid 1 \leq i \leq n\}$. If L is the set of languages used in the multilingual document then parallel multilingual document is the collection of several monolingual documents $D^L = \{d^l \mid l \in L\}$. With this granularity we will focus on consistency of multilingual content at a sentence level. We refer to [4] for basic concepts in automata theory. Next we will present state transition model to define states, actions and state transitions. Then we will define inconsistency detection rules to check inconsistent states.

3.1.1 State Transition Model

The state transition model is described as a tuple: $M = (S, \Sigma, \delta, S_0)$ where, (1) $S = \{Q, NQ, T\}$ is the set of states of sentences corresponding to Qualified, Non-Qualified and Translated states respectively. $S_0 = \{Q, NQ\}$ is the set of initial states, (2) $\Sigma = \{modify, qualify, translate\}$ is the set of actions performed on sentences and (3) δ is the state transition function given by $\delta : S \times \Sigma \rightarrow S$.

States. To define states S in multilingual content we need to consider (i) relation of content originating in one language with content derived from translation in another language and (ii) change in relation as the content is modified with either contextual changes (addition or deletion of facts or information) or surficial changes (e.g. paraphrasing the text).

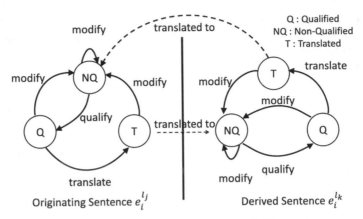

Fig. 2 State transition diagram of a parallel aligned sentence $(e_i^{l_j}, e_i^{l_k})$

- **Qualified:** A sentence e_i^l in the multilingual document is said to be in Qualified state Q if the sentence holds updated facts or new information. Such sentence is eligible for translation to other languages.
- **Non-Qualified:** A sentence e_i^l in the multilingual document is said to be in Non-Qualified state NQ if the sentence holds paraphrased text, grammatical corrections or derived information from another language. Such sentence do not require translation.
- **Translated:** A sentence e_i^l in the multilingual document is said to be in Translated state T if the sentence is translated into another language.

Transition Function. The state transition diagram of parallel aligned sentence $e_i^{l_j}$ (originating) and $e_i^{l_k}$ (derived) in Fig. 2 shows the change in states for actions corresponding to *modify, qualify* and *translate*. Multilingual Document d^{l_j} and d^{l_k} have several such parallel aligned sentences and information about their states.

3.1.2 Inconsistency Detection Rules

To design rules we will use the combination of states between parallel aligned sentences in documents, $d^{l_j} = \{e_i^{l_j} \mid 1 \leq i \leq n\}$ and $d^{l_k} = \{e_i^{l_k} \mid 1 \leq i \leq n\}$. Table 1 illustrates case of interest *content omitted, content updates not propagated* and *content conflict* represented as rules using state combination. For example the presence of Qualified Q states in both parallel aligned sentences $e_i^{l_j}$ and $e_i^{l_k}$ corresponds to content conflict as both sentence holds updated information. The rules presented here are naturally extended in the case of parallel multilingual documents ($|L| \geq 2$) meaning more than two languages. The tabular representation of aligned sentences and their states in [10] highlights the ease in tracking inconsistencies.

Table 1 Inconsistency detection rules

Rules description for inconsistent cases	State combination of parallel aligned sentence $(e_i^{l_j}, e_i^{l_k})$
(i) Content Omitted $\forall e_i^{l_j}, e_i^{l_k} : isCreated(e_i^{l_j}) \Rightarrow isInconsistent(e_i^{l_j}, e_i^{l_k})$	$(Q, \_)(\_, Q)$
(ii) Content Updated not Propagated $\forall e_i^{l_j}, e_i^{l_k} : isStateOf(e_i^{l_j}, Q) \wedge (isStateOf(e_i^{l_k}, NQ)$ $\vee isStateOf(e_i^{l_k}, T)) \Rightarrow isInconsistent(e_i^{l_k}, e_i^{l_j})$	$(Q, NQ)(NQ, Q)$ $(Q, T)(T, Q)$
(iii) Content Conflicts $\forall e_i^{l_j}, e_i^{l_k} : isStateOf(e_i^{l_j}, Q) \wedge isStateOf(e_i^{l_k}, Q)$ $\Rightarrow isInconsistent(e_i^{l_j}, e_i^{l_k})$	(Q, Q)

3.2 Experimental Evaluation

Setup. We referred to edit histories of multilingual articles titled "2013 ICC World Cricket League Division Three" (referred as Article 1) and "2014 ICC World Twenty20" (referred as Article 2) available in English and Nepali languages. We extracted 71 parallel contents in Article 1 from May 4 to May 9 and 72 parallel contents in Article 2 from March 16 to April 6, the duration of tournament. Content directly copied and appearing as English text in Nepali articles are ignored. We then labeled 30 modification actions from Wikipedia Edit Summary Legend as qualifying and non-qualifying modification.

Evaluation. We compared inconsistencies detected applying the proposed technique with inconsistencies identified from manual inspection to compute precision and recall. For Article 1 overall precision of 94% and recall of 85% is achieved. Precision is higher due to detection of majority of missing contents in Nepali article. The missing content (*matches between Nepal-America, Nepal-Uganda, Nepal-Oman* in Nepali article, Revision Id: 337549) is detected as missing content in English article. For Article 2 the overall precision achieved is 82% and the recall is 87%. Inconsistency between content "Round 1 Group B" in English Article (Revision Id: 600298773) and Nepali article (Revision Id: 384275) is detected as updated content (*match entries to Netherland vs. Zimbabwe*) is not propagated to Nepali article. However, the decrease in precision for Article 2 accounts from the absence of content processing involved in checking semantic relatedness in parallel content. Content conflict due to updating same content in both languages is also detected. The content (*entries for score points for Nepal*) in English article (Revision Id: 600444676) and Nepali article (Revision Id: 384304) is detected as conflicting content and hence inconsistent. With the proposed technique for detecting inconsistency in the selected articles, we find an average precision of 88% and recall of 86% which is satisfactory in detecting inconsistency given that only user editing actions are used.

The result can be improved if integrated with NLP to apply semantics to confirm content consistencies. Towards leveraging knowledge equally the proposed approach requires minimal language processing and hence support resource poor languages. When supplemented with advanced NLP techniques the accuracy can be improved. Next section will highlight knowledge sharing involving community preferences.

4 Customize Knowledge Sharing

Several managerial strategies are adopted by organization in their business processes, content management and so on. Centralization is exercised to control and dictate business activities from headquarter office. Knowledge sharing is unidirectional where what content is to be published for a certain market, what is to be translated, what not to be translated are all decided by the central authority. There are ample chances to lose relevance yet the main focus is to create unified brand presence worldwide. Decentralization on the other hand encourages country offices to independently execute their business activities. Inconsistent branding, fragmented localization, inappropriate content published in the absence of well-defined guidelines are some problems associated with knowledge sharing. Hybrid strategy ensures brand preservation while country offices develop local programs that complies with corporate goal and standards. From a technical standpoint, collaborative tools that support global consistency and local flexibility is required. This is where the need to customize knowledge sharing is crucial so that content consistency is imposed only where relevant. Customization is also attributed to cultural [13] and non-cultural [6] differences when sharing content features such as corporate information, communication/customer support, financial information and so on in websites. Past studies have also depicted cultural differences among geographic regions in the use of instant messaging [8] and stimuli to website effectiveness. This raise an important concern whether there exists preferences when sharing content categories with specific regions. This section will explore the relation of content categories and their scope in publication to specific geographic regions.

4.1 Propagation Based Approach

Our work is based on the concept of *analyzing propagation of content* occurring among communities during knowledge sharing and use it to determine their preferences when sharing specific content categories and to specific geographic regions. We then infer information about 'scales' and 'coupling' in sharing to generalize required content consistency policy. Country-specific websites managed by global brands is an ideal example of cross country propagation in knowledge sharing. The managerial challenge in such knowledge sharing remains difficulty in propagating content updates where required, which leads to inconsistent cross-site content. By comparing content in webpages belonging to country-specific websites and analyzing their propagation allows us to understand preferences when sharing specific content categories and for specific geographic regions.

Propagation. Propagation is said to occur between websites w_1 and w_2 managed in a global brand if webpages $p_a \in w_1$ and $p_b \in w_2$ have exactly same or comparable content. This literally means comparing webpages to check whether exactly same text or comparable (paraphrased text with same information) or completely different text appears between websites. Since comparable content has to be checked between webpages, manual effort is needed to examine their propagation among websites which means existing text-based method cannot be applied. We base this notion of propagation in network of websites and their affiliated regions.

4.1.1 Website Graph and Website Pair

Website graph is a structure that interconnects all country-specific websites. The concept here is to examine propagation occurring to and from all interconnected websites. If timestamp information is available it can be used to assign the source website producing content and follow its propagation to remaining websites. Else we consider each country-specific website as a potential source for publishing content in a webpage shared with the remaining websites, as in this chapter. Propagation in all interconnected potential sources websites is represented as a website graph in Fig. 3a. The purpose is to examine 'scales' in sharing for specific content categories. The scale is represented with three options of propagation to (i) *all country-specific websites* meaning tendency for being global (ii) *some country-specific websites* meaning tendency for being regional and (iii) *no propagation* meaning tendency for being local. The purpose of applying concept of propagation in website pair as in Fig. 3b is to examine 'coupling' between websites when sharing specific content categories. The higher occurrences of (i) *propagation* in website pair meaning high coupling between websites and (ii) *no propagation* meaning low coupling between websites.

4.1.2 Within and Among Geographic Region

Since country-specific websites also represent specific geographic regions, abstracting the concept of propagation at this level, expands our understanding of preferences when sharing within and among specific regions. Figure 3d illustrates intra-regional propagation occurring in websites of India and Australia, both countries within Asia Pacific. Coupling among countries within a region is measured by the occurrence of propagation and no propagation among websites. Figure 3c represents inter-regional propagation occurring among countries in Asia Pacific (India, Australia) and Europe (UK and Ireland), in a structure which is a subset of website graph. Coupling among regions is again determined from occurrences and no occurrence of propagation. In the subsequent sections, we will determine community preferences when sharing

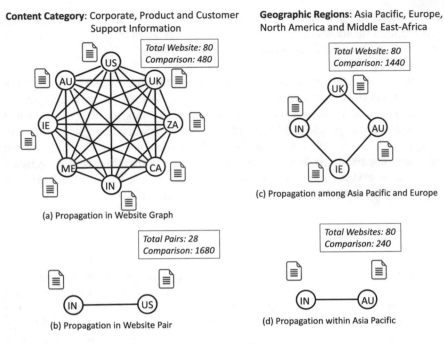

Content Category: Corporate, Product and Customer Support Information

Geographic Regions: Asia Pacific, Europe, North America and Middle East-Africa

Total Website: 80
Comparison: 480

Total Website: 80
Comparison: 1440

(a) Propagation in Website Graph

(c) Propagation among Asia Pacific and Europe

Total Pairs: 28
Comparison: 1680

Total Websites: 80
Comparison: 240

(b) Propagation in Website Pair

(d) Propagation within Asia Pacific

Fig. 3 Propagation in content categories and geographic regions

specific content categories and specific geographic regions by analyzing propagation in website graph, website pair, within and among geographic region.

4.2 Content Preferences

Websites from 10 global brands ranked highly in the web globalization report card (Yunker 2014) are selected for this study. Sample of 8 country-specific websites from each brand representing countries: India (IN), Australia (AU), United Kingdom (UK), Ireland (IE), United States (US), Canada (CA), Middle East (ME) and South Africa (ZA) and representing geographical regions: Asia Pacific, North America, Europe and Middle East-Africa are chosen. A total of 80 country-specific websites are collected as the source for webpages to be used for comparison. From 8 country-specific websites, we also have 28 possible websites pairs representing content sharing in country pairs such as (IN, AU), (IN, UK) and so on.

Webpages offering content in '*English*' language are selected. Content categories used for sampling webpages are: (a) *Corporate Information*: webpages that provide background information of a company such as mission statements, history and its people (b) *Product Information*: webpages on description, usage, and specification of product and (c) *Customer Support Information*: webpages on ways to contact company or find answer to queries. We then manually label webpages to their specific content categories. From each global brand we collected 48 webpage samples making a total of 480 webpage samples. We applied propagation-based approach to check for content propagation in website graph and website pair. A total of 480 webpages are qualitatively compared for their propagation in website graph. For each website pair there are 60 comparisons of webpages making a total of 1680 comparison for all 28 website pairs.

4.2.1   Propagation in Website Graph

Table 2 illustrates that out of 160 comparisons of webpages in "Corporate Information", 50% of cases are identified in which propagation occurs among all country-specific websites while 32% of cases in which propagation occurs in some websites and 18% of cases in which no propagation occurs among the websites. As for more than 80% cases propagation occurs from at least a single country-specific website, it can be agreed that the suitability of content related to "Corporate Information" at a global scale. This means the dissemination of up-to-date knowledge is required globally. Only 15% cases in which propagations occur in all websites are identified for "Product Information" which strongly suggest that such content are not globally suitable. However, 36% cases of propagation to some websites and 49% cases of no propagation are comparable which infers "Product Information" may be suitable both regionally and locally among countries. This means the dissemination of up-to-date knowledge is either restricted among several countries within and across regions or limited to specific country. Contrary to this 66% cases of no propagation among countries strongly suggested that in "Customer Support Information" is locally suitable within a country. Local scale also suggests for synchronization of content updates to occur in local languages within a country. For example, content synchronized in official languages (English and French) within Canada.

4.2.2   Propagation in Website Pair

Table 2 illustrates that out of 560 comparisons of webpages in "Corporate Information" 71% of cases with propagation occurs in website pairs. This suggests high

Table 2 Results of comparing webpages with content categories

Content category	Propagation in website graph			Propagation in website pair	
	All (%)	Some (%)	None (%)	Yes (%)	No (%)
(i) Corporate information	80 (50)	52 (32)	28 (18)	397 (71)	163 (29)
(ii) Product information	24 (15)	57 (36)	79 (49)	200 (36)	360 (64)
(iii) Customer support information	32 (20)	23 (14)	105 (66)	142 (25)	418 (75)

coupling when sharing content related to corporate information. Consistency has to be strictly enforced as such content are more likely to be updated frequently. 75% of cases with no propagations are identified for "Customer Support Information". This suggest low coupling in websites and consistency is not strictly enforced except in local languages. The coupling in a website pair while sharing content for "Product Information" tends to be neutral (no significant difference in occurrence of propagation and no propagation). This suggest that policy for consistency to be moderately enforced while sharing product related information. This section expanded our understanding of community preferences in sharing that differs for specific content categories. Next we will detail customization involving geographic regions.

4.3 Geographic Preferences

As with previous setup we categorized country-specific websites from the global brands into four geographic regions: Asia Pacific, North America, Europe and Middle East-Africa. We again sampled webpages related to "Corporate Information", "Product Information" and "Customer Support Information". A total of 480 webpages samples were manually labeled to their specific content categories and geographic regions. We applied propagation-based approach to check for content propagation within geographic region and among geographic regions. A total of 240 comparisons of webpages are performed to check for propagation occurring within all four geographic regions. A total of 1440 comparisons of webpages are performed to check for propagation among geographic regions.

4.3.1 Propagation Within Geographic Region

From Table 3 we found that the number of occurrences of propagation and no propagation among websites are comparable within Asia Pacific and Middle East-Africa. But for websites within North America, the majority of cases 67% show no propagation. This suggest low coupling in sharing content among countries in North America. In contrast the majority cases of propagation almost 60% occur among country-specific websites in Europe. This means high coupling in websites among countries in Europe.

4.3.2 Propagation Among Geographic Region

As in Table 3 there tends to be noticeable differences in the number of occurrences of propagation and no propagation while sharing content with countries in North America. More than 60% cases of no propagation in websites for sharing content from Asia Pacific, Europe and Middle East-Africa with customer in North America. This suggest low coupling in websites when sharing content with North America meaning

Table 3 Results of comparing webpages with geographic regions

Propagation among geographic region	Yes (%)	No (%)
(i) Asia Pacific, Europe	107 (45)	133 (55)
(ii) Asia Pacific, North America	78 (33)	162 (68)
(iii) Asia Pacific, Middle East-Africa	105 (44)	135 (56)
(iv) Europe, North America	83 (35)	157 (65)
(v) Europe, Middle East-Africa	110 (46)	130 (54)
(vi) North America, Middle East-Africa	87 (36)	153 (64)
Propagation within geographic region	Yes (%)	No (%)
(i) Asia Pacific	29 (48)	31 (52)
(ii) Europe	35 (58)	25 (42)
(iii) North America	20 (33)	40 (67)
(iv) Middle East-Africa	32 (53)	28 (47)

websites within North America tend to have less interaction with websites from other region. Content categories wise we find that the occurrences of propagation tends to be higher among regions Asia Pacific, Europe and Middle East-Africa for sharing corporate related information in comparison to North America. This suggests high coupling among regions except with North America. Also corporate related information tend to be globally suitably. Higher occurrences of no propagation among region while sharing "Product Information" suggest that such content tend to be region specific and either locally or regionally suitable. In fact more than 70% no propagation cases occur for product related with North America meaning region specific product information is mostly preferred. The differences in the occurrences of propagation and no propagation for "Customer Support Information" seem to be consistent among all regions suggesting websites in all regions are more likely to prefer locale content. Next we will summarize the findings of this chapter.

5   Discussion

In designing a multi-language knowledge sharing system, we first shifted our focus from stating consistency rules explicitly to highlight source of inconsistency. Cases such as *content omitted, content updates not propagated* and *content conflicts* were considered as they are obvious in collaborative setting. Their occurrences in real world example of country-specific websites managed in a global brand also shed light on some of the consequences such as (a) community bias, (b) global and local inconsistency and (c) regional discrepancies. By no means are the mentioned cases trivial; the complexity to detect their presence meaning inconsistency increases with the number of languages and communities participating in knowledge sharing. Then we touched on an important issues about consistency constraints due to opposing knowledge sharing goals of communities. We made following contributions.

1. *Approaches for consistency adhering to knowledge sharing goals.* We proposed a process-based approach to detect inconsistency in multilingual content when leveraging knowledge equally. The concept is to synchronize user editing activities realized with a state transition model and design of rules to detect inconsistent states. We evaluated approach to be satisfactory with an average precision of 88% and a recall of 86% in detecting cases of inconsistency. We also proposed a propagation-based approach to determine scales and coupling a key indicator for community preference in customized knowledge sharing. We used propagation in website graph, website pair, within and among geographic region to show preferences for sharing content categories/geographic regions.

2. *Guidelines to enforce content consistency.* We suggested guidelines for content consistency. We showed that community prefer to share corporate related information globally, customer support related information locally and product related information regionally. Implication is 'global consistency policy' for corporate related, 'local consistency policy' for customer support related information is required. Patterns of sharing Internationalization, Regionalization and Localization in [12] are useful to propagate updates consistently based on scales. We showed that community prefer high coupling when sharing corporate related and low coupling when sharing customer support related information. High Coupling means frequent interaction for sharing content, more vulnerable for inconsistency and higher priority for consistency policy required. Websites in Europe tend to be more dependent due to high coupling and share most content compared to websites in North America. Websites inside North America tend to be autonomous and participate less in sharing. This means customer inside European region is more vulnerable to 'intra-regional discrepancies', a higher priority for 'intra-regional consistency policy' for European countries. High coupling among Asia, Europe and Middle East-African countries suggest higher priority for 'inter-regional consistency policy'. We also revealed that websites in North America have higher preferences for specialized product related information not shared with other region; while customer support related information are specialized inside all regions and not shared; for both cases 'intra-regional consistency policy' is suited. Details also examined in [11].

3. *Support for resource poor language communities.* We proposed approaches that require minimal language processing and supported knowledge sharing for resource poor communities. The problem surfacing limited support of existing approaches to content consistency in resource poor languages is scarce linguistic corpuses to perform advance NLP operations. Better results can be anticipated when proposed approaches is integrated with NLP at a preliminary stage of inconsistency management and using framework such as Language Grid [7].

6   Conclusion

This chapter addressed two important issues in multi-language knowledge sharing: (i) impracticality in stating consistency rules explicitly in advance and (ii) constraint in content consistency. We showed that even minor cases such as *content omitted*, *content updates not propagated* and *content conflicts*, when considered as potential cause for inconsistency, it leads to undesirable consequences: *community bias, global and local inconsistency* and *regional discrepancy*. We also showed that opposing knowledge sharing goals impose consistency requirements from rigid to non-rigid. To avoid inconsistencies while adhering to knowledge sharing goals of communities, we contributed in the design of multi-language knowledge sharing system with (a) process-based approach for multilingual content synchronization to leverage knowledge equally and (b) propagation-based approach to analyze community preferences when sharing specific content categories/geographic regions, to customize knowledge sharing. We also extended support to resource poor language communities by basing our approach on minimal language processing requirements.

Acknowledgements   This research was supported by the Grant-in-Aid for Scientific Research (S) (24220002, 2012–2016) from Japan Society for the Promotion of Science (JSPS).

References

1. Adar, E., Skinner, M., Weld, D.S.: Information arbitrage across multi-lingual Wikipedia. In: Proceedings of the Second ACM International Conference on Web Search and Data Mining, pp. 94–103. ACM (2009)
2. Al Assimi, A.B., Boitet, C.: Management of non-centralized evolution of parallel multilingual documents. In: Proceedings of Internationalization Track, 10th International World Wide Web Conference, Hong Kong, pp. 1–8 (2001)
3. Hartley, A., Paris, C.: Multilingual document production from support for translating to support for authoring. Mach. Transl. **12**(1), 109–129 (1997)
4. Hopcroft, J.E., Motwani, R., Ullman, J.D.: Automata theory, languages, and computation. Int. Ed. **24** (2006)
5. Huberdeau, L.P., Paquet, S., Désilets, A.: The cross-lingual wiki engine: enabling collaboration across language barriers. In: Proceedings of the 4th International Symposium on Wikis, WikiSym '08, pp. 13:1–13:14. ACM, New York (2008)
6. Huizingh, E.K.: The content and design of web sites: an empirical study. Inform. Manage. **37**(3), 123–134 (2000)
7. Ishida, T.: The Language Grid: Service-oriented Collective Intelligence for Language Resource Interoperability. Springer Science & Business Media, Berlin (2011)
8. Kayan, S., Fussell, S.R., Setlock, L.D.: Cultural differences in the use of instant messaging in Asia and North America. In: Proceedings of the 2006 20th Anniversary Conference on Computer Supported Cooperative Work, pp. 525–528. ACM (2006)
9. Monz, C., Nastase, V., Negri, M., Fahrni, A., Mehdad, Y., Strube, M.: Cosyne: a framework for multilingual content synchronization of wikis. In: Proceedings of the 7th International Symposium on Wikis and Open Collaboration, pp. 217–218. ACM (2011)
10. Pariyar, A., Lin, D., Ishida, T.: Tracking inconsistencies in parallel multilingual documents. In: 2013 International Conference on Culture and Computing (Culture Computing), pp. 15–20. IEEE (2013)

11. Pariyar, A., Murakami, Y., Lin, D., Ishida, T.: Content sharing in global brand from geographic perspective. In: 2015 International Conference on Culture and Computing (Culture Computing), pp. 151–158. IEEE (2015)
12. Pariyar, A., Murakami, Y., Lin, D., Ishida, T.: Content sharing in global organization: a cross-country perspective, pp. 1–10 (2015)
13. Robbins, S.S., Stylianou, A.C.: Global corporate web sites: an empirical investigation of content and design. Inform. Manage. **40**(3), 205–212 (2003)
14. Tonella, P., Ricca, F., Pianta, E., Girardi, C.: Restructuring multilingual web sites. In: International Conference on Software Maintenance, 2002. Proceedings, pp. 290–299. IEEE (2002)

Supporting Non-native Speakers' Listening Comprehension with Automated Transcripts

Xun Cao, Naomi Yamashita and Toru Ishida

Abstract Various language services exist to support the listening comprehension of non-native speakers (NNSs). One important service is to provide NNSs with real-time transcripts generated by automatic speech recognition (ASR) technologies. The goal of our research is to explore the effects of ASR transcripts on the listening comprehension of NNSs and consider how to support NNSs with ASR transcripts more effectively. To reach our goal, we ran three studies. The first study investigates the comprehension problems faced by NNSs, and the second study examines how ASR transcripts impact their listening comprehension, e.g., what types of comprehension problems could and could not be solved by reading ASR transcripts. Finally, the third study explores the potential of using eye-tracking data to detect their comprehension problems. Our data analysis identified thirteen types of listening comprehension problems. ASR transcripts helped the NNSs solve certain problems, e.g., "failed to recognize words they know." However, the transcripts did not solve problems such as "lack of vocabulary," and indeed NNS burden was increased. Results also show that from eye-tracking data we can make reasonably accurate predictions (83.8%) about the types of problems encountered by NNSs. Our findings provide insight into ways of designing real-time adaptive support systems for NNSs.

Keywords Non-native speakers (NNSs) · Listening comprehension problems
Automatic speech recognition (ASR) transcripts · Eye-tracking

X. Cao (✉) · T. Ishida
Department of Social Informatics, Kyoto University,
Kyoto 606-8510, Japan
e-mail: xun@ai.soc.i.kyoto-u.ac.jp

T. Ishida
e-mail: ishida@i.kyoto-u.ac.jp

N. Yamashita
NTT Communication Science Labs, 2-4 Hikaridai, Seika-cho, Soraku-gun,
Kyoto 619-0237, Japan
e-mail: naomiy@acm.org

1   Introduction

Non-native speakers (NNSs) often face comprehension difficulties when listening to the speech of native speakers (NSs) [3]. To support NNS comprehension in real-time communication, various language services have been provided. One notable service infrastructure built for NNSs is the Language Grid, which enables users to use multiple services more efficiently [11, 12, 18]. Among the various language services provided by the Language Grid, this chapter focuses on automatic speech recognition (ASR) technologies in order to support NNSs' listening comprehension.

Previous research has suggested that real-time transcripts generated by ASR technologies hold the potential to help NNSs improve their listening comprehension by providing them supplemental information to understand the speech [20, 25]. However, we still lack a detailed understanding of how NNSs benefit from ASR transcripts (e.g., what types of listening comprehension problems could be solved) and what are the difficulties of using them.

Our goal is to explore the effects of ASR transcripts on listening comprehension of NNSs and how to support NNSs with ASR transcripts more effectively. To reach our goal, we conducted three studies. Figure 1 provides an overview of the three studies.

The first study investigated the types of comprehension problems faced by NNSs. 40 NNSs engaged in a listening task. The participants pressed a button whenever they encountered a comprehension problem, and explained each problem in the subsequent interview. From our data analysis, we identified thirteen types of listening comprehension problems. The second study examined how the ASR transcripts impacted their listening comprehension, e.g., what types of comprehension problems

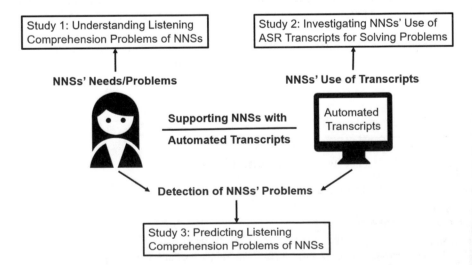

Fig. 1 Overview of our research

could be solved by reading ASR transcripts. 20 NNSs engaged in two listening tasks, each in different conditions: (C1) audio only and (C2) audio + ASR transcripts. Same as study 1, the participants pressed a button when they encountered a comprehension problem and described them in their interviews. From the second study, we found that ASR transcripts helped NNSs solve certain problems, e.g., "do not recognize words they know." We also found that NNSs often tried to solve problems which were unsolvable by reading ASR transcripts. In such cases, the transcripts seemed to only pose burden on them. For such unsolved problems, if a system can automatically detect the problem type and provide appropriate support (e.g., showing a translated word for a vocabulary problem), the listening comprehension of NNSs might be further improved. In Study 3, we explored the potential of using eye-tracking data for such detection. We collected gaze data from NNSs who engaged in listening tasks, and we also gave them ASR transcripts. By applying machine learning techniques, our study shows that we can make reasonably accurate predictions (83.8%) about the types of problems encountered by NNSs using eye-tracking data.

In the remainder of this chapter, we first review previous work and then describe our three studies in further details.

2 Background

2.1 Real-Time Listening Comprehension Problems of NNSs

Researchers have examined the problems faced by NNSs from different perspectives. Most of the previous studies explored the factors that influence second language listening [3, 22]. A representative work by Rubin extensively reviewed the research on second language listening comprehension and attributed the factors that affect listening comprehension into five characteristics: text characteristics, interlocutor characteristics, task characteristics, listener characteristics, and process characteristics [22]. On the other hand, Goh investigated NNSs' listening comprehension from a different perspective. She classified the listening comprehension problems faced by NNSs into ten categories (Table 1). In her study, 40 non-native students wrote weekly diaries and explained the listening comprehension problems they faced during lectures [9].

2.2 Providing NNSs with Real-Time ASR Transcripts

According to previous research, real-time transcripts generated by ASR technologies hold the potential to facilitate the listening comprehension of NNSs [20]. ASR transcripts provide textual information that can complement audio speech and improve the comprehension of NNSs [10, 25]. Pan et al. investigated how the quality of ASR

Table 1 Listening comprehension problems identified in Goh's work [9]

Problems
1. Do not recognize words they know
2. Unable to form a mental representation from words heard
3. Cannot chunk streams of speech
4. Neglect the next part when thinking about meaning
5. Do not understand subsequent parts of input because of earlier problems
6. Concentrate too hard or unable to concentrate
7. Understand words but not the intended message
8. Confused about the key ideas in the message
9. Miss the beginning of texts
10. Quickly forget what is heard

transcripts impact comprehension and found that a 20% word-error-rate (WER) was the critical point for transcripts to be acceptable, and at a 10% WER, comprehension performance significantly improved compared to a no-transcript condition [20]. Yao et al. compared the NNS comprehension performance among three conditions (no-transcript, perfect transcripts with a 2-s delay, and transcripts with a 10% WER and a 2-s delay). The comprehension performance in the latter two conditions was significantly better than that in the no-transcript condition [25]. Despite the positive effects of introducing ASR transcripts, previous research also reported that NNSs sometimes get overwhelmed when they simultaneously listen to speech and read ASR transcripts that contain errors and delays [8, 25].

Overall, the previous studies identified the usefulness of ASR transcripts for supporting NNS listening comprehension and the risk of placing an extra burden on NNSs. However, we still lack a detailed understanding of how NNSs benefit from ASR transcripts (e.g., what types of listening comprehension problems could be solved) and what are the difficulties of using them.

2.3 Eye-Tracking and NNSs' Use of Textual Information

Eye-tracking data are a valuable source of information when designing an adaptive system because they provide information about a person's focus or intentions [1].

In the field of intelligent tutoring systems, researchers have used eye-tracking data to predict the effectiveness of learning [15], emotions relevant to learning [13] and user attention patterns [7].

Another research area lies in the field of information visualization. Many researchers in this field have investigated the potential of leveraging eye-tracking data to design user-adaptive information visualization systems. For example, Steichen et al. showed that a user's eye gaze can be used to infer what he/she is doing in real-time as well as predicting her cognitive abilities. Their results show that simple machine learning techniques on simple eye-tracking metrics are useful, even when only partial data has been observed. Their findings provide insights for designing systems that can adapt to the individual user in real-time [23].

Our research builds on previous works on adaptive interfaces and focuses on how to instantly detect the listening comprehension problems of NNSs from eye movements while following ASR transcripts.

3 Study 1: Understanding Listening Comprehension Problems of NNSs

In this study, we investigate the types of comprehension problems encountered by NNSs while listening [5]. We focus on the problems that occur during the NNSs' cognitive processing of speech input. Our work builds on Goh's research, which also focused on the cognitive aspects of NNSs' listening comprehension problems. Note that our study covers transient problems, which were not covered by Goh's work. Transient problems are problems that tentatively confuse the NNSs but are eventually resolved or quickly forgotten.

RQ1: What types of listening comprehension problems arise when NNSs listen to native speech?

3.1 Method

We developed a tool that logs the participants' listening comprehension problems in real time. During the listening task, participants pressed a button when they encountered a comprehension problem. Pressing the button marked (in the lecture transcripts) specific places that were to be visited later to explain the details of the problems. We chose this "pressing a button" method because it has low-overhead, as suggested by previous work [14]. In addition, the method allows us to record the problems faced by NNSs in real time while simultaneously keeping the task close to actual listening experience.

We recruited 40 non-native English speakers as participants, including 22 females and 18 males. Among these NNSs, 20 were native Japanese speakers and 20 were native Chinese speakers. Their mean age was 30.4 (SD = 9.97). Their Test of English for International Communication (TOEIC) scores ranged from 650 to 960 (M = 828, SD = 95.18).

Five audio clips from the Test of English as a Foreign Language (TOEFL) were chosen as task materials. Two clips were conversations, and the other three were lectures. The length of the clips ranged from two to five minutes. One of two out of the five audio clips were randomly assigned to each participant.

The experimental procedure was as follows.

- *Step 1 (real-time listening).* The participants listened to the audio clip. While listening, they pressed a button whenever they encountered a comprehension problem.
- *Step 2 (retrospective listening).* The participants listened to the same clip again. The computer automatically stopped at the places where they pressed the button in Step 1. At this point, the participants briefly explained the type of problem they faced. This step helped them re-experience Step 1 and recall their comprehension problems.
- *Step 3 (interview).* The participants were handed perfect transcripts of the audio clip with markings that indicated their comprehension problems. Based on the marked-up transcripts, they explained the problems they faced during the listening task.

To identify each type of listening comprehension problem faced by the participants during the listening task, we transcribed the interview data and classified the problems into ten categories based on Goh's work. We created a new problem category if a problem did not belong to any of the ten categories. The interview data were coded independently by two coders. Discrepancies were discussed until an agreement was reached.

3.2 Results

RQ1 asked what types of listening comprehension problems arise when NNSs listen to native speech. To identify all of the listening comprehension problems faced by non-native participants, we counted the number of times problems occurred based on the markups (times they pressed the button). In a few cases when participants described two problems with one markup, the occurrences of problems were counted as two. 513 problem occurrences were initially identified by the NNSs; 366 were "cognitive problems," 144 were due to their lack of vocabulary, and the rest reflected situational factors (e.g., unable to distinguish different speakers). The average number of problem occurrences identified by each non-native participant was 2.8 times per minute.

Note that Goh's study excluded the NNSs' lack of vocabulary when identifying their listening comprehension problems because their main focus was to propose an effective learning method to improve listening skills. Our study aims to provide effective technological support for NNS comprehension in real-time communication. Since "lack of vocabulary" problems can be solved by providing a dictionary function in ASR transcripts [8], we included them in our study.

Table 2 shows sample excerpts extracted from our interviews, the number and percentage of the occurrences of each problem (i.e., number of times each problem occurred/total number of occurrences). Among them, item 5 ("confused about unexpected word appearance") and item 9 ("unsure about the meaning of words") were newly identified in our study, as we describe in further detail below.

Table 2 Example, number, and percentage of each listening comprehension problem faced by non-native participants

Problem	Example interview excerpt	Number	Percentage (%)
1. Lack of vocabulary	I simply didn't know the word "respiration." (NNS 6)	144	28.2
2. Do not recognize words they know	Since I misheard "slides" as "five," I couldn't understand it. If I had read it, I would've understood it. (NNS 2)	97	19.0
3. Unable to form a mental representation from words heard	I didn't really understand "bubble gas." Although I caught both words, I couldn't form a picture of them. (NNS 6)	73	14.3
4. Cannot chunk streams of speech	I couldn't catch "cause you loved them too much." I couldn't divide that chunk into separate words. (NNS 9)	56	11.0
5. Confused about unexpected word appearance	"Commercially" came out of the blue. I got confused when I heard it because I thought they were talking about stuff happening in a lab. (NNS 1)	25	4.9
6. Neglect the next part when thinking about meaning	While I was wondering what "bubble gas" meant, I missed the subsequent words. They just drifted away, so I gave up. (NNS 10)	20	3.9
7. Do not understand subsequent parts of input because of earlier problems	I couldn't understand this part: "scientist decided that the best place to see a whole root system would be to grow it, where." Maybe the lecturer is asking a question, but since I couldn't get that part, I also couldn't understand the answer to it. (NNS 13)	19	3.7
8. Concentrate too hard or unable to concentrate	I couldn't concentrate. I was almost panicking. (NNS 19)	18	3.5
9. Unsure about the meaning of words	When I heard "root system," I wasn't sure what it meant. I came up with many possibilities. It could be the roots of plants, but when combined with "system," I got confused. I thought it might have something to do with a Linux file system or something related to a chart in linguistics. (NNS 10)	18	3.5
10. Understand words but not the intended message	I could understand the meaning. But I couldn't understand why he repeated the words. It seems that I didn't get the point.... (NNS 32)	15	2.9
11. Confused about the key ideas in the message	Until now, the lecturer has been talking about "growing stuff in water," "bubble gas through water," and "growing plants in soil." Now, she's saying that giving too much water will kill a plant ...I don't understand. What on earth did they want to say? (NNS 19)	14	2.7
12. Quickly forget what is heard	When I heard "bubble gas," I thought I understood. But when the lecturer continued to the next sentence, I suddenly forgot what it was. I got confused whether it was gas or gassed water. (NNS 16)	5	1.0
13. Miss the beginning of texts	I wasn't quite ready and missed the beginning of the lecture. (NNS 10)	6	1.2

Confused about unexpected word appearance. In our experiment, participants reported that they got confused about the appearance of a word or phrase that seemed unrelated to the current context. People generally use information from a prior discourse to rapidly predict specific upcoming words as the discourse unfolds [19]. However, a prediction failure often hinders the processing of an unexpected word or phrase [24].

Unsure about the meaning of words. Some participants in our study got confused about the correct meaning of words/phrases that carried multiple meanings. Especially when such words/phrases were keywords that appeared repeatedly in the speech, the problem nagged them until they determined the correct meaning. Most of our participants gradually resolved their doubts using context information. Participants also reported confusion when they encountered homonyms. Although they had a guess or multiple candidates in mind, they were not sure if their guess was correct, or which candidate was correct. As a result, they had to expend too much mental energy to resolve the problem by listening to subsequent speech, which burdened them and sometimes triggered other problems.

4   Study 2: Investigating NNSs' Use of ASR Transcripts for Solving Problems

In Study 1, we identified thirteen types of listening comprehension problems faced by NNSs [5]. Among all the problems identified, we expect that certain types of problems such as "do not recognize words they know" could be solved using ASR transcripts, but others will not. In addition, due to transcript errors and delay, the problem solving process might not be successful and could place an extra burden on NNSs. We are interested in understanding how NNSs are burdened during such a process. Thus, we pose the following research questions:

RQ2: What types of listening comprehension problems can be solved by reading ASR transcripts?

RQ3: Do ASR transcripts place an extra burden on NNSs when they fail to solve their listening comprehension problems?

4.1   Method

We conducted a laboratory experiment with participants who engaged in two listening tasks in different conditions [6]. Under the without-transcript condition, only audio was provided. Under the with-transcript condition, both audio and ASR transcripts were provided. In each condition during the listening task, the participants pressed a button to indicate when they encountered a comprehension problem. The experiment used a within-subject design. Its conditions were counterbalanced across subjects to minimize the order effects.

We recruited twenty non-native English speakers for our study, including ten females and ten males. Their mean age was 25.9 (SD = 2.41). All spoke Chinese as their first language. Their TOEIC scores ranged from 690 to 950 (M = 823, SD = 95.05).

Four audio clips from the TOEFL exam were chosen as task materials. The length of the clips varied from two to five minutes. Two clips (one conversation and one lecture) were randomly chosen for each experiment condition. Real-time transcripts of each audio clip were generated by Google speech recognition API.

The procedure for each condition basically followed that of Study 1. To better understand how NNSs used the ASR transcripts, under the with-transcript condition, they were also asked if they tried to solve their problems using the ASR transcripts and if the ASR transcripts were helpful.

4.2 Results

4.2.1 Listening Comprehension Problems Generally Solved by ASR Transcripts

RQ2 asked what types of listening comprehension problems can be solved by reading ASR transcripts. To answer these questions, we first identified the listening comprehension problems faced by NNSs in each condition and investigated the types of problems that significantly decreased when ASR transcripts were provided.

We did the same count and categorization as in Study 1 for the listening comprehension problems faced by NNSs. Table 3 shows the distribution of the listening comprehension problems faced by non-native participants under the without- and with-transcript conditions. Item 14 covers problems caused by ASR errors. The problem occurrences identified under the without- and with-transcript condition were 372 and 267 separately.

To compare how the ASR transcripts changed the distribution of the problem occurrences, we first counted the problem occurrences of each participant. Next, we conducted a paired t-test (two-tailed) to see whether the average number of problem occurrences per minute changed between the two conditions. Results showed that the NNSs faced significantly fewer problems in the with-transcript conditions for three types of problems: "do not recognize words they know" ($P < 0.01$), "cannot chunk streams of speech" ($P < 0.01$), and "confused about unexpected word appearance" ($P < 0.05$).

One common element to these three problems is that they occur in the early stage of speech comprehension. In other words, they all occur during the cognitive processing phases of perception in language comprehension, which deals with the encoding of acoustic messages [2]. ASR transcripts benefit NNSs in perceptual processing by transforming acoustic information into textual information.

Table 3 Listening comprehension problems faced by NNSs under different conditions

Problems	Without-transcript		With-transcript		p-value
	Number	Percentage (%)	Number	Percentage (%)	
1. Lack of vocabulary	114	30.6	121	45.3	0.567
2. Do not recognize words they know	77	20.7	9	3.4	**0.000**
3. Unable to form a mental representation from words heard	59	15.9	46	17.2	0.400
4. Cannot chunk streams of speech	41	11.0	19	7.1	**0.005**
5. Understand words but not the intended message	14	3.8	10	3.7	0.448
6. Concentrate too hard or unable to concentrate	14	3.8	7	2.6	**0.135**
7. Neglect the next part when thinking about meaning	12	3.2	12	4.5	0.897
8. Confused about unexpected word appearance	12	3.2	3	1.1	**0.034**
9. Unsure about the meaning of words	11	3.0	7	2.6	0.498
10. Do not understand subsequent parts of input because of earlier problems	10	2.7	13	4.9	0.349
11. Confused about the key ideas in the message	4	1.1	7	2.6	0.044
12. Quickly forget what is heard	2	0.5	3	1.1	0.745
13. Miss the beginning of texts	2	0.5	0	0.0	0.163
14. Confusion caused by ASR errors	0	0.0	10	3.7	**0.005**

4.2.2 Issues of Using ASR Transcripts to Solve Problems

RQ3 asked about the burdens placed on NNSs when they read ASR transcripts but failed to solve their problems. Note that we focus on the problems reported by the NNSs, which means that we discounted the problems which were solved by reading the transcripts. "Response time (T(res))" was considered to be a rough measure for NNS workload. Response time is the time taken to press a button when the NNS recognized a comprehension problem. The longer it took to press the button, the heavier the burden is. We calculated the response time by counting the number of words spoken from where the problems started to where the NNSs pressed the button.

Table 4 shows the average response time of each listening comprehension problem under the without- and with-transcript conditions. The response times of the four types of listening comprehension problems significantly increased (t-test, two-tailed): "lack of vocabulary" ($P < 0.01$), "do not recognize words they know" ($P < 0.05$), "unable to form a mental representation from words heard" ($P < 0.01$), and "cannot chunk streams of speech" ($P < 0.01$).

This result suggests that even though NNSs tried to solve certain problems by reading the transcripts, these problems were not necessarily solved, rather their burden was increased. For example, although the "lack of vocabulary" problems tend to be unsolved by reading the transcripts, NNSs seemed to read the transcripts to check whether they actually were unsolvable; this did not help them resolve the problem but only increased their workload.

Table 4 Response times of each listening comprehension problem under without- and with-transcript conditions

Problem	Without-transcript	With-transcript	p-value
1. Lack of vocabulary	3.6	5.4	**0.000**
2. Do not recognize words they know	4.3	6.7	**0.023**
3. Unable to form a mental representation from words heard	7.4	15.0	**0.000**
4. Cannot chunk streams of speech	6.4	12.3	**0.004**
5. Understand words but not the intended message	19.9	15.1	0.241
6. Concentrate too hard or unable to concentrate	25.9	27.3	0.845
7. Neglect the next part when thinking about meaning	17.4	15.8	0.631
8. Confused about unexpected word appearance	5.1	4.7	0.831
9. Unsure about the meaning of words	6.3	6.9	0.759
10. Do not understand subsequent parts of input because of earlier problems	23.5	19.7	0.437
11. Confused about the key ideas in the message	32.3	35.1	0.842
12. Quickly forget what is heard	29.5	31.7	0.905
13. Miss the beginning of texts	16.5	0.0	·

5 Study 3: Predicting Listening Comprehension Problems of NNSs

In the two previous studies, we found that NNSs encountered various types of comprehension problems when listening to native speech [5]. ASR transcripts helped the NNSs solve certain problems, e.g., "do not recognize words they know." However, certain issues such as vocabulary problems or sentence-level problems remained unsolved [5, 6].

For such unsolved problems, additional support is necessary. Different types of problems require different types of support. For vocabulary problems (e.g., not knowing a word or an idiom), providing a dictionary translation might be helpful. For sentence-level problems (e.g., confusion about the key ideas in the message), since NNSs often don't have enough time or cognitive resources to carefully read the transcripts while listening, a support that helps them reduce their burden and follow the speech might be useful. For example, showing them keywords to highlight the speech's topic transition may be helpful.

Study 3 examines whether we can automatically detect the types of problems (i.e., vocabulary vs. sentence-level problem) faced by NNSs by using eye-tracking data. We pose the following research question:

RQ4: How accurately can we predict the type of listening comprehension problems being experienced by NNSs from their eye gaze data?

5.1 Method

We collected the gaze data of 32 NNSs about their use of ASR transcripts while listening. The participants were given real-time ASR transcripts while they engaged in listening tasks. During the task, they pressed a button whenever they encountered a comprehension problem. They didn't need to press the button if the problem was immediately solved by reading the ASR transcripts.

32 non-native English speakers with normal vision participated in our study. All spoke Chinese as their first language. Among them, 6 participants' eye movement data were excluded due to low eye-tracking accuracy (lower than 70%). As a result, the eye movement data of 26 participants (11 females and 15 males) were subjected to data analysis. Their mean age was 25.1 (SD = 2.61). Their TOEIC scores ranged from 690 to 965 (M = 826, SD = 82.29).

Four audio clips from the TOEFL exam were chosen as listening task materials. The length of the clips ranged from two to five minutes. Each participant was assigned two randomly chosen audio clips whose real-time transcripts were generated by Google speech recognition API. The WER of the ASR transcripts averaged about 10%.

We recorded the participants' eye movements during the task using a Tobii TX300 eye-tracker, which is composed of an eye-tracker unit and a 23-inch, 1920×1080 wide-screen monitor (Fig. 2). The eye-tracker collects gaze data at 300 Hz and allows large head movements.

Fig. 2 Participant sitting in front of a screen-based eye-tracker

Before the listening tasks, the participants completed a 9-point calibration. The tasks were divided into two steps.

- *Step 1 (real-time listening).* The participants listened to the audio clip and pressed a button whenever they encountered a problem.
- *Step 2 (retrospective listening).* They listened to the same audio clip again. The computer automatically paused at the places where they pressed the button during Step 1. At each pause, the participants answered whether their problem was caused by a lack of vocabulary or a different issue. Participant eye movements in Step 1 were also shown at the top of the ASR transcripts. After explaining the problem, the participants were further asked to explain their own eye movements while they encountered the problem. Specifically, they were asked the following questions: Did you try to solve your problems using the ASR transcripts? Why didn't the ASR transcripts help?

5.2 Classification Experiments

We transcribed the interview data and classified each problem into two types (vocabulary or sentence-level) based on the explanations of the NNSs. Note that we removed the following problems from our pool: (1) cases where they pressed the button once but indicated both vocabulary and sentence-level problems; (2) problems caused by ASR errors. The interview data were coded independently by two coders. Discrepancies were discussed until an agreement was reached. In total, we collected 142 problems: 88 vocabulary problems and 54 sentence-level problems.

Eye-gaze information is normally described in the form of fixations (i.e., gaze maintained at one point on the screen) and saccades (i.e., a quick gaze movement from one fixation point to another), which can be analyzed to understand the reader's attention pattern [23].

Four basic gaze measures were used in our study, as described in Table 5. The fixation count indicates the number of fixations, and the fixation duration indicates the time of individual fixations. The saccade length indicates the distance between two fixations that delimit the saccade (d in Fig. 3). The regressive saccade count indicates the number of eye movements backwards in x coordinate in the text. These features were chosen because they are potentially useful in detecting reader difficulties (e.g., failure to understand a word or a sentence) [21].

Table 6 describes the gaze features that were used for our analysis; they were obtained by computing statistics such as average, standard deviation, and the maxima of the basic gaze measures.

The gaze features in Table 6 may contain irrelevant or redundant features. Some features could even degrade the classification performance. Since we want to select an optimal subset of features that yields the best classification performance, we employed a wrapper-based feature selection technique. This technique selects a subset of the available features by incrementally adding features to the classification model and testing its performance until no added feature improves the performance [16].

All of our classification experiments tested the accuracy of the learning models using logistic regression and wrapper-based feature selection. We selected logistic regression after testing it alongside support vector machine, random forest, decision

Table 5 Description of basic gaze measures

Basic gaze measures	Description
Fixation count	Number of fixations
Fixation duration	Duration of individual fixations
Saccade length	Distance between two fixations delimiting the saccade (d in Fig. 3)
Regressive saccade count	Number of eye movements backwards in x coordinate in the text

Fig. 3 Saccade-based eye measures: dots indicate fixation positions; numbers in dots represent fixation order; lines between fixations represent saccades

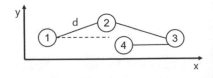

Table 6 Description of gaze features

Gaze features	Description
Fixation num	Number of fixations
Fixation duration mean	Mean of fixation durations
Fixation duration SD	Std. deviation of fixation durations
Fixation duration max	Max. of fixation durations
Saccade length mean	Mean of saccade length
Saccade length SD	Std. deviation of saccade length
Saccade length max	Max. of saccade length
Regressive saccades num	Number of regressive saccades

tree, multilayer perceptron, and naive Bayes classifiers because it had the highest overall accuracy. This result is also consistent with previous works which suggested that logistic regression is the best performing classifier for experiments involving eye gaze data [4, 23]. We used the WEKA data mining toolkit for model learning as well as our evaluation. A ZeroR classifier was used as a baseline classifier; it always predicts the majority category (class). To test the effectiveness of our classifier, we employed a commonly used 10-fold cross-validation test [17].

5.3 Results

RQ4 asked to what extent a NNS's current listening comprehension problem be predicted from eye gaze data.

As described earlier, we used a wrapper-based feature selection technique to determine which classification features to include in the logistic regression classification model. Among the eight gaze features described in Table 6, five were selected: (1) max. of fixation durations; (2) mean of saccade length; (3) std. deviation of saccade length; (4) max. of saccade length; and (5) number of regressive saccades.

With the selected features and the best performing classifier, our classifier yielded reasonably accurate predictions (83.8%) for the type of problems encountered by NNSs using eye-tracking data, significantly better than the majority class baseline classifier of 62.0%.

6 Conclusions

We reported three laboratory studies. The first investigated listening comprehension problems of NNSs and identified thirteen types of listening comprehension problems. The second study explored the types of problems that could be solved by using ASR transcripts. We found that the transcripts helped the NNSs solve certain problems, e.g., "failed to recognize words they know." However, the transcripts did not solve problems such as "lack of vocabulary," and indeed NNS burden was increased. In the third study, we explored whether it is possible to detect NNSs' problems from eye-tracking data. Results showed that we can make reasonably accurate predictions (83.8%) about the types of problems encountered by NNSs from eye-tracking data. Our findings provide insight into ways of designing real-time adaptive support systems for NNSs.

Acknowledgements This research was partially supported by a Grant-in-Aid for Scientific Research (A) (17H00759, 2017–2020) from Japan Society for the Promotion of Science (JSPS).

References

1. Aaltonen, A., Hyrskykari, A., Räihä, K.J.: 101 spots, or how do users read menus? In: Proceedings of the SIGCHI Conference on Human Factors in Computing Systems, pp. 132–139. ACM Press/Addison-Wesley Publishing Co. (1998)
2. Anderson, J.R.: Cognitive Psychology and Its Implications. WH Freeman/Times Books/Henry Holt & Co., New York (1990)
3. Bloomfield, A., Wayland, S.C., Rhoades, E., Blodgett, A., Linck, J., Ross, S.: What makes listening difficult? Factors affecting second language listening comprehension. Technical Report, DTIC Document (2010)
4. Bondareva, D., Conati, C., Feyzi-Behnagh, R., Harley, J.M., Azevedo, R., Bouchet, F.: Inferring learning from gaze data during interaction with an environment to support self-regulated learning. In: International Conference on Artificial Intelligence in Education, pp. 229–238. Springer (2013)
5. Cao, X., Yamashita, N., Ishida, T.: How non-native speakers perceive listening comprehension problems: Implications for adaptive support technologies. In: International Conference on Collaboration Technologies, pp. 89–104. Springer (2016)
6. Cao, X., Yamashita, N., Ishida, T.: Investigating the impact of automated transcripts on non-native speakers' listening comprehension. In: Proceedings of the 18th ACM International Conference on Multimodal Interaction, pp. 121–128. ACM (2016)
7. Conati, C., Jaques, N., Muir, M.: Understanding attention to adaptive hints in educational games: an eye-tracking study. Int. J. Artif. Intell. Educ. **23**(1–4), 136–161 (2013)
8. Gao, G., Yamashita, N., Hautasaari, A.M., Fussell, S.R.: Improving multilingual collaboration by displaying how non-native speakers use automated transcripts and bilingual dictionaries. In: Proceedings of the 33rd Annual ACM Conference on Human Factors in Computing Systems, pp. 3463–3472. ACM (2015)
9. Goh, C.C.: A cognitive perspective on language learners' listening comprehension problems. System **28**(1), 55–75 (2000)
10. Hautasaari, A., Yamashita, N.: Do automated transcripts help non-native speakers catch up on missed conversation in audio conferences? In: Proceedings of the 5th ACM International Conference on Collaboration Across Boundaries: Culture, Distance and Technology, pp. 65–72. ACM (2014)
11. Ishida, T. (ed.): The Language Grid: Service-Oriented Collective Intelligence for Language Resource Interoperability. Springer, Heidelberg (2011)
12. Ishida, T.: Intercultural collaboration and support Systems: a brief history. In: International Conference on Principle and Practices in Multi-Agent Systems (PRIMA 2016). Invited Paper, pp. 3–19 (2016)

13. Jaques, N., Conati, C., Harley, J.M., Azevedo, R.: Predicting affect from gaze data during interaction with an intelligent tutoring system. In: International Conference on Intelligent Tutoring Systems, pp. 29–38. Springer (2014)
14. Kalnikaitė, V., Ehlen, P., Whittaker, S.: Markup as you talk: establishing effective memory cues while still contributing to a meeting. In: Proceedings of the ACM 2012 Conference on Computer Supported Cooperative Work, pp. 349–358. ACM (2012)
15. Kardan, S., Conati, C.: Exploring gaze data for determining user learning with an interactive simulation. In: International Conference on User Modeling, Adaptation, and Personalization, pp. 126–138. Springer (2012)
16. Kohavi, R., John, G.H.: Wrappers for feature subset selection. Artif. Intell. **97**(1–2), 273–324 (1997)
17. Kohavi, R., et al.: A study of cross-validation and bootstrap for accuracy estimation and model selection. In: Ijcai, vol. 14, pp. 1137–1145. Stanford, CA (1995)
18. Murakami, Y., Lin, D., Ishida, T.: Service-oriented architecture for interoperability of multilanguage services. In: Towards the Multilingual Semantic Web, pp. 313–328. Springer (2014)
19. Otten, M., Van Berkum, J.J.: Does working memory capacity affect the ability to predict upcoming words in discourse? Brain Res. **1291**, 92–101 (2009)
20. Pan, Y., Jiang, D., Yao, L., Picheny, M., Qin, Y.: Effects of automated transcription quality on non-native speakers' comprehension in real-time computer-mediated communication. In: Proceedings of the SIGCHI Conference on Human Factors in Computing Systems, pp. 1725–1734. ACM (2010)
21. Rayner, K., Chace, K.H., Slattery, T.J., Ashby, J.: Eye movements as reflections of comprehension processes in reading. Sci. Stud. Reading **10**(3), 241–255 (2006)
22. Rubin, J.: A review of second language listening comprehension research. Mod. Lang. J. **78**(2), 199–221 (1994)
23. Steichen, B., Carenini, G., Conati, C.: User-adaptive information visualization: using eye gaze data to infer visualization tasks and user cognitive abilities. In: Proceedings of the 2013 International Conference on Intelligent User Interfaces, pp. 317–328. ACM (2013)
24. Van Petten, C., Luka, B.J.: Prediction during language comprehension: benefits, costs, and ERP components. Int. J. Psychophysiol. **83**(2), 176–190 (2012)
25. Yao, L., Pan, Y.X., Jiang, D.N.: Effects of automated transcription delay on non-native speakers' comprehension in real-time computer-mediated communication. In: IFIP Conference on Human-Computer Interaction, pp. 207–214. Springer (2011)

Translation Agent

Chunqi Shi, Toru Ishida and Donghui Lin

Abstract When applying Language Grid for multilingual communication support, it is important to understand the effects of the machine translation service. To support the users in multilingual communication, it is recognized that machine translation service used is not a perfect transparent-channel to users. We present agent metaphor as a novel interactive way to promote the efficiency of communication in using machine translation service. It will reduce the communication breaks caused by translation errors. We propose to shift from the transparent-channel metaphor to the agent metaphor, which motives the interactions between the users and the machine translator. Following this paradigm shifting, the agent should encourage the dialog participants to collaborate, as their interactivity will be helpful in reducing the number of translation errors. We examined the translation issues raised by multilingual communication, and analyzed the impact of interactivity on the elimination of translation errors. We proposed an implementation of the agent protocol for interactivity promotion. We designed the architecture of our agent, analyzed the interaction process, and provided an example of preparing repair strategy. We conducted an English–Chinese communication task experiment on tangram arrangement. The experiment shows that compared to the transparent-channel metaphor, our agent metaphor reduces human communication effort by 21.6%.

Keywords Machine translation mediated communication · Interactivity · Repair

C. Shi (✉) · T. Ishida · D. Lin
Department of Social Informatics, Kyoto University,
Kyoto 606-8501, Japan
e-mail: shi@ai.soc.i.kyoto-u.ac.jp

T. Ishida
e-mail: ishida@i.kyoto-u.ac.jp

D. Lin
e-mail: lindh@i.kyoto-u.ac.jp

© Springer Nature Singapore Pte Ltd. 2018
Y. Murakami et al. (eds.), *Services Computing for Language Resources*,
Cognitive Technologies, https://doi.org/10.1007/978-981-10-7793-7_11

1   Introduction

Machine translation (MT) plays an important and promising role in multilingual communication. When MT-mediated communication is used for a cooperation task, the translation of the task-oriented dialog should be accurate. Generally speaking, a communication dialog can be tagged as task-oriented, emotion-oriented, or both [10]. However, the translation errors continue to be the barrier for this MT-mediated communication. Providing various translation services, Language Grid is used in multilingual communication [6–8]. In the MT-mediated communication, the focus is not only the translation quality but also the communication efficiency. This chapter provides concrete analysis of how translation errors break communications and how to promote the communication by repairing translation errors with support from both users and various services [11]. Based on the better understanding of repairing translation error in the communication, the translation agent will be a novel way to design service for multilingual communication.

In MT-mediated communication, translation errors lead to miscommunication. Analyzing miscommunication in different levels of granularity (phrase, sentence, and dialog) is popular in machine-mediated communication research. The MT-mediated communication environment is affected by both translation channel and users. From the perspective of multilingual communication users, there are existing works on translation errors in these levels: *phrase-level*, *sentence-level*, and *dialog-level*. The analysis of translation errors can be different in whether user can use them to actively correct translation or not. For example, in phrase level, highlighting inaccurate words will facilitate user modification [13]. In sentence level, back-translation will provide certain information of translation result [12]. In dialog level, prediction of potential translation inconsistency prevents user using an improper shortened reference of the previous concept [21]. We summarize these mistranslation found in existing works. It not only shows that mistranslation often happens and can lead to communication breaks, but also there are existing works on user perspective dealing with variable situations of translation errors.

We have to mention two characteristics of complex MT-mediated communication. One is the variable quality of machine translator output. The other is that, two messages from different people expressing the same information can have widely different translation quality by the same machine translator. Second, in the transparent translation channel, the *activeness* of the user is ignored. Activeness plays an important role in interactivity between people and translation channel. For example, certain people get better translation results than others because they can craft expressions that suit the characteristic of that machine translator. Inspired from this difference, we carefully designed a translation agent metaphor to promote interactivity, provided the interaction protocol, and implemented an interactivity-promoted prototype in this MT-mediated communication environment.

In the following, we will analyze the paradigm shifting from transparent translation channel to agent metaphor, including examples for studying the interactions that can eliminate those translation errors. We will propose an interactivity model, including the interaction process, interaction simple model and interactivity level analysis. Furthermore, we will describe the design of the agent metaphor, including its architecture and functions. In order to evaluate our prototype, we conduct a wizard of OZ experiment on the multilingual task-oriented dialog. Finally, we summarize what has been learned before discussing the limitations of current design and implication.

2 Beyond Accuracy Promotion

2.1 Limitation of Transparent Translation Channel

To show the translation errors leading to miscommunication, we will give one concrete example for each of the phrase, sentence, and dialog level. These translation errors are picked out from English–Chinese machine translation mediated dialogs, in which the English instructs the Chinese to arrange tangram.[1] Using these examples, we show the communication breaks occasioned by different translation errors. In first example (see Fig. 1), due to phrase concept mistranslation, the Chinese receiver cannot understand. The word "square" in the geometry domain was translated into "plaza" of another domain, because the word "square" is polysemous. The machine translator just provides the everyday meaning of the word, but its true meaning depends on the domain of communication task.

In the second example (see Fig. 2), the mistranslated sentence is an imperative sentence that requests the receiver to conduct an act ("put something someplace"). This sender describes actions in imperative sentences, such as requests and commands.

The last example (see Fig. 3) is the mistranslation of inconsistent phrases. The abbreviated reference ("the light one") is not translated accurately, and it is unnatural to stick to exactly the same expression globally. Such inconsistency easily leads to translation errors.

From above, once machine translators cannot guarantee the translation accuracy; communication will break due to those translation errors. From the above examples, the translation errors can not be interpreted by the users, and thus break the multilingual communication. Though the accuracy promotion in machine translation function is really important, the high accuracy still can not be guaranteed, due to the limits of current research on machine translation.

We will not assume the accuracy of the machine translation is perfect. Moreover, seeking out a perfect transparent translation channel ignores the linguistic and social nature of the users. We will pay attention to the interactivity motivation. For example, the level of user's foreign language skill will affect this multilingual communication. We will show how interactivity helps to reduce translation errors.

---

[1] http://en.wikipedia.org/wiki/Tangram.

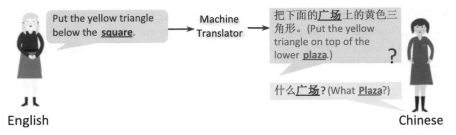

Fig. 1 In English–Chinese tangram arrangement communication, the Chinese receives inaccurately translated phrase and the communication breaks (In this figure or following figures, the parentheses indicate references of Chinese-to-English translation.)

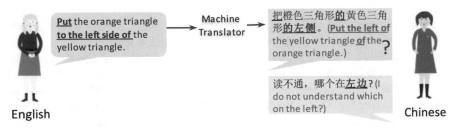

Fig. 2 In English–Chinese tangram arrangement communication, the Chinese receives a disfluent translation and the communication breaks

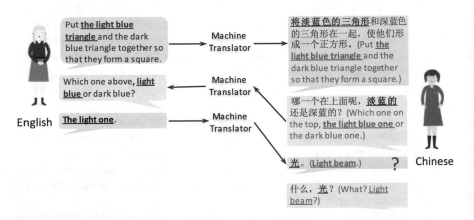

Fig. 3 In English–Chinese tangram arrangement communication, the Chinese receives an inconsistent translated phrase and the communication breaks

2.2 Benefit of Interactivity Promotion

We introduce three interactions motivating users to repair the translation errors in previous examples. In the first repair (see Fig. 4), the "square" is main direct object and polysemous. Based on the dictionary, the multiple target concepts were sent to the sender, who selected one target concept. The target phrase was integrated into the translation. This translation error can also be solved through existing works on domain adaptations and disambiguation. The difference is that this interaction is an online model and user-oriented, while the domain adaptations are offline models and machine-oriented works.

In the second repair (see Fig. 5), based on the morphological analyzer, the sentence was detected as an imperative sentence. Thus, the sender was suggested to rewrite it into declarative version, because machine translators often fail to translate imperative sentences as well as declarative sentences.

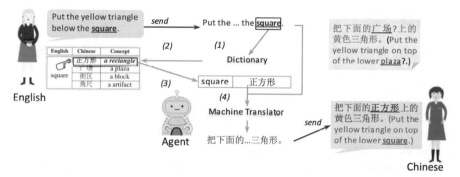

Fig. 4 Interaction to handle inadequately translated phrase: (1) check the feature that the word, "square", has one-to-many dictionary results, (2) suggest the sender select the correct concept, (3) the sender chooses the target concept, (4) translate by the dictionary translator composite machine translator

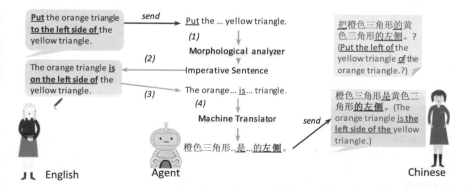

Fig. 5 Interaction to handle mistranslated sentence: (1) check the feature that it is an imperative sentence starting with a verb, (2) suggest the sender rewrite the sentence into declarative version, (3) rewrite the sentence, (4) translate by the machine translator

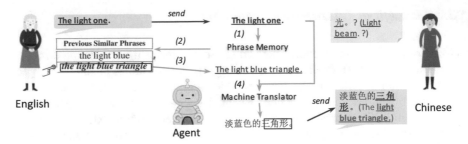

Fig. 6 Interaction to handle inconsistently translated phrase: *(1)* check the feature of similar phrases existing in previous dialog, *(2)* suggest selection of appropriate previous phrase, *(3)* choose a replacement of the previous phrase, *(4)* translate by the machine translator

The last repair (see Fig. 6) suggested a phrase memory to keep and retrieve the similar phrases. An automatic suggestion for replacement can solve the inconsistency of varied reference problem.

Communication "repair", one type of interactions between users and machine translator, is the word referring to the human effort to fix the communication breakdown. Here in MT-mediated communication, "repair" is to refer the human effort to fix translation errors that causes communication breakdown [11]. Machine triggered user adaptation to machine translation will be our strategy in handling translation errors. Such strategies are formalized as specific repairs to particular situations. We want to study an abstract interaction process for repairing MT-mediated communication. By solving previously mentioned communication breakdowns (see Figs. 1, 2, and 3), we showed interactions for repairing those translation errors. When translation errors could be eliminated through collaborating with the users, one goal of the machine translators is to encourage the proper interactions.

Thus, given the assumption of quality limitation of machine translators, we will go beyond the accuracy promotion and motivate the interactivity. We will analyze the interactivity model of MT-mediated communication, and design an agent protocol (interaction process abstraction) to motivate the interactions (repair strategies).

3 From Interactivity Motivation to Agent Metaphor

3.1 Interaction Protocol and Agent Metaphor

With interactivity, once unacceptable translation is detected, an interaction process will be applied to motivate users to repair the translation errors [19]. A unanimous interaction process is necessary to integrate different *repair strategy*. The proposed interaction process consists of four steps (see Fig. 7):

1. Agent's move to check the *feature* of current message.
2. Agent's move to *suggest* repair tips to the sender.

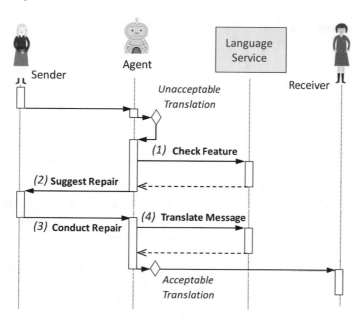

Fig. 7 Four steps of the interaction process for one repair strategy: *(1)* Check Feature, *(2)* Suggest Repair, *(3)* Conduct Repair (Sender), and *(4)* Translate Message

3. Sender's move to conduce the repair.
4. Agent's move to translate the repaired message, and output an improved translation result.

Repair strategy is the concrete interactions for motivating users to conduct translation errors repair. Given that there are multiple repair strategies, the agent has to decide the cause of the failure, and send the appropriate repair suggestion to the sender. Different types of repair strategies, such as selecting phrases based on the prediction of available information [3], rephrasing based on back-translation results and sentence rewriting [13], should be used in the same abstract process.

Obviously, if the agent can initiate interactions properly, many translation errors can be eliminated. But, we have to mention that the sensibility of users does not necessarily lead to the elimination of translation errors, because of the unpredictability of the machine translation function, and the uncertainty of the human repair action. Thus, the interactivity between the agent and people must be carefully designed to motivate them by making their actions easy, even for monolingual neophytes.

Accordingly, we propose simple three-interaction model (see Fig. 8). From the above interactions, the interaction message varies among different repairs, but the *intent* of these interactions is clear.

We describe three typical categories of interactions based on the analysis of their intent. The typical categories include:

Fig. 8 Three-interaction modeling of agent metaphor for machine translation mediated communication

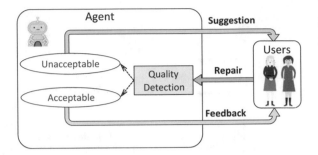

1. *Suggestion*: when translation is found unacceptable, the repair suggestion will be sent to the participants. As mentioned previously, more than one repair can be available. To initiate a suggestion, the repair strategy has to be decided and the tips should be prepared.
2. *Repair*: the users conduct the repair to resolve the miscommunication. It can be an adaptation to machine translation, such as pre(post)-editing [17], or other ways to improve translation quality, such as paraphrase word [2], split sentence, or even ways to improve understanding, such as the redundant supplementary information [20]. It should be noticed that the users can conduct the repair without any suggestion. It can be an agent-initiated repair or a user-initiated repair.
3. *Feedback*: after the quality detection, the quality can be either unacceptable or acceptable, and it will be fed back to users. Back-translation is often used for the quality evaluation [12]. Other quality evaluations can also be considered.

From the modeling, it is obvious that built-in translation quality detection is important for understanding whether translation quality is acceptable or not. Without quality detection, it is difficult for the agent to notify users the translation quality, not to mention motivating them repair the errors. Besides, it allows the reiteration of these interactions. In reiteration, the repair suggestion implies the quality.

3.2 Interactivity Levels

From the interaction process, we analyzed the *intent* of interactions and proposed three-interaction model. We propose interactivity levels based on the analysis of *initiation* of interactions, mainly the suggestion or repair interactions. The ability of agent in motivating users to conduct a repair is tightly related to this initiation. We clarify three typical interactivity levels (see Fig. 9), which is inspired by the taxonomy of interactivity from the work of Schwier [18]:

1. Reactive: it is the user-initiated repair. The agent gives feedback on the quality after repair. It depends on user's experience in repairing translation errors. Because the agent does not have to interpret and initiate the repair suggestion,

Fig. 9 Interactivity Levels:
Reactive (participant-
initiated repair), Proactive
(agent-initiated repair), and
Mutual (agent-initiated
collaborative repair)

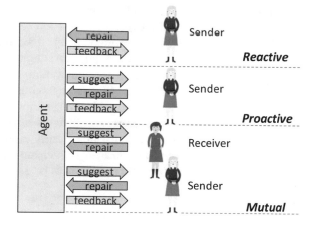

we call it a reactive level. Agent could feedback the quality of the user-initiated repairs.

2. Proactive: it is the agent-initiated repair. The users listen to and follow the suggestion to conduct the repair. To provide a suggestion, agent has to interpret the translation error, decide the repair strategy and give tips. It is called proactive level, because agent guides the repair process.

3. Mutual: it is an agent-initiated collaborative repair. Agent will initiate interaction to both sender and receivers. The agent will provide suggestion and activate collaborative repair. It represents agent's ability to coordinate both the receiver and sender together.

An example in the reactive level is to repair the mistranslation of the polysemous word "square". After knowing that the quality is unacceptable, the sender initiated the repair rephrasing the word using a more specific word "foursquare". Obviously, such rephrase action indeed requires the knowledge or experiences from the sender. The sender has to decide the proper repair upon his/her own knowledge. An example in the proactive level is to repair the mistranslation of the imperative message *"Put the orange triangle to the left side of the blue triangle"* (see Fig. 5). Agent detected the feature "an imperative sentence", and decided the repair strategy rewriting it into declarative version. The sender received this suggestion and conducted the rewriting. An example in the mutual level is to repair the same mistranslation of the imperative message. The repair is divided into two subtasks that (1) the agent asks the receiver to concrete the translation problem "It is not clear which is on the left" and (2) the agent asks the sender to rewrite message using the receiver's information "The orange triangle is on the left side of the blue triangle".

The interactivity level will be helpful in understanding existing related works. For example, the self-initiate repair, which well falls into the reactive level of our proposal, shows its weakness in the face of the changes of translation function [12]. The repair support agent proposed a back-translation mechanism to deal with the anticipatory inadequacy [13]. It belongs to the proactive, but with limited repair methods available. Another is collaborative translation, which has protocol to coordinate both users [14]. Still it expects changes and better easiness to motivate users [5]. It provides a coarse-grain description of agent's ability.

Moreover, the interactivity level implies simple user modeling for human-interpreter agent. In MT-mediated communication, the users are often described as experienced/novices user, and bilingual/monolinguals. The reactive, proactive, mutual levels have ability to deal with bilingual/monolingual experienced users, bilingual/monolingual novice users, monolingual novice users. Considering such user modeling and the built-in translation quality evaluation, a proper translation agent can be designed with concrete agent-participant interactions to elicit the repair suggestion with machine translation techniques [16].

4   Design of Translation Agent

We propose an agent metaphor for the interactivity. According to the interactivity model, the proactive interactivity needs agent's initiation to repair translation error. We have proposed the interactions process of applying repair strategies. Thus, we will design the agent to initiate the repair using the interaction process. We discuss why the agent metaphor is needed to establish the proactive interactivity. Basically, to apply the agent metaphor, we have to define the agent sophistication and the role of the agent. In this study, we want to clarify them through *flexible autonomous behavior* and *decision support function* of our agent metaphor.

Flexible Autonomous Behavior: An agent enables flexible autonomous translation and repair, which is much more efficient for multilingual communication. Because online translation and interactions need variable actions, such as dictionary retrieval or morphological analysis, a proactive agent has the ability to avoid unnecessary operations. On the contrary, for example, process protocol based collaborative translation [5] is potentially inefficient to go through the complete preset process flow.

Decision Support Functionality: Decision support enables dealing with complex environment of MT-mediated communication, such as translation error candidates, repair suggestions or extra translation improvement actions. A simple premise of such decision should be drawn from current translation environment. Through further design enhancement, the agent metaphor will gather not only translation accuracy, but also additional quality estimates or information from the users. Thus, the agent metaphor has to sense the environment like the quality of current translations, build common awareness among users about current translation, and pass proper repair suggestions to users.

4.1 Agent Architecture

We will focus an agent metaphor for the proactive interactivity, because this level covers all the interaction categories: suggestion, repair, and feedback. Once we have the agent metaphor for the proactive interactivity, it will be adapted to other two levels. Our translation agent is designed around three agent phases: observation, decision, and action (see Fig. 10). Observation phase will perceive the translation quality, which is needed for the decision phase. Decision phase will make a plan of actions. The action phase will follow the plan and fulfill the actions.

Observation Phase: the translation quality will be discerned by an *evaluation* module and it will be passed to the next phase. The translation quality contains not only the accuracy but also quality features. The accuracy will be used for decision of translation acceptable or not. While the quality feature will be used for decision of taking which repair strategy. For accuracy, popular evaluation methods such as BLEU, METEOR, compare the lexical similarity between the translation result and a standard reference to calculate an evaluation score. Previous studies use back-translation to predict potential translation errors [5]. In this chapter, back-translation and the BLEU method (maximum 3-gram, smoothed) are used as a simple way to estimate accuracy. About quality features, many quality estimation approaches can be considered. In this chapter, we developed own quality features in the development of repair strategies.

Decision Phase: a real time *planner* is necessary for online communication. A knowledge base is needed to keep experience and/or policy. The planner is critical to establishing autonomous behavior and decision support, by describing the experience, policy, or decision in rules. The activities of the users might provide uncertain results, because of their limited ability to generate correct repair actions and the machine translation quality of each message is unpredictable. Accordingly, the planner should provide online planning and decision support to counter this uncertainty. The knowledge base will save and allow access to experience and policy.

Action Phase: three types of actions are needed. First, to help the users get an idea of current quality, a *notification* action is needed. Second, the detection of an unacceptable translation triggers the *repair suggestion* action. The repair suggestion

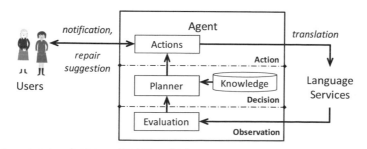

Fig. 10 Architecture design of translation agent

is the key to interactivity. Last, *translation* actions are needed to implement the different repair strategies. Both notification and repair suggestion demand that the agent and dialog participants talk. We use a simple meta-dialog for this purpose. It includes five meta-dialog acts: INFORM, SUGGEST, REPEAT, ACCEPT, and CANCEL. This means that the agent can inform the sender and receiver status of detected translation quality, pass repair tips to the sender, repeat the process until accept the repaired message or terminate the process if improvement proves to be impossible. The meta-dialog rule, <IF, THEN, PRIORITY>, is enough to trigger one meta-dialog and properly sequence the several triggered meta-dialogs. Based on the five meta-dialog acts, the agent is able to finish the actions of notification and repair suggestion.

For the actions of notification and repair suggestion, the demand is that the agent and dialog participants talk. We use a simple meta-dialog for this purpose. For the translation actions, the repair strategies in the observations of the last section require the dictionary service result, and the dictionary translator composition service (see Fig. 4). These services will be provided through the Language Grid, a service-oriented platform. Through Language Grid, several categories of atomic language services are available, including dictionary, parallel text, morphological analyzer, dependency parser, machine translators, etc. Meanwhile, several composite services are available, including dictionary-translator composite translation, multi-hop machine translation, and back-translation. Language Grid also provides a client that supports the invocation of both atomic and composite language services [15]. People can develop their own version of services based on this client using Java programs. Language Grid allows translation actions to be realized and invoked flexibly.

4.2   Repair Strategy Example

An example of issuing the repair strategy "split", is explained. Here, we picked one rule from the AECMA Simplified English Standard [1], which is for technical manual preparation, and tried using it as the basis of a repair strategy, because simplified writing is effective in enhancing machine translation quality according to Pym's study [17].

Simplified Writing Rule: use short sentences. Restrict sentence length to no more than 20 words (procedural sentences) or 25 words (descriptive sentences). Inspired by this rule, we developed the repair strategy "split". *Repair Strategy Split*: when an unacceptable translation is detected, if the message is a long and complex sentence, the repair tip is to split the source sentence into two sentences. *Feature of Split Strategy*: the literal length of the sentence is not directly used here. Instead, we choose the syntax-tree-width of its non-leaf syntax tree (see Fig. 11). For example, the English message from the tangram arrange task, "Please place the blue triangle upside down into the middle of two given triangles.", is parsed into a constituency structure tree. The non-leaf part nodes form a non-leaf syntax, and its width is 5. Compared to the literal message length, this syntax-tree-width better represents the complexity of sentence structure.

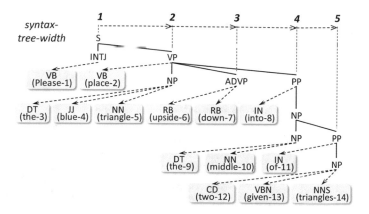

Fig. 11 The *syntax-tree-width* feature of the repair strategy *split*: a width of non-leaf part of its constituency structure tree

Repair Suggestion: the tips are provided to help the sender undertake the repair. In this repair strategy, the core of the message, which is the main elements of the sentence with low depth (less than 4) in the dependency structure tree, is picked out for the sender (see Fig. 12). This meta-dialog shows that, if the repair strategy is "split", then the suggestion and repair tips are passed to the sender (see Fig. 13). The priority value is 0.5. It means that this will be the first message shown to the sender, if there is no higher priority meta-dialog defined for the IF premise. Both the constituency parse tree and dependency parse tree are from Stanford Parser, which is an open source Java implementation of natural language parsers [9].

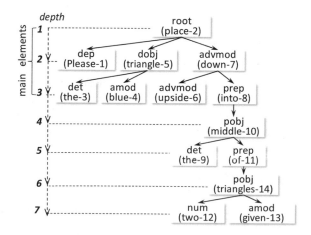

Fig. 12 The *tips* for the repair strategy *split*: the core of the message, defined as the main elements of low depth (less than 4) in the dependency structure tree

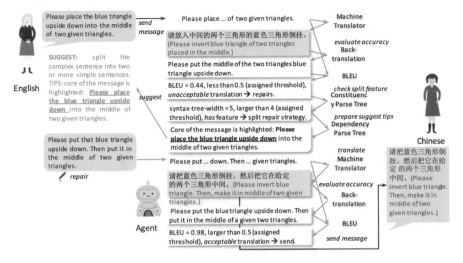

Fig. 13 Example of agent's split strategy. Agent will follow the decision of sending message to receiver or starting repair strategy. Back-translation and BLEU evaluate translation quality (*accuracy*). The process steps of the repair strategy (see Fig. 7) are given: check split feature, *the syntax-tree-width* (see Fig. 11); suggest split with tips, *the core of the message* (see Fig. 12); human repair; and translate the repaired message. Then, the evaluation shows that it becomes accepted

5 Evaluation

In order to evaluate the impact of the agent metaphor, we conducted a controlled experiment, which compared the machine translator mediated transparent channel approach to the proposed agent metaphor approach.

5.1 Experiment Preparation

An English–Chinese tangram arrangement communication task was conducted: an English user instructs a Chinese user how to arrange a tangram. When the tangram is complex, this task is generally difficult to finish through text based messages, even for two native speakers. We set two limitations to make this task easier to finish. *Only use convex figures*[2]: there are only 13 convex figures. It is much easier to construct a convex figure. *Share initial state of tangram pieces*: both participants start with the same piece arrangement. With these two limitations, tangram arrangement focuses on communication.

We examine the elimination of translation errors raising the efficiency of communication. Higher efficiency means that the information is transferred with fewer messages. According to conversation analysis, the *turn* is the basic unit interaction in

---

[2]http://en.wikipedia.org/wiki/Tangram.

the communication [4]. The tangram arrangement task can be divided into seven sub-tasks; there are seven pieces to be arranged. For each arrangement, the information transferred per turn unit, includes piece, rotation type, and position. The *number of human messages per turn unit* is defined as the number of messages sent by the human participants during one turn unit of the multilingual communication. It reflects the participants' effort to transfer the task information. For better data collection, after one message is sent, the participants were asked to wait for feedback before issuing the next message.

Normally, a turn unit consists of two messages: one information message from the sender and one feedback message from the receiver. Here, to transfer the square's position information, 4 messages are needed (the number of human messages is 4) because the translation error misleads the message receiver, and the receiver has a query. It should be noted that, in the agent metaphor, the repaired message from the sender is counted, for example, the number of human messages in the turn unit is 2 (two messages from the English sender) in the split strategy example (see Fig. 13).

For each tangram, we conducted the task using a single machine translator, a translation agent prototype, and bilingual translators. We randomly selected 5 tangram figures from the 13 convex figures. Two English and 2 Chinese participants, and 1 English–Chinese bilingual joined this experiment. In this experiment the agent prototype knew three repair strategies; the *split* strategy of the last section, and the two repair strategies of Figs. 4 and 5: *phrase* and *rewrite*.

5.2   Result and Analysis

Each group was asked to finish 5 figures. The number of human messages and the average number of human messages in each turn were collected (see Fig. 14). The average number of human messages in each turn in human-mediated communication is 2.2 (see Table 1). This shows that human-mediated communication is pretty efficient. The average number of human messages in each turn in machine translator mediated communication was 3.7. This shows that using machine translation almost doubles the participants' effort. Our prototype agent held the average number of human messages in each turn to 2.9, a **21.6%** improvement in communication efficiency.

Next, the total number of repair strategies in the English–Chinese dialogs was determined (see Table 2). First, the two different message senders had different repair strategies. Sender E_2's messages triggered more repair suggestions. The phrase and split strategies were used to almost the same extent. Second, different repair strategies took different amounts of time to complete. Here, the phrase strategy and split strategy were not activated as frequently as rewrite. This might be because there were few polysemous words, and the sentence structures were not too complex. We note that the senders used many imperative messages in the first instance.

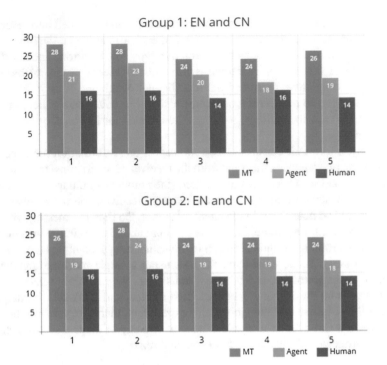

Fig. 14 Number of human messages in each turn unit of the 5 English–Chinese communication tasks in the Tangram experiment of English–Chinese (EN and CN) tangram arrangement through machine translator (MT), agent prototype using the wizard of OZ (Agent), and human bilingual (Human). There are 2 groups of participants, Group 1 (E_1-and-C_1) and Group 2 (E_2-and-C_2) for this tangram arrangement experiment

Table 1 The average number of human messages in each turn unit of the English–Chinese communication tasks of 2 groups

Medium	Average Number of human messages		Average number of human
	E_1-**and**-C_1	E_2-**and**-C_2	**Messages / Turn**
MT	26.0	25.2	3.7
Agent	20.2	19.8	2.9
Human	15.6	14.8	2.2

5.3 Discussion

We want to consider the scalability and limitation of the proposed agent metaphor. Only one controllable experiment has been studied here, but the agent metaphor will be applicable to other task-oriented MT-mediated communication. People in the task-oriented communication share similar topic structures, task actions and domain

Table 2 The total times of the repair strategies

Sender	Total times of the repair strategies		
	Phrase	Rewrite	Split
E_1	6	21	9
E_2	5	17	10

knowledge. Thus, it will be easier to design repair strategies in each of dialog, sentence and phrase levels. For example, in the multilingual communication task about road directions, certain repair strategy such as pictograph We provided the implementation framework of agent metaphor. It allows customization on different multilingual communication application to gain better communication efficiency. But for more general agent for any multilingual communications, current research has many limits on such as larger amount of repair strategy collection, more flexible experience analysis and training on the planner, and more intensive user modeling on monolingual or foreign language learning users.

6 Conclusion

The translation agent metaphor is proposed in the machine translation mediated communication environment. Given the assumption of limited translation quality, we learned that interactivity between people and translation function reduces communication breakdowns. Based on the design of interaction protocol, three-interaction agent model and interactivity levels are proposed. After that, we proposed the agent architecture and the lessons to build up a repair strategy. Finally, we described our English–Chinese communication experiments on a tangram arrangement task. The results showed that the wizard-of-OZ prototype of our agent metaphor improved communication efficiency in the face of translation errors. The agent does save users' effort to solve translation errors to promote the communication efficiency.

Acknowledgements This research was partially supported by Service Science, Solutions and Foundation Integrated Research Program from JST RISTEX, and a Grant-in-Aid for Scientific Research (S) (24220002) from Japan Society for the Promotion of Science.

References

1. AECMA: A Guide for the Preparation of Aircraft Maintenance Documentation in the Aerospace Maintenance Language. AECMA Simplified English. Brussels (1995)
2. Callison-Burch, C., Koehn, P., Osborne, M.: Improved statistical machine translation using paraphrases. Proc. HLT-NAACL **2006**, 17–24 (2006)

3. Carl, M., Way, A., Schler, R.: Toward a hybrid integrated translation environment. Machine Translation: From Research to Real Users. Lecture Notes in Computer Science, vol. 2499, pp. 11–20. Springer, Berlin / Heidelberg (2002)
4. Goodwin, C., Heritage, J.: Conversation analysis. Annu. Rev. Anthropology **19**, 283–307 (1990)
5. Hu, C., Bederson, B.B., Resnik, P., Kronrod, Y.: Monotrans2: a new human computation system to support monolingual translation. In: Proceedings of the CHI 2011, pp. 1133–1136. ACM (2011)
6. Ishida, T.: Communicating culture. IEEE Intell. Syst. Special Issue Future AI **21**(3), 62–63 (2006)
7. Ishida, T. (ed.): The language grid: Service-oriented collective intelligence for language resource interoperability. Springer Science & Business Media (2011)
8. Ishida, T.: Intercultural Collaboration and Support Systems: A Brief History. International Conference on Principle and Practices in Multi-Agent Systems (PRIMA 2016). Invited paper, pp. 3–19 (2016)
9. Klein, D., Manning, C.D.: Fast exact inference with a factored model for natural language parsing. In: In Advances in Neural Information Processing Systems 15 (NIPS, pp. 3–10. MIT Press (2003)
10. Lemerise, E.A., Arsenio, W.F.: An integrated model of emotion processes and cognition in social information processing. Child Dev. **71**(1), 107–118 (2000)
11. Lin, D., Ishida, T., Murakami, Y., Tanaka, M.: Qos analysis for service composition by human and web services. IEICE Trans. Inf. Sys. **E97.D**(4), 762–769 (2014)
12. Miyabe, M., Yoshino, T.: Accuracy evaluation of sentences translated to intermediate language in back translation. In: Proceedings of IUCS 2009, pp. 30–35. ACM (2009)
13. Miyabe, M., Yoshino, T., Shigenobu, T.: Effects of repair support agent for accurate multilingual communication. In: Proceedings of the PRICAI 2008: Trends in Artificial Intelligence, vol. 5351, pp. 1022–1027. Springer, Berlin (2008)
14. Morita, D., Ishida, T.: Designing protocols for collaborative translation. In: PRIMA 2009, pp. 17–32. Berlin, Heidelberg (2009)
15. Murakami, Y., Lin, D., Ishida, T.: Service-Oriented Architecture for Interoperability of Multi-language Services, pp. 313–328. Springer Berlin Heidelberg, Berlin, Heidelberg (2014)
16. Pascual-Nieto, I., Santos, O.C., Perez-Marin, D., Boticario, J.G.: Extending computer assisted assessment systems with natural language processing, user modeling, and recommendations based on human computer interaction and data mining. Proc. IJCAI **2011**, 2519–2524 (2011)
17. Pym, P.J.: Pre-editing and the use of simplified writing for mt: an engineer's experience of operating an mt system. In: Translating and the computer, pp. 80–96. London (1990)
18. Schwier, R., Misanchuk, E.: Interactive multimedia instruction. In: Englewood Cliffs, NJ: Educational Technology Publications, pp. 19–33 (1993)
19. Shi, C., Ishida, T., Lin, D.: Translation agent: a new metaphor for machine translation. New Generation Computing **32**(2), 163–186 (2014)
20. Siddharthan, A., McKeown, K.: Improving multilingual summarization: using redundancy in the input to correct mt errors. Proc. HLT **2005**, 33–40 (2005)
21. Yamashita, N., Ishida, T.: Effects of machine translation on collaborative work. In: Proceedings of the 20th CSCW 2006, pp. 515–524. ACM (2006)

Gaming for Language Services

Yuu Nakajima, Ryutaro Otsuka, Reiko Hishiyama, Takao Nakaguchi
and Naoyuki Oda

Abstract Service-oriented computing environments (SoCEs) such as the Language Grid can be regarded as the synthesis of their individual services. However, to make sustainable SoCEs, the user will want assurance that the billing structure is valid of and apportionment of cost burden among users is fair. To analyze the factors involved, we conduct donation and investment games for a machine translation service, where the service users participate in gaming. The results confirm the existence of users that actively try to make donations and social investments, users that remain passive to this kind of service, as well as users who tend to free ride on other users. Furthermore, we find that setting bonuses based on the total amount of donation and investment is effective in incentivizing some players to donate and invest. We also show how to reduce the cost of developing and executing gaming exercises for domain practitioners or experts. We define a game as a workflow of collaborative tasks executed by players. We develop game definition criteria to simplify game descriptions. We develop a gaming environment that enables web-based games to be implemented by using the game definitions.

Y. Nakajima (✉) · N. Oda
Faculty of Science, Toho University, Chiba, Japan
e-mail: yuu.nakajima@is.sci.toho-u.ac.jp

N. Oda
e-mail: 6515003o@nc.toho-u.ac.jp

R. Otsuka · R. Hishiyama
Faculty of Science and Engineering, Waseda University, Tokyo, Japan
e-mail: amadareisiugatu@ruri.waseda.jp

R. Hishiyama
e-mail: reiko@waseda.jp

T. Nakaguchi
Department of Web Business Technology, The Kyoto College of Graduate Studies
for Informatics, Kyoto, Japan
e-mail: ta_nakaguchi@kcg.edu

© Springer Nature Singapore Pte Ltd. 2018
Y. Murakami et al. (eds.), *Services Computing for Language Resources*,
Cognitive Technologies, https://doi.org/10.1007/978-981-10-7793-7_12

Keywords Gaming · Participatory simulation · Sustainable service design
Public goods game

1 Introduction

Service-oriented computing environments (SoCEs) such as the Language Grid [1] are characterized by the provision of many non-profit and highly public services by private/non-profit organizations. SoCEs should, of course, be provided free of charge if at all possible, but service maintenance will inevitably incur costs. Therefore, how such costs are distributed among the service users is a key issue.

For analyzing how service users will perceive and respond to cost sharing, we apply a gaming environment in which not only agents, but also people participate in simulations a virtual space. The goal is to recreate a SoCE whose operation incurs specified costs. To achieve this, the following three issues are addressed.

- **Creation of game definition criteria**
  Gaming examines the relationships between individuals, or between individuals and the environment. It typically involves the cooperation of several persons to carry out tasks. A mechanism that can easily describe such a process is needed.
- **Implementing gaming systems**
  Experts with domain knowledge of game-oriented problems are often not software engineers. Therefore, it is necessary to have a system that makes it easy to implement a game using the given game definition.
- **Analyzing cost burden sharing system by gaming**
  We assumed service operational model which is highly public and social in nature and user behavior will be investigated by combining incentive effect, its nature as a social investment and its nature as Donationware where the payment of compensation for use is left to the user's judgement. We conduct donation and investment games for a machine translation service with our proposed system.

2 Gaming

Various perspectives exist on the nature of gaming (or gaming simulations); e.g., a simulation tool for interpreting a system, a method to describe the expansion of game theory, a way to understand the correlation between social processes through role play, a method to achieve interdisciplinary integration, popular entertainment, and an educational technique. Richard D. Duke, who wrote a systematic commentary on gaming in 1974, concluded that gaming is "a form of communication" [2].

In gaming, the experimenter extracts the essential parts of a problem and presents them to the participants as a game to elucidate people's behavior and the reasons for such behavior. The participants are assigned roles in the problem, with the intention of encouraging them to treat the game as a personal experience. This is expected to provide a near-exact feel of the experience at the problem site. Gaming can allow the participants to experience the social and organizational problems associated with the assigned roles. For the experimenter, it serves as a means to deepen the understanding of the problem through observation of the participants' behavior in the game and analyzing the feedback.

A multiagent based simulation is executed by agents described as software. Attempts are being made to analyze and understand social problems by analyzing social interactions in areas dealing with decision-making mechanisms [3]. A multi-agent model that models each individual as an agent and calculates the interactions between people is suitable for analyzing such problems.

Gaming is executed by real players (human) and agent players who are described by the experimenter and controlled by a computer program. In this respect, gaming can be said to be a form of multiagent simulation for role-playing games. In the multiagent based simulation research field, some studies describe simulations which include not only agents, but also humans [4, 5].

Furthermore, implementing a game requires a strong insight into society and the ability to describe the roles and contexts of people and organizations. In this regard, it is essential to collaborate with practitioners or researchers in the field.

In this study, we design an environment that uses just simple game definitions to implement games related with social interactions. This advance is significant as people with domain knowledge of the applied problem are not always computer experts.

3 Game Definition

In this study, the multiagent-based game model is regarded as "processes in which multiple players with different roles collaborate to carry out pre-defined tasks." In this section, we introduce descriptive criteria that we use to define the process of such games. The game definition criteria consist mainly of two parts: (1) The game scenario, which describes the game process workflow; and (2) the player's internal model and the environment model, which calculate the player behavior and environmental changes.

3.1 Game Scenario

The game scenario describes the process in which the players cooperatively perform the task as a workflow. In other words, the game scenario describes the actions that a player should take and their order of execution.

Figure 1 shows how a player is controlled according to the game scenario. The game scenario's interpreter interprets the workflow and requests the player to execute

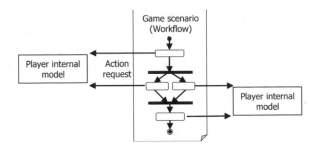

Fig. 1 Interaction between game scenario and player internal model

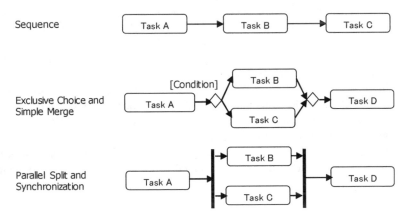

Fig. 2 Basic control patterns of workflow

the action. The player's internal model is responsible for processing the action-execution request.

Business-process workflows are generally illustrated using the Unified Modeling Language (UML) 2.0[1] or the Business Process Model and Notation (BPMN).[2]

van Der Aalst et al. [6] identified Sequence, Parallel Split and Synchronization, and Exclusive Choice and Simple Merge as examples of the Basic Control Patterns of workflows. Figure 2 uses UML activity diagrams to illustrates these examples.

Since gaming is intended to replicate real-world task-execution processes, the Basic Control Patterns that describe the workflow are also considered effective for describing a game scenario. Therefore, the concepts of tasks, stages, and rounds were created to incorporate these control structures into the game scenario.

- **Task**

  A task represents an action. Tasks can be executed by the player or by the environment. These correspond to actions in the activity diagram.

---

[1] UML 2.0: http://www.omg.org/spec/UML/2.0/.

[2] BPMN: http://www.bpmn.org/.

- **Stage**
  Since a stage controls task execution, it is a bundle of several tasks or stages. Stages are executed in the described order. Three stage types represent different execution controls: the Sequence stage, the Parallel Split and Synchronization stage, the Exclusive Choice and Simple Merge stage. The Sequence stage represents a set of ordered tasks. When this stage starts, the first task is executed. On its completion, the next task is executed. The process is repeated until all the tasks are completed. When the Parallel Split and Synchronization stage starts, the process path is divided into multiple paths, so multiple tasks are executed simultaneously. On completion of all the tasks in the stage, the divided paths recombine and the parallel paths are synchronized. The Exclusive Choice and Simple Merge stage represents a set of tasks, but the only one task that meets the specified conditions will be executed. In this stage, the process path is divided into as many paths as there are tasks, and the task corresponding to the condition is exclusively executed. When task execution is completed, the divided paths are combined into a single path.
- **Round**
  A round is a bundle of several stages. Rounds are executed in the described order. While the task execution is controlled in stages, the stages are conceptually grouped in rounds. A game scenario is defined as a set of rounds.

A detailed description example is given in Sect. 3.3.

3.2 Player Internal Model and Environmental Model

The player's internal model and environmental model are implemented as actors of actions requested by the game scenario.

The player object stores the individual information of each player; whereas, the environmental object is only one of the objects shared in the game. A player object can deliver synchronous messages to other players. The delivered messages are stored in the message box of the target player. Data transfer between players is effected by the giving and receiving of these messages.

When implementing the player internal models of participants, it is important to inform the players about the game's context (environment) so they can make "realistic" decisions. This was achieved by displaying an HTML form in the participants' Web browsers and preparing interfaces to gather the results.

Swarm,[3] artisoc,[4] etc. have simulation models that are strongly oriented towards spatial coordinates. The spot-oriented agent-role simulator (SOARS) [7], which is deeply connected with institutional design, has a simulation model in which an abstract field based on the concept of a spot. In contrast, the game definition in the present study describes the process by which players collaborate to carry out tasks as a workflow.

---

[3] Swarm: http://www.swarm.org.

[4] artisoc: http://mas.kke.co.jp/.

The Q language has a model in which a scenario with a written interaction protocol is assigned to a monolithic agent; the agent interacts with the environment and other agents according to the protocol [8]. The scenario written in Q is different from the game scenario in this study in that it describes only the interaction protocol of each agent and not the scenario of the entire agent group.

3.3   Game Definition Example: Ultimatum Game

We select the ultimatum game as a game definition example as it is a well-known model for examining why people undertake acts such as donating as opposed to the selfishness of "rational economic people" [9].

The experiment setting of the ultimatum game is as follows. First, some money is given to person P_1 by the experimenter, and P_1 divides it between himself and another person R_1. P_1 can decide how to share the amount, but if R_1 rejects the proposal, neither of them receives anything.

Consider an extension of this ultimatum game, where "the number of recipients is increased to two players, R_1 and R_2. P_1 gives each of them the ultimatum, and shares the money with each one" (Fig. 3). The game scenario would then be written as follows.

```
(define (def:game-scenario)
  (def:round
    (def:stage 'ultimatum
      (def:task 'P1 'issue-ultimatum))
    (def:parallel-stage 'response
      (def:task 'R1 'vote-yes-or-no)
      (def:task 'R2 'vote-yes-or-no))
    (def:stage 'divide
      (def:task 'divide-money)))))
```

The ultimatum game is composed of and is executed in the order of ultimatum stage, response stage, and divide stage.

The ultimatum stage is a Sequence stage. In the def:stage function, the task's first argument is the stage name, and the subsequent variable-length arguments are sequentially executed. In this stage, P_1 issues the ultimatum (issue-ultimatum). In the def:task function, the first argument is the name of the function that represents the acting entity (the environment, if abbreviated) and the second argument is the name of the function that represents the internal model of the acting entity.

The response stage is a Parallel Split and Synchronization stage. In other words, both R_1 and R_2 simultaneously respond (vote-yes-or-no) to the ultimatum. In the def:concurrent-stage function, the task's first argument is the stage name, and the subsequent variable-length arguments are executed in parallel.

At the divide stage, divide-money is executed by the environment.

The experimenter can define the game as demonstrated above and conduct web-based gaming simply by uploading it to the Web system described in the next section.

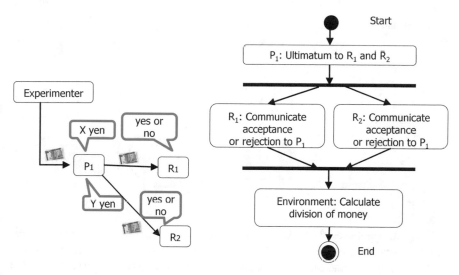

Fig. 3 Flow and game scenario of extended ultimatum game

4 Gaming System

In studies of gaming, specific gaming environments are often developed to suit individual problems. For researchers and practitioners who wish to examine hypotheses and theories of social problems by themselves, easy-to-use tools are a necessity. However, multiagent model based gaming systems are rather complicated, and development costs are inevitable and significant.

Several simulation languages and toolkits have been provided to facilitate multiagent simulations. Although these can help reduce the cost of implementing a multiagent simulator, there is still a large difference between a simulator and a gaming system.

In some environments, games can be easily generated by restricting games to model problems in specific areas, e.g., management games, thereby reducing the development and implementation costs of the gaming environment [10]. They reduce the development cost of gaming but game applicability is limited.

Using the game definition mentioned in the preceding sections, we have developed the MAGCruise[5] gaming system environment to execute web-based gaming [11]. This environment reduces game development and execution costs. Figure 4 shows the structure of the gaming environment.

In MAGCruise, the experimenter inputs a game definition to the game interpreter[6] and triggers the start of the game. The game interpreter is in control of game execution. The game interpreter creates a game session and enlists participants.

---

[5]MAGCruise: https://www.magcruise.org/.

[6]The game definition interpreter was implemented using Scheme interpreter Kawa (https://www.gnu.org/software/kawa/).

Fig. 4 Structure of gaming system

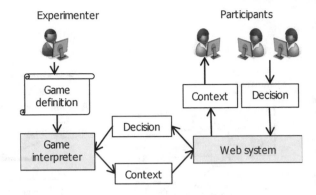

The participants access the Web system using Web browsers. Once the necessary players have been gathered, the game begins. Participants receive the game context via the Web system and input their decisions in response to the requests made. This interaction is repeated until the game scenario is finished.

After the game is over, the experimenter can browse the setting information and the game results stored in the database on the Web system.

5 Gaming for Design of Sustainable Services Computing Infrastructures

We shall now explain the exploratory gaming for design of sustainable services computing infrastructures.

5.1 Overview

For an SoCE, configurable computing resources including network and server, storage and application software and contents are provided by many different stakeholders and shared by multiple users. This arrangement has the merit of lower service maintenance cost than is possible with the conventional computing environment. However, as the SoCE is shared amongst unspecified numbers of users, payment models for fair billing are required.

There are various payment models, for instance, perpetual license, pay-as-use, and donation. With the spread of SOA and cloud computing, the pay-as-used, subscription-based, and hybrid pricing models are becoming mainstream [12]. In service collaboration and cloud computing systems, each provider/user may constitute multiple entities. In the past, this has led to problems regarding resource pricing, cost burden, and profit sharing [13, 14]. However, there has been no research on the problem of the cost burden from the standpoint of providing services in public.

Some mechanism that can manage the cost burden/sharing of users is required for web services that are provided through voluntary resources and services such as the Language Grid. We assumed the service operational model with voluntary resources and services, which is highly public and social in nature and investigated user behavior by combining two incentive effects: (1) its nature as a social investment and (2) its nature as Donationware, where the compensation payment for use is left to each user's judgement.

As the confirming experiment, we use MAGCruise to conduct donation and investment games for a machine translation service.

5.2   Design of Game

Subjects were organized into groups of four people. At the beginning of every round, the original sentence was displayed. Subjects received 100 tokens of in-game currency, and determined how much to donate or invest independently. At the end of a round, the usage rights (return) were determined and equally divided among the players in a group, and the sum of the usage rights and the amount of money left over were taken as each player's profit. Each player could view a table listing his or her own accounts, donations/investments, usage rights, and the translation result of all previous rounds. The players could not know how much the other members paid.

In this experiment, 25 rounds constituted one game. One round is each time all the players act. Each set, five rounds, used identical rules. After five rounds, the set changed. Table 1 shows the settings of the experiments. The settings were explained to the subjects before the experiments. The flow of all rounds and the game scenario are written in Fig. 5.

We now explain each set in the game. Sets 1 and 2 are donation games asking how much each player would like to donate to the machine translation service. Usage rights are always rewarded with 200 tokens, regardless of whether or not subjects donate and how much they give. When player i has an initial budget of 100 tokens and elects to donate g_i, profit u_i is given by:

$$u_i = 100 - g_i + 200. \tag{1}$$

Sets 3–5 are investment games in which the usage rights change. The public goods game framework is used to design these sets [15]. When player i has a budget of 100 tokens and elects to pay g_i, the profit u_i is given by:

$$u_i = 100 - g_i + 0.5 \sum_{j=1}^{4} g_j. \tag{2}$$

Table 1 Summary of the settings of the experiments

Set	Investment (tokens)	Usage rights (token)	Use of services when there is no investment	Translation destination
1	0 or 100	200	Possible	Korean
2	0–100	200	Possible	Korean
3	0–100	Total investment in group ×2/4	Possible	Korean
4	0–100	Total investment in group ×2/4	Possible with limited function	Chinese, English or Korean (depending on total investment in group)
5	0–100	Total investment in group ×2/4	Impossible	Japanese, Chinese, English, or Korean (depending on total investment in group)

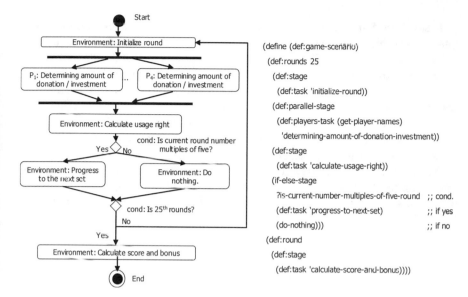

Fig. 5 Flow and game scenario of the financial support game

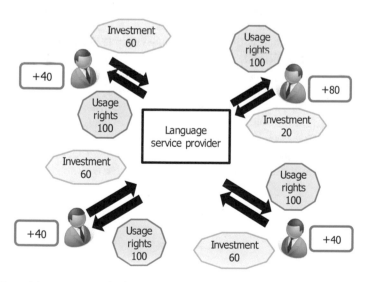

Fig. 6 Financial support game for language service management and maintenance

For example, if three out of four people invest 60 tokens and one invest 20 tokens, the total investment in the group is 200 tokens. By doubling the total investment in the group and dividing by 4 people, the usage right of the language service per person is 100 tokens. A player who pays 60 tokens gains 40 tokens, but a player who pays 20 tokens gains 80 tokens (Fig. 6).

In sets 4 and 5, the language of the translation destination changes according to the total investment within the group. The language is Chinese when the total investment in the group is from 0 to 199, English when the investment is 200–299, and Korean when the investment is 300–400. The subjects were told that in this scenario, the value of information is high if the quality of translation is good. Scores are assigned according to the quality of the translation result, with one point for the lowest quality Chinese, two points for English, and three points for the best quality Korean. In set 5, no translation is performed when there is no investment by the group; thus, the translation result is in Japanese, and the score is 0 points.

At the end of the game, a bonus is determined from the sum of the scores of the translation results of sets 4 and 5. Subjects receive 0 tokens when the total is 0–5 points, 1000 tokens for 6–10 points, 5000 tokens for 11–20 points, and 10,000 tokens for 21–30 points.

5.3 Settings of Experiment

We conducted experiments using 32 subjects (12 people for experiment 1, 12 people for experiment 2, and 8 people for experiment 3). The group members did not know who the other members are. We recorded data for 16 groups in each experiment, as the games were repeated with different group compositions. We distributed and explained the scenario, instructed the subjects on the games, and then conducted the games. The games were anonymous and we explained that all participants would remain anonymous to simulate donation and investment.

In this experiment, the following scenario was presented to the participants.

Machine translation services are provided publicly in the Language Grid. There is no license fee and it is designed to be used for free. However, we ask for contributions because support is required to maintain the service. In other words, payment is not obligatory, but donations are welcome (i.e., shareware, but with no specified donation amount).

5.4 Result

After the games were finished, the subjects completed a questionnaire. They were required to indicate their motivation for donating to the language service on a scale of 1–5 (1 is lowest motivation and 5 is highest motivation) in each set.

Figure 7 shows the correlation between the players' actual donation and investment behavior and the questionnaire survey results for each set. To indicate the characteristics of different players, we named the 32 subjects P1–P32.

First, we examine the behavior of P3 and P27, whose motivation and donation/investment amount remained the same throughout the experiments. P3 always donates or invests 100 tokens. In the questionnaire, P3 stated that "I thought I'd pay

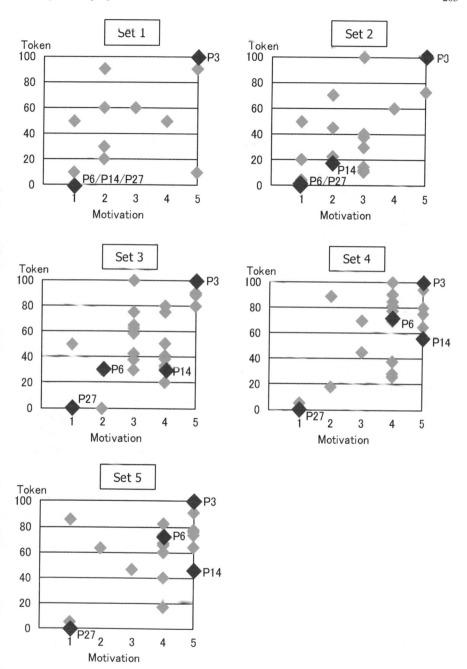

Fig. 7 Correlation between actual donation/investment and motivation in each set

for the translation service" regarding sets 1 and 2 and "I tried to maximize the profit of everyone" regarding sets 3–5. Therefore, P3 is always a cooperative player. P27 did not donate or invest any tokens throughout the experiments. P27 answered that "I tried to maximize my profit" for all sets. P27 is thus always an uncooperative player.

Next, we look at P6, whose motivation and donation amount were low in sets 1 and 2 but increased in sets 3–5. P6 stated that "I did not have enough money to donate" in sets 1 and 2. Regarding set 3, P6 answered "As people in the group are investing, I invested", and then, in sets 4 and 5, "I made a minimum investment to earn a bonus." This player made donations and investments in response to the incentive of a bonus.

P14 is similar to P6, because the motivation for sets 3–5 is higher than in sets 1 and 2. However, the investment amount remained small. The reason for this was "Because I thought that members would not invest unless I invested." This player paid only a small amount, even though he felt motivated to donate and invest.

From the above, we classified the players into four categories.

1. Always cooperative players
2. Always uncooperative players
3. Players who donate and invest according to incentives
4. Players who only pay a small amount, even if they feel motivated to donate and invest

These experiments assumed the services operational model which is highly public and social in nature, and user behavior was investigated by experimental gaming in combination with the incentive effect, its nature as a social investment and its nature as Donationware where payment of compensation for use is left to the judgement of the user. As a result, we could confirm the existence of users actively trying to make donations and social investments, the existence of users who were constantly passive to this kind of act, and users oriented to free riding on to other users. Furthermore, the bonus, which was based on the total amount of donation and, was effective in incentivizing some players to donate and invest.

In the future, a system to restrain the behavior of free riders and a rule to encourage donation and investment behavior while heightening the satisfaction level of the user, will be examined.

6 Conclusion

To create sustainable service-oriented computing environments, which are highly public and social in nature, such as, for example, the Language Grid, the revision of rules will be examined so that validity of the billing structure and the fairness of cost burden amongst users are made obvious to the users.

Multiagent model based gaming is used to analyze and understand the manifold problems in society, with a focus on social problems. For analyzing how service users participate in cost burden sharing, we applied the technology of gaming in a services computing infrastructure where the operation has a predetermined cost burden. To achieve this analysis, we addressed the following three issues.

- **Design of game definition criteria**
  We regarded the game as a process of multiple player coordinated tasks, and designed a simple mechanism to describe this. We formulated a method of describing the game process from the perspective of writing the game as a workflow.
- **Building a gaming system**
  We created a web-based gaming system that could interpret the game definition. This will help to reduce the cost of developing and executing web-based gaming by researchers and practitioners who are not software engineers.
- **Analyzing cost burden sharing system by gaming**
  We conducted a game involving the donation and investment for a machine translation service, and analyzed the players' behavior under various rules to consider sustainable system design.

Acknowledgements This work was supported by a Grant-in-Aid for Scientific Research (S) (24220002, 2012-2016) from the Japan Society for the Promotion of Science (JSPS).

References

1. Ishida, T. (ed.): The Language Grid: Service-Oriented Collective Intelligence for Language Resource Interoperability. Springer Science & Business Media (2011)
2. Duke, R.: Gaming: The Future's Language. Sage Publications, Halsted Press, New York (1974)
3. Ishida, T., Hattori, H., Nakajima, Y.: Multiagent simulation. In: Field Informatics, pp. 89–105. Springer Berlin Heidelberg (2012)
4. Hattori, H., Nakajima, Y., Ishida, T.: Learning from humans: agent modeling with individual human behaviors. IEEE Trans. Syst. Man Cybern.-Part A: Syst. Hum. **41**(1), 1–9 (2011)
5. Torii, D., Ishida, T., Bousquet, F.: Modeling agents and interactions in agricultural economics. In: Proceedings of the Fifth International Joint Conference on Autonomous Agents and Multiagent Systems (AAMAS 2006), pp. 81–88 (2006)
6. van Der Aalst, W.M., Ter Hofstede, A.H., Kiepuszewski, B., Barros, A.P.: Workflow patterns. Distrib. Parallel Databases **14**(1), 5–51 (2003)
7. Tanuma, H., Deguchi, H., Shimizu, T.: SOARS: spot oriented agent role simulator—design and implementation. In: Agent-Based Simulation: From Modeling Methodologies to Real-World Applications, pp. 1–15. Springer (2005)
8. Ishida, T.: Q: a scenario description language for interactive agents. Computer **35**(11), 42–47 (2002)
9. Güth, W., Schmittberger, R., Schwarze, B.: An experimental analysis of ultimatum bargaining. J. Econ. Behav. Organ. **3**(4), 367–388 (1982)
10. Terano, T., Suzuki, H., Kuno, Y., et al.: Understanding your business through home-made simulator development. Dev. Bus. Simul. Experiential Learn. **26**, 65–71 (1999)
11. Nakajima, Y., Hishiyama, R., Nakaguchi, T.: Multiagent gaming system for multilingual communication. In: 2015 International Conference on Culture and Computing, pp. 215–216 (2015)
12. Kansal, S., Singh, G., Kumar, H., Kaushal, S.: Pricing models in cloud computing. In: Proceedings of the 2014 International Conference on Information and Communication Technology for Competitive Strategies, ICTCS '14, pp. 33:1–33:5. ACM, New York, NY, USA (2014)
13. Upadhyaya, P., Balazinska, M., Suciu, D.: How to price shared optimizations in the cloud. In: Proceedings of the VLDB Endowment, vol. 5, pp. 562–573. VLDB Endowment (2012)

14. Wang, H., Jing, Q., Chen, R., He, B., Qian, Z., Zhou, L.: Distributed systems meet economics: pricing in the cloud. In: 2nd USENIX Workshop on Hot Topics in Cloud Computing (Hot-Cloud'10), vol. 10, pp. 1–6 (2010)
15. Fischbacher, U., Gächter, S., Fehr, E.: Are people conditionally cooperative? evidence from a public goods experiment. Econ. Lett. 71(3), 397–404 (2001)

Youth Mediated Communication: Knowledge Transfer as Intercultural Communication

Toshiyuki Takasaki, Yumiko Mori, Toru Ishida and Masayuki Otani

Abstract Transferring knowledge to other people in different languages is difficult because of gaps in languages and cultures. It makes the knowledge transfer more difficult when the recipient is young, because the comprehension and language ability of the young are incomplete. To better understand and design language services, this chapter introduces a communication protocol that meets requirements of agriculture support in rural areas, and fully delineates the communication environment by elucidating the field issues comprehensively; solutions are considered. The field experiment conducted involves agriculture support in Vietnam. In the context of agriculture support in rural areas, there exist several issues such as the requirement of timely knowledge transfer with high translation quality, and multilingual communication between youths and experts where gaps in language ability and expertise should be considered and addressed.

Keywords Knowledge communication · Multilingual communication · Youth
Rural development

T. Takasaki (✉) · Y. Mori
NPO Pangaea, Zou Bldg.301, 509 Kyogokucho, Kyoto 600-8035, Japan
e-mail: toshi@pangaean.org

Y. Mori
e-mail: yumi@pangaean.org

T. Ishida
Department of Social Informatics, Kyoto University,
Kyoto 606-8501, Japan
e-mail: ishida@i.kyoto-u.ac.jp

M. Otani
Department of Informatics, Faculty of Science and Engineering, Kindai University,
3-4-1 Kowakae, Osaka 577-8502, Japan
e-mail: otani@info.kindai.ac.jp

© Springer Nature Singapore Pte Ltd. 2018
Y. Murakami et al. (eds.), *Services Computing for Language Resources*,
Cognitive Technologies, https://doi.org/10.1007/978-981-10-7793-7_13

1 Introduction

Infrastructure of ICT, Information Communication Technology, has been developed quite rapidly even in rural areas of developing countries. However, people in such area still have not found meaningful way to use them in their daily lives compared to people in cities. Though literacy rate of adult is still low, many countries are now putting their efforts to provide good education system to their children and literacy rate has improved significantly for younger generation. In many cases of ODA, Official Development Assistance, to support agriculture, environment, or health care in developing countries, programs do not employ ICT environment, but rather experts travel to these locations physically and implement effective ODA programs. Because the local people cannot read or write, it is difficult to accumulate knowledge from experts in the local community. As an alternative approach to support rural communities in developing country, Mori proposed the communication method called YMC, Youth Mediated Communication, to support illiterate workers (non-experts) through their children who are literate and computer-literate, especially in rural areas in developing countries [11]. In order to verify the proposed YMC model, this chapter shows a field research to implement YMC model in rice farming domain in Mekong delta area of Vietnam.

The purpose of this chapter is to create an intercultural communication environment that links Youth and Expert to support agriculture in developing countries. Agriculture knowledge is transferred from Expert to Youth in different languages. It is difficult to achieve this because the issues include knowledge gaps as well as language gaps. As for intercultural communication, many previous studies have described the utilization of machine translation technology. The goal considered here, that of knowledge transfer, requires very high translation quality required. Because translation quality of machine translations is not perfect, we need to design appropriate language services that can combine machine translation and human support in the most efficacious manner. Note that key issue is to well address the knowledge gap between Expert and Youth. Previous studies on interdisciplinary communication among people with different expertise have been reported. The research in this chapter takes an empirical approach, which means that we design a communication protocol by exhaustively extracting field problems and identifying solutions. Then, we implement a communication system environment, and conduct a field experiment in a rural area in Vietnam. Finally, we evaluate the effectiveness of the communication environment in countering each field problem.

Two issues must be addressed in order to implement interdisciplinary and intercultural communication environments wherein young adults and agriculture experts can communicate by using their mother tongue. The first issue is the communication difficulty raised by language differences and knowledge differences. There has been research on interdisciplinary communication among people with different expertise, and there has been research on intercultural communication among people with different languages. As for interdisciplinary communication, because there is a difference of knowledge, you need to be aware of the knowledge difference when communicating with your counterpart. It may be necessary to strengthen communication by, for example, adding more explanations of technical terms [2, 3]. There may be a misunderstanding or lack of understanding if the you use words in different meaning from your counterpart's use. In order to facilitate interdisciplinary communication, it is necessary to apply a mechanism to identify the situation of misunderstanding and lack of understanding. Also, it is important to apply a mechanism to support knowledge transfer and bridge the knowledge gap.

The second issue is the difficulty of implementing an intercultural communication environment supported by machine translation that creates high quality translations while easing the loads placed on the users. There has been research on intercultural communication to realize social communication via email or chat systems that is supported by machine translation [1, 6]. For example, one study compared the productivity and degree of understandings between communication based on machine translation, and communication within the same language group. Technical issues in machine translations that interfere with social communication have been analyzed [16]. In the case of machine translation among Asian languages, or between an Asian language and a European language, pivot translation via English is utilized [15]. Because pivot translation cascades multiple machine translation engines, translation quality is lower than is true with a single machine translation engine. Our research proposes to enhance the translation quality in pivot machine translation by applying a context-based approach to communication [13]. The focus of this chapter is translating knowledge and thus high quality translations are necessary, so using only machine translation is not good enough. On the other hand, human translators are expensive; that is especially true of experts. In addition, it is difficult to retain those human resources continuously.

2   YMC (Youth Mediated Communication) Model

We discuss a communication method of multilingual knowledge transfer. We assume the scenario in which that Japanese agriculture experts assist, online and in a timely manner, farmers who live in rural areas of developing countries. In previous similar situations, agricultural experts had to visit the local rural areas physically, and they taught the farmers directly or local extension workers, who are in a position to instruct local farmers, with human interpreter support. Unfortunately, the cost of dispatching experts was so high that this approach is now seldom used. Also, it is difficult for local farmers to retain the experts' knowledge to utilize in the next farming stage, because local farmers are illiterate and they are unable to record the knowledge.

Mori proposed the communication method called YMC, Youth Mediated Communication, to support illiterate workers (non-experts) through their children who are literate and computer-literate, especially in rural areas in developing countries [11]. Figure 1 shows the conceptual diagram of YMC. YMC is a means of communication that transfers expert knowledge from the expert to a non-expert via a young adult of the same rural community.

Fig. 1 Diagram of youth mediated communication

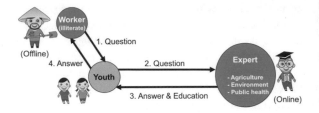

3 System Design

3.1 Requirement Analysis

In order to investigate the YMC method, an intercultural communication environment between agriculture experts and youths was designed and implemented to support agriculture farming in rural areas. The online communication system is called "YMC System." Question and answer communication between youths and remote experts was assumed to be the main communication path. In designing the YMC System, we had to comprehensively identify which field problems were caused knowledge gaps and which by language gaps. Multiple solutions were developed for each field problem and the best solutions were chosen. The design process is conducted by experts in agriculture, education, machine translation, as well as farmers, practitioners in intercultural activities, and system engineers. These field problems are utilized to understand the field experiments. Table 1 shows field problems and corresponding research issues.

Table 1 Field problems and research issues

ID	Field problem	Research issue
1	High quality translation is required, because there is a possibility of serious damage to agriculture crop due to miscommunication of knowledge	Language difference
2	Prompt response by expert is necessary, because questions are posted from time to time in agricultural crop growth process	Language difference
3	Expressions by expert are difficult for youth	Language difference Knowledge difference
4	Composing question sentences is difficult for youth	Knowledge difference
5	Knowledge transfer from youth to parent (farmer) at home is difficult	Knowledge difference
6	It is difficult for expert to answer to each question from youth due to a lack of paddy information	Knowledge difference

3.2 Interaction Design

Problem 1 is the requirement of high quality translation in agriculture knowledge transfer. This is essential because the agriculture crop can be seriously damaged to due to miscommunication of knowledge. One of the solutions is to utilize human translators for all information transfers (Solution 1–1). Another solution is to prepare and utilize an agriculture knowledge database holding bilingual parallel texts (Solution 1–2). The other solution is to improve a machine translation quality by human support (Solution 1–3). As for (Solution 1–1), it is costly to continuously keep bilingual translators of Vietnamese and Japanese in the field. As for (Solution 1–2), it is difficult to prepare answer parallel texts that cover all questions. On the other hand, as in (Solution 1–3), Lin et al. showed that refining machine translation texts by humans was cheaper than translating all texts by humans [8, 10]. As a result, this study adopted (Solution 1–3).

Problem 2 is the need for prompt responses by Expert. In some situations, such as the emergence of an infectious plant disease, urgent treatment is necessary. Agriculture experts suggested that a farmer should be answered as soon as possible, within a week at latest. This, unfortunately, places excessive loads on Expert and the people responsible for refining the machine translations. So, the sooner we require a response, the more costly. One of the solutions is to prepare an FAQ (Frequently asked questions) system (Solution 2–1). Another solution is to increase the number of Experts by utilizing crowdsourcing (Solution 2–2). The other solution is to prepare an online system that allows the Expert to compose answer messages by combining his typed messages (Free-text) with bilingual parallel text (Solution 2–3). As for Solution 2–1, it is difficult to prepare a truly comprehensive FAQ database. Even when huge FAQ database is prepared, it is difficult for some Expert users to find the right FAQ due to ICT literacy. As for Solution 2–2, the problem is the limited number of agriculture experts. As a result, Solution 2–3 is selected.

Problem 3 is the difficulties Youth face in understanding the Expert's answers. One of the solutions is to demand that all answers be comprehensible to Youth (Solution 3–1). Another solution is to employ local staff who have some agriculture background and ask them to explain the answer message to Youth verbally in face-to-face meetings (Solution 3–2). The other solution is to place staff online who can modify the Expert's answers into Youth friendly expressions (Solution 3–3). As for Solution 3–1, youth use more colloquial expressions and abbreviations than adults so that machine translation quality is worse. It is too much load for Expert to require the youth friendly expression. Solution 3–2 is not practical due to the limited human resources of local staff with agriculture background. So, we adopt Solution 3–3 and add to the translation flow a "smoothing" task that modifies the answers into more Youth-friendly expressions.

Problem 4 is the difficulty for Youth to ask pertinent questions due to their limited language ability. One of the solutions is to allocate adult staff who can support Youth in writing questions (Solution 4–1). Another solution is to ask Youth to select their questions from the parallel texts held by the agriculture question database (Solution

4–2). We select Solution 4–2 due to the limitation of human resources. Thus the agriculture question database must have a structure and user interface that make it easy for Youth to find what they would like to ask.

Problem 5 is the difficulty for Youth in transferring the Expert's knowledge to their parents or elders. It is assumed that they cannot access the Internet at home. One of the solutions is to give each Youth a smartphone or tablet device that holds agricultural digital materials, to explain what their understanding of what the Expert said to their parents (Solution 5–1). Another solution is to give an agriculture technical book to Youth and let them read aloud the book to their illiterate parents (Solution 5–2). The other solution is that Youth writes down what they learn from Expert and they bring home written notes of agriculture advice (Solution 5–3). Though Solution 5–1 is an ideal solution, there are a couple of concerns. The first concern is the issue of the cost of the mobile device, and the second is the risk of theft. Such mobile devices are expensive given the standard of living in the rural areas of Vietnam. As for Solution 5–2, though we surveyed available agriculture books in the field, discussions with local agriculture experts reached the conclusion that there was no appropriate material. Textbooks for beginners don't cover agriculture knowledge in enough detail to support this project, and technical books for experts are too difficult for Youth understand. As a result, we selected Solution 5–3.

Problem 6 is the difficulty of Expert has in answering Youth questions appropriately due to a lack of site (paddy) information. In the design phase, agriculture experts indicated the necessary information for this project was rice plant height, leaf color, bugs in paddy, photo of rice plants, temperature, humidity, and weather. One solution is to acquire this field data from remote-sensing and the sensors of a field-monitoring system (Solution 6–1). Another solution is to ask farmers (parents) to gather the data in their daily paddy work (Solution 6–2). The other solution is to ask Youth to visit their parents' paddy and gather the data (Solution 6–3). When we interviewed agriculture experts in the design phase, they pointed out that Solution 6–2 and Solution 6–3 were better than Solution 6–1, because the accuracy and data density of field data gathered by humans is better than that collected by machines. For example, it is difficult and expensive to measure accurate rice height automatically. Youth can master data gathering more quickly than their parents, who are always busy with manual work, and come to see this as a fun activity. As a result, we select Solution 6–3.

3.3 Language Service Design

Language services are designed to meet the field needs of the project. Expert composes an answer message by combining preset "parallel texts" and "free text" in the Experts' mother tongue. Because the highest possible translation quality is required, the translation flow is designed as a combination of machine translation and human refinement. This communication model requires Bridgers for each language as shown in Fig. 2. Lin & Ishida described the detail design process of the translation service [7].

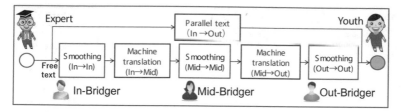

Fig. 2 Translation flow in YMC (In: input language, Mid: middle language, Out: output language)

The Bridger who is responsible for the input language is called In-Bridger. The In-Bridger's role is to edit the Expert's original text into machine-translator friendly text by correcting typographical errors and splitting long sentences into smaller sentences to achieve higher translation quality. This editing process of the In-Bridger is called smoothing. Mid-Bridger, who is responsible for the pivot language, refines the machine translation output of In-Bridger's smoothed text. English is the intermediate language in many cases. The Out-Bridger, who is responsible for the output language, rewrites the machine translation result of the Mid-Bridger's smoothed text to enhance fluency and add youth friendly expressions.

4 Implementation

4.1 Overview of YMC System

YMC System was implemented as a Web-based application written in the PHP programming language. Users access the system from PC web browsers. Youth can access from cell phone web browser only when they submit field data to the system. System diagram is shown in Fig. 3. Analog materials called YMC Tools, which are described later, are also shown in the system diagram to show the whole view of the project. Information shared among Youth and Expert via the YMC System is shown in Fig. 4.

4.2 User Interface

In the YMC System, in order for Youth to post a question message, question category is selected first, and then the corresponding question parallel texts are shown from which one or more can be selected as shown in the left of Fig. 5. These operations need only mouse clicks. On the other side, Expert composes an answer message by using both/either answer parallel text and/or free text in the YMC System as shown

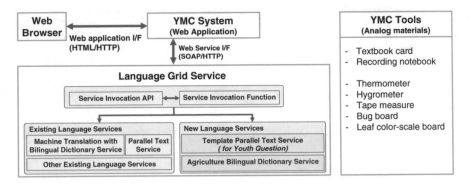

Fig. 3 System diagram of YMC system and YMC tools

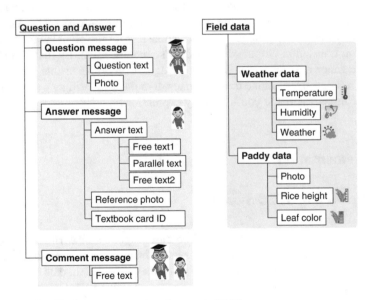

Fig. 4 Shared information among youth and expert in YMC system

in Fig. 6. More than two answers can be combined when necessary. The In-Bridger, Mid-Bridger, and Out-Bridger smooth the answer message. Back translation results are shown in the Bridger's screen for comparison with the original text and back-translated texts to confirm the translation quality. The In-Bridger also adds reference IDs of the related Textbook cards to the answer messages as well as related photos when necessary as supplemental information. Only after the smoothing process is finished by Out-Bridger can Youth see the answer message as shown in the right of Fig. 5.

Fig. 5 A screenshot of question input page (left) and answer view page (right)

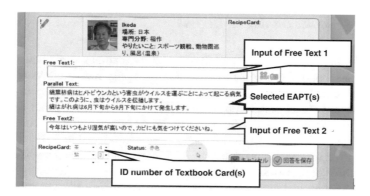

Fig. 6 A screenshot of expert answer composition page

4.3 Language Services

In order to improve machine translation quality, machine translation was combined with multilingual dictionaries using the Language Grid service [4, 5, 12]. The Agrovoc Dictionary, the Rice Dictionary, and the YMC Community Dictionary were linked. The Agrovoc Dictionary has 58,577 agriculture technical terms in English and Japanese, and the Rice Dictionary has 441 rice farming technical terms in English, Japanese, and Vietnamese. Both are existing dictionaries created by third-parties. The YMC Community Dictionary has 2514 entries in English, Japanese, and Vietnamese. It was constructed by our experiment team based on project-related words and includes YMC Tools, names of stakeholders, popular youth words, agriculture words found in parallel texts, and so on. Words were added during the preparation phase and even the experimental phase.

Two types of parallel text, Expert Answer Parallel Text (EAPT) and Youth Question Parallel Text (YQPT), were also prepared. Both have English, Japanese, and Vietnamese word equivalents. EAPT was prepared in order to reduce the loads placed on Experts in composing answer messages to Youth. It is a general agriculture knowledge database in the rice farming domain with 932 entries such as "Big, fat and dense grain is good as seed rice." It is used when Experts compose answer messages in the YMC System. YQPT was prepared to support Youth in composing question messages and accurately deliver the intention of the question to Expert. It is a database with 1904 entries (question texts). All parallel text entries belong to one of the YMC Categories and are used for resource development management as well as parallel text searches of the YMC System. YMC Category is about rice farming domain and the experiment and has a three-layer hierarchical structure; 184 categories were defined by the experiment members, especially Experts.

4.4   YMC Tools: Analog Materials

Prior to the field experiment, YMC Tools such as Textbook cards and Recording notebook to support Youth in the experiments were prepared. Youth were also supplied with a tape to measure rice height and a cell phone to field data to the YMC System and take photos of the crop and paddy. Textbook cards are paper-based cards that show rice farming knowledge visually. Youth take them home and use them in explaining the Expert answer to their parents as shown in Fig. 7. Each Textbook card explains a specific knowledge topic such as rice diseases and pesticides. Each Textbook card belongs to an agriculture category and is color-coded and given an ID number. Expert answer message may include, for example, "Please take the Red-7 Textbook card home." For the experiment, 41 kinds of Textbook cards were prepared.

Each participating Youth was given a Recording notebook intended as an observation diary of his/her parents' rice field. The Recording notebook has preprinted tables for recording temperature, humidity, rice height, and leaf color. It also has "rice calendar" tables to hold the dates of farming processes such as rice seeding,

Fig. 7 Examples of textbook cards

fertilizer use, harvesting and so on. Youth is expected to enter the field data into the Recording notebook. There are also interview sheets that Youth fills out indicating what knowledge his/her parent would like to get from Experts.

5   Field Experiment

5.1   YMCViet Project

YMCViet project was conducted with the cooperation of Vietnamese central and local governments, a team of agricultural Experts in Japan, and Bridger teams in Japan and Vietnam. It lasted four months, starting from December 2011 in Thien My commune, Vinh Long province, Vietnam. 30 youths from 29 farmer households, aged from 8 to 15, participated in the experiment. During the experiments, 378 questions were posted by Vietnamese Youth and 378 questions were answered by Experts via the YMC System. 303 of the 378 answer messages had a reference to a Textbook card.

In the experiment, Youth was active in the home, rice field, and YMC Center. First, Youth interviewed his/her parents or family members at home on what they would like to ask Experts about rice farming. Youth took entered the responses into an interview sheet page of Recording notebook. Youth measured temperature and humidity at home and sent the data together with weather information from his/her cellphone every day. He/she visited the family's rice field once or twice a week to measure rice height and leaf color as well as checking for insects; the information was written down in the Recording notebook. In the rice field, he/she took photos of the rice plants and field with his/her cell phone as shown in the left of Fig. 8. Youth visited the YMC Center once or twice a week and accessed the YMC System via computer as shown in the middle of Fig. 8. He/she used Recording notebook entries when sending the field data such as rice height and leaf color, and posted questions to Expert of the YMC System. Youth could read the Experts' answer about a week after the question was posted. Youth could reply to Expert by sending a comment message. Youth also wrote down the answer in the Recording notebook as shown on

Fig. 8   Using YMC system in YMC center (left), taking photos at rice field (center), and writing down an expert answer in the recording notebook (right)

the right of Fig. 8, and took home Textbook cards indicated in the Expert answer, from the YMC Center. At home, Youth checked the Expert answer/message in Recording notebook and explained it orally to parents by showing photos or illustrations on the Textbook cards.

5.2   Evaluation

We evaluate the field experiment with regard to *Problem 1* to *Problem 5* in Table 1. *Problem 6* is not discussed here because it is not related to the design of language services; Togami et al. discusses this in detail [14].

Problem 1 We designed the translation flow to combine parallel texts and free texts. Because it is translated by humans in advance, translation quality of parallel text is guaranteed. The free text is refined by the Bridgers to improve translation quality. We set five levels of translation quality (5: includes all information, 4: includes most of the information, 3: includes a lot of the information, 2: includes only some information, 1: no information). According to Lin et al., the translation quality of Japanese-Vietnamese machine translation is 1.36 [9]. On the other hand, the evaluation result of translation quality in the field experiment was 4.34. (Eleven Vietnamese sentences, which were randomly selected from the Expert Answer message log data of the experiment, were evaluated by four Vietnamese subjects.) Therefore, the proposed translation flow yielded translation quality that was good enough to include "most information" of the original sentences.

Problem 2 The average turnaround time, delay between the time of posting a question and the time of getting an answer, was 107.2 h (SD: 72.28). In addition, 98.7% (373 out of 378) of the responses were returned within a week (168 h). However, the YMC system failed to cover emergencies such as infectious diseases. In the experiment, the disease of rice blast was observed. In such case, spraying the appropriate agricultural chemical would quickly save the crop, but the delay between disease observation and Expert response was too long.

Problem 3 We introduced the role of the Bridgers, people who refined Expert answer messages so that Youth could more readily understand. All communication logs among all 265 responses were analyzed excluding answers of only example parallel translations and corrections of example parallel translations among the 378 responses, Bridger smoothing was mainly applied to expressions that were easy for children to understand. There were 47 modifications and 16 suggestions of interactivity. Out of the 378 Expert answer messages logged, 265 messages contained free texts. Of these 265 Expert answer messages, 47 messages were refined by the Bridgers for easier understanding by Youth. Sixteen messages were Bridger modified in order to facilitate interaction between Expert and Youth. The modifications made to enhance Youth understanding can be characterized as summarizing, adding supplemental knowledge, and simplifying redundant expressions. As one example, Bridger added the general recommendation "You should not put fertilizers outside, because fertilizers are degraded by rain, wind, and sunlight" at the beginning of an

Expert original answer message consisting of five sentences. Bridger added some supplemental knowledge when the Expert answer lacked full information, or when the Expert answer had difficult technical terms. For example, Youth questioned "Rice stems are bitten. Who bites them?", and Expert answered, "If the lower part of the rice stems are bitten, it is probably by rats." Bridger added "It is necessary to deal with the situation appropriately according to its cause." to suggest action was needed. Also, Bridger added example expressions so that Youth could understand well. On the other hand, to facilitate interaction, Bridger added greeting messages such as "Hello, XXX" and comment messages such as "Your question is interesting." According to an interview of Bridgers, these personal sentences were added because they wanted to facilitate social communication and thus develop a good relationship with Youth.

Problem 4 After selecting the question category, we proposed and introduced a question input method to combine multiple example translations composed of sentence fragments by mouse operation to create question texts. We proposed and introduced the new question input method for Youth so that they could create question texts by combining multiple fragments of bilingual parallel texts by mouse operation without keyboard input. The experts were able to answer all questions from the children. Meanwhile, an interview of Youth who participated in the experiment found that some wanted to use free text for question input, because their search for parallel texts failed or was ineffective. YMC System allows Youth to send free text messages by using the comment input field. According to the log data of the experiment, 86 free text comments were posted. Two of them were questions to Expert and the remaining 84 comments were greetings and gratitude expressions.

Problem 5 In order to support Youth in transferring information to their parents at home, we proposed and introduced Textbook cards that Youth could take home from the YMC Center. In the field experiment, 303 (80.2%) of the Expert answer messages included a reference to one or more Textbook cards. Also, after the experiment, we submitted a questionnaire to all 30 Youth and asked "Please choose what you think is useful (multiple answers allowed)." The choices were six items such as "posting questions via YMC System," "explanation to parents by Textbook cards," "field survey observation," "temperature and humidity measurement." As a result, ten Youth answered "explanation to parents by Textbook cards," followed by "posting questions via YMC System" by 12 respondents which is the most answered item. In the questionnaire, Youth were also asked "Why do you think so?," and they answered such as "Because I can clearly explain to my parent what I got from Expert with Textbook cards" and "Because I can tell my parents how to raise rice."

6 Conclusion

The experiments in this chapter exemplified the difficulty of intercultural communication between people with different levels of subject matter expertise and proficiency in different languages. First, a communication environment with language services was designed to investigate the Youth Mediated Communication method. The design combined multilingual text information with peripheral data feedback, visual information, and paper-based materials. Second, a communication system was implemented to provide language services. The combination of parallel text and free text input contributed to decrease the loads placed on the Japanese rice farming experts. Finally, a field experiment was conducted. The target was rice farming households in the Mekong Delta, Vietnam; 30 youths from 29 local households participated. The evaluation of the experiment verified the positive effect of the communication system, though some issues remain. For example, the system was unable to identify and respond to emergency situations.

According to the Ministry of Agriculture and Rural Development of Vinh Long province in Vietnam where the project took place, the average rice yield of participating farmers was 0.3–0.5 tons per hectare larger than that of non-participating farmers in the area (Average yield in the area was 6.8 tons per hectare). In addition, due to the reduction in pesticide use, which was suggested by Expert, rice production cost decreased, while the rice yield increased. Thus, the revenues of participating farmers increased. This verifies the positive effect of the project in agricultural support.

Acknowledgements The field experiment in this research was funded by the Ministry of Internal Affairs and Communications, Japan, as part of its interest in Information and Communication Technology model projects in three priority areas in developing countries called "Ubiquitous Alliance Project." This research is partly supported by Service Science, Solutions and Foundation Integrated Research Program from JST RISTEX and a Grant-in-Aid for Scientific Research (A) (17H00759, 2017–2020) from Japan Society for the Promotion of Science (JSPS).

References

1. Climent, S., Mor, J., Oliver, A., Salvatierra, M., Snchez, I., Taul, M., Vallmanya, L.: Bilingual newsgroups in catalonia: a challenge for machine translation. J. Comput.-Mediated Commun. **9**(1) (2003)
2. Fruchter, R.: Conceptual, collaborative building design through shared graphics. IEEE Expert Intell. Syst. Appl. **11**(3), 33–41 (1996)
3. Fruchter, R., Clayton, M.J., Krawinkler, H., Kunz, J., Teicholz, P.: Interdisciplinary communication medium for collaborative conceptual building design. Adv. Eng. Softw. **25**(2), 89–101 (1996). Computing in Civil and Structural Engineering. http://www.sciencedirect.com/science/article/pii/0965997895001069
4. Ishida, T. (ed.): The Language Grid: Service-Oriented Collective Intelligence for Language Resource Interoperability. Springer Science & Business Media (2011)
5. Ishida, T.: Intercultural Collaboration and Support Systems: A Brief History. International Conference on Principle and Practices in Multi-Agent Systems (PRIMA 2016). Invited paper, pp. 3–19 (2016)
6. Jiang, H., Singley, K.: Exploring bilingual, task-oriented, document-centric chat. In: Proceedings of the ACM 2009 International Conference on Supporting Group Work, GROUP '09, pp. 229–232. ACM, New York (2009)
7. Lin, D., Ishida, T.: Participatory service design based on user-centered qos. In: Proceedings of the 2013 IEEE/WIC/ACM International Joint Conferences on Web Intelligence (WI) and Intelligent Agent Technologies (IAT) - vol. 01, WI-IAT '13, pp. 465–472. IEEE Computer Society, Washington, DC (2013)

8. Lin, D., Ishida, T.: User-Centered Service Design for Multi-language Knowledge Communication, pp. 309–317. Springer, Tokyo (2014)
9. Lin, D., Ishida, T., Murakami, Y., Tanaka, M.: Qos analysis for service composition by human and web services. IEICE TRANS. Inf. Syst. **97**(4), 762–769 (2014)
10. Lin, D., Murakami, Y., Ishida, T., Murakami, Y., Tanaka, M.: Composing human and machine translation services: language grid for improving localization processes. In: Proceedings of the Seventh International Conference on Language Resources and Evaluation (LREC'10), pp. 500–506. European Language Resources Association (ELRA), Valletta (2010)
11. Mori, Y.: Youth Mediated Communication Model: New Challenge to Bring Youths for Better World. Phase i Agriculture. Asia-Pacific Advanced Network (APAN2009) (2009)
12. Murakami, Y., Lin, D., Ishida, T.: Service-Oriented Architecture for Interoperability of Multi-language Services, pp. 313–328. Springer Berlin Heidelberg, Berlin (2014)
13. Tanaka, R., Murakami, Y., Ishida, T.: Context-based approach for pivot translation services. In: IJCAI, pp. 1555–1561 (2009)
14. Togami, T., Ninomiya, S., Yamamoto, K., Mori, Y., Takasaki, T., Okano, Y., Ikeda, R., Takezaki, A., Kameoka, T.: Field and weather monitoring with youths as sensors for agricultural decision support. Agric. Inf. Res. **21**(3), 65–75 (2012)
15. Wu, H., Wang, H.: Pivot language approach for phrase-based statistical machine translation. Mach. Transl. **21**(3), 165–181 (2007)
16. Yamashita, N., Ishida, T.: Effects of machine translation on collaborative work. In: Proceedings of the 2006 20th Anniversary Conference on Computer Supported Cooperative Work, CSCW '06, pp. 515–524. ACM, New York (2006)

Author Index

© Springer Nature Singapore Pte Ltd. 2018
Y. Murakami et al. (eds.), *Services Computing for Language Resources*,
Cognitive Technologies, https://doi.org/10.1007/978-981-10-7793-7

Printed in the United States
By Bookmasters